The 2016 Book of Baby Names

Hannah Crawford

Copyright © 2015 Hannah Crawford

All rights reserved. No part of this publication may be reproduced, stored in a retrieval system, or transmitted in any form or by any means, electrical, mechanical, photocopying, recording, or otherwise, without the prior written permission of the copyright owner.

ISBN:151739421X

ISBN-13: 978-1517394219

Penguinies@outlook.com

DEDICATED

This book is dedicated to my son Troy and to my unborn baby due in 2016. I would also like to thank Alexander Oliver Brawn for his photograph.

Introduction

The 2016 Book of Baby Names has over 1700 first names to help you to decide on the right name for your baby. There is a wide variety to choose from with both modern and classic names listed alphabetically. With pronunciations, origins and meanings all included to give you a better understanding of each name.

The 2016 Book of Baby Names can help you to pick a suitable baby name that suits your baby and family surname. Each name is divided into easily readable sections. Agreeing on a special baby name can be one of the most difficult yet rewarding decisions that any parent can make during their lifetime. This book can help make choosing a baby name easy and lots of fun.

Contents

Introduction	4
How to choose a baby name	7
Where to start	8-9
Unique names	9-12
Name meanings & connotations	13
Pronunciation & sound	14
Surnames	14-15
Can you agree on a name?	15-16
Does the name suit your baby?	16-17
Name popularity	17-18
Popular baby names	18-25
Celebrities	25-30
Pop culture names	30-33
Different spellings	33-36
Destination names	36-39
Gender neutral names	39-40
When should I announce the baby name?	41-45
Past trends	45-46

A-Z Baby Boy Names   47-228

A-Z Baby Girl Names   229-448

Banned baby names around the world   449-455

Biblography   457-458

How to choose a baby name

Finding out that you are expecting a baby is one of the most joyous and happiest moments that you can experience in your life. Some parents already have name choices and know what they want to call their baby long before they find out that they are pregnant, however for others this can be a daunting and difficult task.

I know when I was expecting my son that I found it extremely difficult to pick a name that I thought would be perfect for him, and a couple of months before he was born, I finally settled on a name. However, once my son was born and I held him in my arms for the first time, I quickly realised the name that I had spent so many months deciding on didn't seem to suit him and I was back to square one.

Names are a part of everyday life and culture; they can have a great significance to the child who receives the name and also to the societies that give them. A baby name is not only a name that will be with your infant throughout its childhood, it is a name that will stick with them for life. To add to the pressure, there is such a huge range and variety of baby names to choose from and to consider that the task can seem tremendously overwhelming. The 2016 Book of Baby Names have suggested a few helpful tips when it comes to choosing a baby name that is right for you, your child and family.

Where to start

Decide what are the most important factors for you and your partner when choosing a baby name; this may include any family traditions, uniqueness, popularity, celebrity influences, or gender.

It is a good idea to make a list of your favourite baby names and share them with your partner who can do the same with you. Combine your favourite names into one list and use this as a starting point. If you do not have a partner you could make a list with a good friend or a family member and have lots of fun listening to each other's name suggestions. You can add more names along the way; no doubt you will have lots of name suggestions from family members, friends and even from strangers that you can also add to your list of possible baby names.

One popular choice for parents-to-be is to name their newborn baby after a grandparent, relative or an ancestor. Your baby's heritage will always be an essential aspect to who they are as an individual. Choosing a name that is important to you or your family can reflect this. Some families have a strict naming tradition that dates back generations. Although you should never let anybody pressure you into naming your baby something that you are not keen on or really do not like. Instead, you could consider using them as middle names to honour your family traditions. This can make the process a whole lot simpler, however this choice is not for everybody, for me personally this was not an option.

Unique names

For some parents one of the most important aspects when deciding on a name for their baby is the uniqueness of it. The obvious advantage in choosing a unique or unusual baby name is how it can stand out from the crowd and be remembered throughout time. Some people like the shock factor that a unique name can generate for the child. The downside of picking a unique or unusual name is pronunciation; numerous people may struggle to pronounce your child's name which could bring negative attention to your child for all of the wrong reasons. The name may be hard for others to spell and constantly having to correct people who cannot spell or pronounce the name can become tiring, especially for your child when he/she is at school.

Choosing a unique name can allow the parents to use and to also show off their own personal creativity. This could be a lot of fun, albeit if you choose this option you should prepare yourself for being asked numerous questions about your chosen baby name and the reasons behind it. Modern celebrities often pick unusual and unique names for their babies which can generate a lot of publicity for them and their new-born child. Another thing to consider if you are looking for a unique baby name is that the name may sound cute and adorable when the baby is young, although when the child grows up into an adult the name could possibly sound outrageous and somewhat ridiculous. Some parents might feel too embarrassed to consider using a unique baby name for their child and may prefer to opt for a more traditional name instead.

A rising trend with parents who are opting to pick unique baby names for their children is for them to use names that begin with or have the letter 'x' in them. The reason being, that the names are thought to have a unique and edgy style and sound over other baby names. Angelina Jolie facilitated this popularisation by choosing names that had the letter 'x' in them for three of her five children, Pax, Maddox and Knox.

Boys Names with the letter X

1. Alexander
2. Axel
3. Baxter
4. Braxton
5. Bronx
6. Dixon
7. Felix
8. Huxley
9. Jax
10. Lennox
11. Madox
12. Maxim
13. Maxwell
14. Pax
15. Rex

Girls Names with the letter X

1. Alexa
2. Alexandra
3. Alexis
4. Beatrix
5. Dixie
6. Exene
7. Jaxine
8. Moxie
9. Oxsana
10. Phoenix
11. Roxanne
12. Trixie
13. Xena
14. Xenia
15. Xiomara

Name meanings and connotations

Name meanings can be a very important attribute to a family when considering a baby name. Some names have different meanings within different cultures and countries that have evolved from different languages, this can be a little confusing when deciding on a baby name. However, it can also be a positive as the meaning of the name may be more desirable in one culture than it is in another.

Some names may have personal connotations, even though your partner may love one name it might remind you of somebody that you don't get along with, or it could be the same name as an ex-partner or ex-friend etc. You may have found a perfect name that you have always loved and wanted to give to your newborn baby however a friend or family member may have got there first and used the same name for their child. This might put you off from using the name for your own baby. Alternatively you may love the name so much that you might decide to give the name to your baby anyway.

Pronunciation and sound

How to pronounce your baby's name and how it sounds when spoken aloud is often an essential element to all parents when choosing a name for their baby. A name could sound harmonious and pleasant, alternatively it may sound harsh or brash which could be an ultimate decision maker. The name could also be extremely difficult for others to pronounce which could end up completely changing your opinion on the name.

Surnames

Considering your child's surname is a common practice for a lot of parents when choosing a baby name as it can help you to pick the right name. Some parents prefer to avoid names that rhyme with their surnames whilst others favour this option. Names that flow with your baby's last surname can help you to narrow your list down. People can be ever so cruel when it comes to nicknames which are usually given to a person during their adolescent years. This is something that you could consider when choosing a name for your baby, especially when it comes to the initials. Check what the initials spell out, for example, Georgina Imogen Thomas sounds like a nice name, however, the initials are somewhat unfortunate in what they spell out. This is something that could be picked up on by classmates, family members, work colleagues and even by strangers. This could be rather embarrassing and unpleasant for your child to have to experience throughout their life.

Can you agree on a name?

One of the reasons why choosing a baby name can become so difficult for a lot of parents is because it's a decision that both you and your partner often make together. Finding a name that two people like can be tricky and take a lot longer than if it was just one person who was making the decision on their own. However if your partner strongly disagrees with one of your favourite choice names you should listen to their opinions and not force a name that isn't liked or appreciated by both sides as it can cause conflict and resentment. If you both make a list of favourite baby names you can look through each other's lists and then discuss the pros and cons of each one, this could help the process dramatically. You partner may have some really great ideas for names that you hadn't thought about before, therefore it's always good to share your honest thoughts and opinions with one and other.

Does the name suit your baby?

As I mentioned previously, I spent months looking through and researching baby names until I found one that I thought would be perfect for my son just before he was born. When I finally decided on a name that I thought would be ideal for my child I was a hundred percent sure that this was going to be his name for life. However, as soon as my son arrived into this world I quickly realised that the name that I was so certain about before did not suit him or his little personality at all. We spent the next few days thinking up alternative names until we found the perfect one that did suit him to the T. Luckily you are given 42 days after your baby is born to register the name officially in England, Wales and Northern Ireland. This means you could try out alternative names and see which one best suits him/her before you make your final decision.

Name popularity

Names that are already extremely popular and are in the top ten can be a decision maker when deciding on a baby name. Some parents like to pick a popular baby name, whilst others prefer to choose a name that is out of the top ten or even the top hundred baby names category. Celebrities can also have a drastic effect on the popularisation of a baby name. The name Harper has seen the largest rise in girls' names; this is mostly likely due to the celebrity couple Victoria and David Beckham who chose the name for their daughter in 2011. The name Eric rose by 314% in 2014 after celebrity Simon Cowell chose it for his first born son.

The media can also

have a huge influence in popularising baby names in addition to celebrities. The popular television series, *Game of Thrones* has recently inspired some parents with their choice of baby names particularly, those who gave birth to baby girls. Almost two hundred and fifty babies have been named Arya, and fifty-three babies have been named Khaleesi. Although the male names have proven to be less influential they have still been rather popular with eighteen babies being called Theon and seventeen babies named Tyrion. Likewise, the release of a new Disney movie always tends to influence people's choices in baby names. Recently there has been a dramatic rise in babies being named Elsa, which was the name used for the Ice queen in the animated blockbuster 2013 film Frozen.

Popular baby mames

The names Oliver and Amelia were the most popular baby names given to infants that were born in England and Wales in 2014 for the second year running. Amelia has enjoyed a huge increase in popularity since 2012, and the name has been in the top spot since 2011. The name Oliver has been in the top spot since 2013 and has remained an extremely popular choice for baby boy names in Wales. The Office for National Statistics revealed that 6,649 baby boys were named Oliver and 5327 baby girls were given the name Amelia.

The Top Baby Names in England

Girls	Boys
1. Amelia	1. Oliver
2. Olivia	2. Jack
3. Isla	3. Harry
4. Emily	4. Jacob
5. Poppy	5. Charlie
6. Ava	6. Thomas
7. Isabella	7. George
8. Jessica	8. Oscar
9. Lily	9. James
10. Sophie	10. William

The Top Baby Names in Scotland

Girls

1. Sophie
2. Olivia
3. Emily
4. Isla
5. Lucy
6. Ava
7. Jessica
8. Ella
9. Amelia
10. Millie

Boys

1. Jack
2. James
3. Lewis
4. Oliver
5. Daniel
6. Logan
7. Alexander
8. Lucas
9. Harry
10. Charlie

The Top Baby Names in Wales

Girls

11. Amelia
12. Olivia
13. Ava
14. Ruby
15. Emily
16. Poppy
17. Ella
18. Mia
19. Isla
20. Isabella

Boys

1. Oliver
2. Jacob
3. Jack
4. Charlie
5. Alfie
6. Noah
7. Harry
8. Riley
9. William
10. Dylan

The Top Baby Names in Northern Ireland

	Girls	Boys
1.	Emily	Jack
2.	Grace	James
3.	Sophie	Charlie
4.	Ella	Harry
5.	Sophia	Daniel
6.	Lucy	Noah
7.	Aofie	Matthew
8.	Amelia	Ethan
9.	Anna	Jacob
10.	Jessica	Oliver

The top baby names in America

	Girls	Boys
1.	Emma	Noah
2.	Olivia	Liam
3.	Sophia	Mason
4.	Isabella	Jacob
5.	Ava	William
6.	Mia	Ethan
7.	Emily	Michael
8.	Abigail	Alexander
9.	Madison	James
10.	Charlotte	Daniel

The Top Baby Names in Australia

Girls	Boys
1. Charlotte	1. Oliver
2. Olivia	2. William
3. Ava	3. Jack
4. Emily	4. Noah
5. Mia	5. Jackson
6. Amelia	6. James
7. Ruby	7. Thomas
8. Sophia	8. Ethan
9. Chloe	9. Lucas
10. Sophie	10. Cooper

The Top Baby Names in France

Girls	Boys
1. Manon	1. Armand
2. Jade	2. Jules
3. Louise	3. Lucas
4. Alice	4. Léo
5. Camille	5. Gabriel
6. Chloé	6. Arthur
7. Léa	7. Louis
8. Lou	8. Hugo
9. Emma	9. Tom
10. Charlotte	10. Sacha

The Top Baby names in Spain

Girls   **Boys**

1. Lucía   1. Hugo
2. María   2. Daniel
3. Paula   3. Pablo
4. Daniela   4. Alejandro
5. Martina   5. Álvaro
6. Carla   6. Adrián
7. Sara   7. David
8. Sofía   8. Mario
9. Valeria   9. Diego
10. Julia   10. Javier

The 2016 Book of Baby Names predicts another year of vintage baby names hitting the top spots. Our top ten predictions are;

Top Ten Baby Name Predictions for 2016	
1. Amelia	1. George
2. Ava	2. Oliver
3. Emily	3. Harry
4. Poppy	4. William
5. Olivia	5. Jack
6. Jessica	6. Alfie
7. Isla	7. Jacob
8. Ruby	8. Charlie
9. Isabella	9. Lewis
10. Ella	10. James

Celebrities

New baby name trends often emerge once a popular celebrity has a baby. Both celebrities and pop culture can impact and generate a sudden usage of a baby name, creating a remarkable rise in popularity within such a short period of time. Prominence is often given to a name after a celebrity has chosen it for their own child.

Celebrity culture can have a huge impact on people, influencing parents and helping to inspire them with baby names. Some celebrities like to choose traditional and more vintage baby names for their child, whilst other celebrities like to turn their backs on tradition and prefer to pick a unique name that can seem outrageous to some. Celebrities can be feel pressurised and incentivised to create a unique baby name for their child, the use of objects such as Apple and Pilot are becoming frequently used for baby names along with the use of verbs.

Either way celebrities can influence parents across the globe on their choice of baby names. The more popular a celebrity the more influence they are likely to have on the public.

Some of the most talked about celebrity baby names are;

Kim Kardashian and Kanye West

One of the most famous and recent controversial baby names came from the reality TV star Kim Kardashian, and her rapper husband Kanye West. The celebrity couple named their daughter North West in 2013. The name is said to have been chosen as it represents the highest power. The couple are expecting their second child in December 2015. There has already been much speculation about the name for baby number two. The name Easton West seems to be the public's favourite prediction.

Lil' Kim and Papers

Lil' Kim and Papers welcomed their baby girl into the world back in June 2014. They named their daughter Royal Reign, which didn't seem so much of a surprise as rapper Lil' Kim likes referring to herself as the 'Queen Bee.'

Liv Tyler and David Gardner

Liv Tyler and her

boyfriend choose a nautical baby name for the son Sailor Gene Gardner in early 2015.

Tom Fletcher and Giovanna Fletcher

McBusted star Tom Fletcher and his author wife Giovanna Fletcher named their son Buzz Michelangelo. The married couple insists that the name was not inspired by the famous Toy Story character Buzz Lightyear.

Megan Fox and Brian Austin Green

Hollywood stars Megan Fox and Brian Austin Green raised eyebrows after they named their second son Bodhi Ransom in early 2014. The Buddhism-inspired name Bodhi means awakened or enlightenment on the path to Nirvana.

Omarion and Apryl Jones

The R&B singer Omarion and his partner Apryl Jones named their son Megaa Omari Grandberry in 2014. The name is definitely distinctive and one of a kind.

Ciara and Future

Singers Ciara and

Future named their son Future Zahir in 2014. Naming your child after its father has been a popular tradition for centuries. However the name Future was actually taken from his father's stage name.

Holly Madison

Former Playboy model Holly Madison received quite a lot of criticism after she named her daughter Rainbow Aurora in 2013. Holly defended her baby name choice by claiming that she had always loved the name Rainbow because it is such a pretty and unusual name. She also revealed that the name was inspired by somebody that she went to school with who also had the same name Rainbow.

Alicia Silverstone

Hollywood actress Alicia Silverstone named her son Bear Blu back in May 2011. The name is definitely unique and Silverstone claims that most people find the name to be "Super cute".

Nicole Ritchie and Joel Madden

Reality TV star Nicole Ritchie and her musician husband Joel

Madden named their son Sparrow James Midnight. Nicole explained that she really liked the name Sparrow which was influenced by Captain Jack Sparrow from The Pirates of the Caribbean. Madden is said to like the name for different reasons. Nicole also revealed that she liked how the name sounded with her daughter's name, Harlow.

Gwen Stefani and Gavin Rossdale

Although musicians Gwen Stefani and Gavin Rossdale have never disclosed the origins of their sons name, Zuma Nesta Rock. There has been much speculation and theories surrounding their baby name choice. Many people believe that Zuma is named after a beach in Malibu where Rossdale is said to have had an epiphany. Nesta is believed to have come from Gwen Stefani's love of reggae music, as it is also the given name of Bob Marley. Finally, Rock is thought to be inspired by the genre in music.

Nicholas Cage

Possibly due to his love of comics, Hollywood actor

Nicholas Cage notoriously named his son after the Krypton name of Superman, Kal-El.

Penn Jillette

Renowned magician Penn Jillette believes that it is cruel for parents to give a child a name that others already have, therefore he and his wife decided to call their daughter a very unique and rememberable name, Moxie Crimefighter.

Pop culture names

Movies and successful television shows have had a huge influence on baby names, along with books and music for decades. Names that are given to the leading protagonists typically see an instant increase in the popularity of baby names. *The Twilight Saga* has popularised the names, Isabella and Jacob, along with other hugely successful names that have been given to vampires in films and television shows such as *True Blood* and the *Vampire diaries*. Reality television can also have an immense influence on the choice of baby names. Since the Kardashians shot to fame in 2007, there has been a huge rise in baby names beginning with the letter 'K'. The globally successful US television series, *Teen Mom* has sparked a spectacular surge in the popularity of the baby names Maci and Bentley. Maci Bookout is one of the show's original cast members and Bentley is the name of her son.

Disney moves inspire people every day with their faiytale stories and beautiful characters. The unique personalities and the inner qualities that the leading characters boast, quite often influence parents-to-be with a list of baby names. In 2010, the girls name Tiana more than doubled with parents giving this name to their daughters after Disney released *The Princess and The Frog*. Disney princesses have had a huge impact on baby names over the years.

However it is not only the Disney princesses that inspire parents with new baby names, Disney films have featured a succession of unforgettable heroines and heroes which parents are naming their children after.

Disney Princess Names

Anna	Frozen
Ariel	The Little Mermaid
Aurora	Sleeping Beauty
Belle	Beauty and The Beast
Elsa	Frozen
Jasmine	Aladdin
Merida	Brave
Moana	Moana
Mulan	Mulan
Pocahontas	Pocahontas
Tiana	The Princess and the Frog
Tinkerbell	Peter Pan

Disney Male Names

Buzz	Toy Story
Eric	The Little Mermaid
Finn	Cars
Gaston	Beauty and the Beast
Milo	Atlantis
Peter	Peter Pan
Hans	Frozen
Kristoff	Frozen
Remy	Ratatouille
Rex	Toy Story
Sebastian	The Little Mermaid
Woody	Toy Story

Paying homage to a historical figure, classic movie star, musician or celebrity by naming your child after them is a way of demonstrating the admiration and respect that you have for that individual. Hollywood actor Vin Diesel is the latest celebrity to pay homage to a fellow actor by naming his daughter Pauline after the death of his co-star Paul Walker, who tragically died in a car wreck in 2013. Mariah Carey named her daughter Monroe after one of her favourite idols and film stars Marilyn Monroe. Liam Gallagher named his son Lennon after his favourite Beatles star John Lennon.

Different Spellings

Creating new or using different spellings can make your babies name less traditional and also help it to stand out from the crowd. Making up new spellings for a traditional name can also become trendy and quickly generate a new name craze. The name Chloe has seen a modern change in how it is spelled with some parents opting to spell the name with a 'K', Khloe. Swapping the 'c' with a 'k' has become a popular choice for parents as these letters are easily substitutable with one and other.

Names with letter C	Names with the letter K
Cameron	Kamron
Carly	Karlee
Cailyn	Kailyn
Caitlyn	Katelyn
Cassandra	Kassandra
Catalina	Katalina
Chloe	Khloe
Danica	Danika
Dominic	Dominik
Eric	Erik
Jacob	Jakob
Lucas	Lukas
Mackenzie	Makenzie
Michaela	Makayla
Marcus	Markus
Nicholas	Nickolas
Zachary	Zakary

Changing or mixing up the vowels, A, E, I, O, U & sometimes Y can create a brand new version of a traditional name. Very occasionally will the vowel from the first letter of a name be changed, it is frequently more common for parents to change the vowels within the name.

Vowel changes	
Aiden	Aidyn
Jayden	Jaiden
Lauren	Lauryn
Reagan	Regan
Zoe	Zoie

One of the most popular ways to modify a name is to add or to remove one or more of the consonants within the name. This is particularly common with baby girl names. Adding or removing consonants can create a whole new vibrant name.

Adding or removing consonants	
Alana	Alannah
Austin	Austyn
Ava	Avah
Eliana	Elianna
Giselle	Gisselle
Hannah	Hanna
Isabelle	Izabelle
Jackson	Jaxson
Jason	Jayson
Liliana	Lillianna
Madison	Maddison

There are no set rules on how to spell a name, however being creative with a name's spelling can cause problems in the long run, constantly having to correct people on spellings and pronunciations, which could also cause confusion and embarrassment throughout your child's life.

Some parents decide to spell their babies name differently from the traditional way as a way to indicate the gender of their child.

Destination Names

Destination names may have depth and personal meaning to the parents who choose to give them to their children. The name might tell a personal adventure or a story as well as being exotic and unusual. A destination name could be a destination where the couple first met or dated, where they grew up, or where the child was conceived. It could just be a location loved by the parents from a holiday or somewhere where that they have always wanted to visit or live. Destination names can also send out a signal that the parents are worldly travelers.

Alicia Keys and her husband Swizz Beatz named their son Egypt. Alicia said that the name was inspired by a trip and personal journey she went on whilst visiting Egypt. Her husband suggested that they should use the name for their baby as the holiday was such a life changing and important time for Alicia. The Beckhams famously named their first son Brooklyn after he was apparently conceived there in the late 90's.

Parents have numerous reasons as to why they choose destination names for their children. Locations can have great significance to people's lives and history. Honouring a city, state, county or a country by giving your baby the same name is a way of telling your story and having it live on through your family tree.

Destination names	
Austin	Lourdes
Boston	Lucia
Bronx	Madison
Brooklyn	Marseille
Carolina	Montana
Catalina	Odessa
Charlotte	Orlando
Chelsea	Oxford
Dakota	Paris
Dallas	Phoenix
Denver	Savannah
Eden (Biblical Garden of Eden)	Shiloh (Biblical city)
Georgie	Sicily
Hamilton	Sonora
Houston	Troy
India	Valencia
Ireland	Venice
Kenya	Vienna
Kingston	Virginia
Lincoln	Zion (Biblical)
London	

Gender neutral names

Gender neutral names are becoming increasingly popular with modern parents. This is most likely due to the fact that there has been a substantial rise with parents who are choosing to raise their child in a gender neutral way with clothes, toys and unisex baby names. Companies and parents are choosing to break away from the traditions and refusing to reinforce gender stereotypes that have been around for millennias.

Blake Lively and her husband Ryan Reynolds chose the name James Reynolds for her daughter in December 2014. Mila Kunis and Aston Kutcher also chose a gender neutral name for their daughter who they named Wyatt Kutcher in September 2014. Some people believe that a masculine sounding name can be a workplace advantage for the child when it is older.

Is a name truly masculine or feminine? Well, a name will always remain a name; therefore, it is whatever your child is. However, time can make a lot of difference when it comes to gender neutral names. Names that are considered unisex today such as Courtney and Casper may not have even been considered for a girl's name twenty years ago. The more creative the spelling the more likely that the name is being used for a girl.

Modern names often start off being unisex and then gradually start being spelled differently, thus creating a female version and a male version. Names that end with –on usually imply that the name is being used for a male, whereas names ending with –ynn tend to imply that the name is being used for a female.

Names can shift from being gender neutral to male or female over time. Therefore, if you decide to pick a gender neutral name for your baby you should be prepared for the name to eventually tilt to being associated with either a male or a female.

When should I announce the baby name?

There is no specific time or rule on when you or your partner should announce your chosen baby name. It is a personal choice and nobody can tell you when you can and can't do it. You should announce the baby's name when you and your partner feel comfortable and certain with your name choice. I announced my son's name-to-be when I was seven months pregnant, however when he was born I didn't go with the name which I had originally chose for him. This did cause some confusion for family and friends, as I ended up giving my son a completely different name which wasn't even considered during my pregnancy.

Some parents decide to announce their babies name during pregnancy whilst others prefer to wait until the baby is born. Whether you decide to announce your babies name before or after the birth you can still have some fun with the announcement. The rise in baby showers has also seen an increase on baby name announcements. You could do this with the use of balloons, cakes or by getting everybody to play a fun guessing game and reveal the baby's name at the very end.

The power of social media has also had a great impact on announcing both pregnancy and baby names. This is because it is an easy and cheap way to make announcements which can also be fun whilst reaching vast amounts of people who may live all over the world.

Photography is a fun and creative way to announce the baby's name. Some mothers like to take a picture of their pregnant bellies with the chosen baby name stuck onto the belly using a name tag. Others like to place objects on top or in front of the belly that spell out the baby's name. Letter bricks are a popular choice for this method.

If you have more than one child, involving any siblings can be an extremely fun and adorable way to announce the babies name to the world. You could have your child wearing a T-shirt with the babies name exhibited on the front, they could be holding up a picture with the baby's name spelled out on a chalkboard, easel painting, box, or even on a tablet device. There any many creative ways that you and your family could do this.

Video announcements have too seen a rise in baby name announcements. Parents are opting to use this method to announce their baby's name, the reasons behind their choice and then explaining the meaning of the name. A video announcement could also make a great family keepsake, you could watch the video together in ten or twenty years' time when your child is all grown up and maybe have some children of their own. It's a good way to look back and remember those special family moments.

A new and rising trend with parents is for them to reserve the baby's full name on social media sites, then revealing the name to family and friends with a picture of their scan or of the newborn baby. The pages are then used to update the child's milestones with close friends and family.

Keepsake announcements have a more traditional feeling to them and can be a great keepsake for your family and friends. This can be done by using paper or card announcements with a picture of your baby, weight and size and, of course, the baby's full name.

Decorations and baby nurseries can be a good way to announce the baby's name, with the use of personalised toys, decoration stickers, wall hangers, and door names.

Being creative with food is a fun choice since buying personalised sweets and candy bars has become easier and, therefore, a fun way to make pregnancy and baby name announcements. You could combine this option with the use of photography and social media. Spelling out your baby's name with candy, alphabet spaghetti or other food items, whilst creating cool and artistic photographs that would make a lovely family keepsake.

The number of parents who are choosing to have a baby naming ceremony to reveal their children's full name has tripled in the past few years. With loved ones gathered together for a non-religious celebration, the name is then presented to family and friends.

Past Trends

Important titles
Names that carry a grand sense of importance such as King, Queen, Prince, and Princess have been a highly popular name choice throughout the times. Although these names tended to decline during the 1950's there has been a recent surge in popularity, this is most likely due to the celebrities who are choosing these names for their own children.

'Y' spellings
Replacing a letter in the name with the letter 'y' has been a popular choice since the early twentieth century. During the 1920's it also became highly desirable to add an 'e' to names that already ended with the letter 'y' for example, Bettye, Bobbye and Rubye.

Gems
For centuries valuable gems and precious stones have been a popular choice for baby names. This includes names such as Beryl, Diamond, Opal, Pearl,

and Ruby. Other signs of preciousness such as Coral and Goldie have also been a fashionable name choice.

Boy names for girls
Choosing traditional male names and using them as female names became trendy during the late 19th century. The most popular boy's names that were given to girls are, Billie, Bobbie, Charlie, Frankie and Tommie.

Last names for first names
The names Coleman, Hilton, Preston, Scott and Spencer are just some of the names that emerged after it became increasingly popular to use surnames as given first names.

A-Z

Baby Boy Names

For

2016

A

Aaden

Pronunciation: Ay-din.
The name originates from Irish Gaelic, origin of the name Aidan. The name means, "fire", "fiery."

Aamir

Pronunciation: Aa-mir
Aamir is a modernised counterpart of the Arabic and Hebrew name Amir, which means "treetop."

Aaron

Pronunciation: Aa-ron
The name Aaron is of Greek origin. The name is also linked to Ancient Egypt. Aaron is a biblical name and appears in the Old Testament borne by the brother of Moses. The name Aaron means "Strong mountain."

Abdul

Pronunciation: AB-dul
The name Abdul is of Arabic origin and means "servant of God", "servant". The name Abdul also signifies a religious service and devotion.

Abdullah

Pronunciation: Ab-dul-ah
Abdullah is of Arabic origin and means "God's servant".

Abraham

Pronunciation: Ay-bra-ham, Ahb-rahm
The name Abraham comes from the Hebrew *av haomon goyim.* The name Abraham means, "Father of a multitude", "many nations". Abraham is a biblical name; borne in the Old Testament and originally named Abram, was bestowed the name of Abraham by God. He is said to be the father of Jewish nations, the great Jewish patriarchs. Abraham received God's promise that

his people would possess the land of Canaan.

Abran
Pronunciation: a-BRAHN
Abran originates from Spain and means, "father of a mighty nation", "father of a multitude", "high father". Abran is a variant the Hebrew name Abraham.

Ace
Pronunciation: Ayce
Ace is of English origin and also an English surname meaning "Noble". The name Ace means, "Number one". Additionally an ace is a playing card with the highest face value in many card games, making the ace the most powerful card to hold.

Achilles
Pronunciation: ah-KILL-eez
Achilles is of Greek origin. Achilles was the son of the sea nymph Thetis and Peleus, King of the Myrmidons. Achilles was a hero of the Trojan War, the central character and a supreme warrior in Homer's Iliad. Famous for his courage and manly beauty, Achilles was invulnerable on all of his body except for his heel. Achilles was dipped in the River Styx by his mother Thetis, she held him by heel which became his one weak point, "Achilles' Heel".

Adair
Pronunciation: ah-DARE
The name Adair is of German origin. The meaning of the name Adair is, "wealthy spear". Adair is also a Scottish surname from the Gaelic word 'doire', which means "oak grove.

Adam

Pronunciation: AD-am

Adam is of Hebrew origin and means "earth". In Hebrew, it is a generic word for "man". Adam is a biblical name; borne in the Old Testament by the father of the human race, he was the first man created from the red earth of Eden by God. Adam and Eve were the first humans and lived in the Garden of Eden until they committed sin.

Adan

Pronunciation: ah-DAHN

The name is of Spanish origin and is a variant of the Hebrew name Adam. The name Adan has the meaning of "earth", "fire". In Spanish, the meaning of the name Adan is "from the red earth".

Adolfo

Pronunciation: ah-DOLE-foh

The name Adolfo is a Latin name. The Latin meaning of Adolfo is "noble wolf", "majestic wolf". Additionally Adolfo is a Spanish and Italian variant of the German name, Adolf.

Adrian

Pronunciation: Ay-dree-an

Adrian is of Latin origin, the name is derived from the Latin name "Hadrianus". The meaning of the name Adrian is "from Hadria", a town in northern Italy which gave its name to the Adriatic Sea. Adrian is also the name of several early Christian saints and Martyrs.

Agustin

Pronunciation: ah-goos-teen

Agustin has Latin origins. The Latin meaning of Agustin is "deserving of respect". Agustin is a popular Spanish name. The Spanish meanings of Agustin are "majestic", "great".

Aidan
Pronunciation: AY-den
Aidan is of Irish Gaelic origins. The meaning of Aidan is "fire". Aidan is the name of several early Irish saints, one of whom established the greatest centres of learning of its time, The monastery of Lindisfarne which is also known as The Holy Island of Lindisfarne.

Ainsley
Pronunciation: AYNS-lee
The name Ainsley is of Old English origin. The meaning of the name is "clearing", "only hermitage wood".

Originally a place name Annesley or Ansley.

Alan
Pronunciation: AL-an
The name Alan is of Celtic origin. In Celtic, the meaning of the name Alan is, "noble", "harmony", "stone". The name could also be derived from the Gaelic name 'Ailin', which means "little rock". Alan was originally a saint's name and was reborn in Britain during the Normal Conquest.

Alasdair
Pronunciation: AL-as-dare
Alasdair is of Greek origin. In Greek, the meaning of the name Alasdair is "defender", "protector of mankind". Other variations of the name include: Alastair, Alistair, Allaster.

Albert

Pronunciation: AL-burt

Albert is a Norman French name of German Origin. The meaning of the name is "noble", "bright". The name was brought to England by the Normans and replaced the Old English name Ethelbert.

Albin

Pronunciation: AL-bin

The name Albin is taken from the Latin name Albinus derived from '*albus*'. The meaning of Albin is "white", "pale-skinned" Albin is also a variant of the name 'Alban'.

Alexander

Pronunciation: al-ek-ZAN-der

The name Alexander is of Greek origin, taken from the Latin form of the Greek name '*alexandros*'. The meaning of Alexander is "man's defender", "warrior". Alexander appears in the Bible as the one who helps Jesus bear the cross on the journey to Calvary.

Alexis

Pronunciation: a-LEX-iss

Alexis is of Greek origin and means "defender". The name is often used a shortened variation of the name Alexander. Although Alexis is traditionally a male name, it is now also used for girls in the modern world. Saint Alexis was a popular saint of Edessa, admired as a 'man of God.'

Alfonso

Pronunciation: al-FON-so

Alfonso is of Spanish and Italian origin. The name Alfonso is a variant of the German word, 'Alphonse' which means "ready for battle. The Spanish meaning of the name Alfonso is "eager for war".

Alfred
Pronunciation: AL-fred
The name Alfred is of Anglo-Saxon origin and means, "name of a king".

Ali
Pronunciation: ah-LEE
Ali is of Arabic origin. Borne by a cousin the prophet of Muhammad, was also known as the first male convert to Islam. The name Ali is also borne by the hero in 'Ali Baba and the Forty Thieves'. The meaning of the name Ali is "excellent", "noble".

Alton
Pronunciation: ALL-tun
Alton is of English origin. The meaning of the name is "old town".

Alvin
Pronunciation: AL-vin
Alvin is of English origin. The meaning of the name is "friend", "magical being".

Amos
Pronunciation: AYM-oss
The name Amos is of Hebrew origin. The meaning of the name is, "to carry", "carried". A biblical name; borne by one of the twelve minor prophets of the Old Testament, who wrote the Book of Amos. It is the oldest of the prophetic books.

Andrew
Pronunciation: AN-droo
The name Andrew is of Greek origin, from the root *andr-*, 'man' giving the meaning "manly", "strong" or "Warrior". English form of the Greek name Andreas. A biblical name; borne by one of the first of Jesus's

disciples, the first chosen of the 12 apostles. Saint Andrew is the patron saint of Scotland, Greece and Russia. His feast day is 30th November.

Angel
Pronunciation: AIN-jel
The name Angel is of Greek origin. The meaning of the name Angel is "messenger of God". A biblical name; borne as the name for the spirit creatures sent to men by God as his messengers. Angel is used for both female and male names. Derived for the Greek "angelos".

Angus
Pronunciation: ANG-guss
Angus is of Celtic origin. The meaning of Angus is "one choice", "one strength". Angus is the anglicized for of the Irish and Scottish Gaelic name Aonghus. In Celtic mythology, Angus Og is a god of love and beauty. Angus is both a first name and surname.

Anthony
Pronunciation: AN-tha-nee
Anthony is of Latin origin, adopted from the Roman family name Antonius. The 'h' was introduced in the 17th century. Ruler of the Roman Empire and lover of Cleopatra, Marcus Antonius (82-30BC) was an early bearer of the name. Saint Anthony was an Egyptian hermit monk renowned for his resistance to the devil and founded the first Christian monastic order.

Apollo
Pronunciation: er-POH-loh
The name Apollo is of Greek origin. The name

comes from *Apollyon*, Greek translation of the Hebrew word "Abaddon". The meaning of the name is "destroyer". A biblical name; borne as one of the early Christian disciples. The name Apollo has come to symbolise the classical and intellectual aspects of thought.

Archer
Pronunciation: AR-cher
Archer is of Latin origin, derived from the Latin *arcus* meaning "bow". Archer is an adopted English surname from medieval times, originally an occupational name for skilled archer.

Archibald
Pronunciation: Ar-chi-bald
Archibald is of Old French and Old German origin. The name Archibald means "genuine", "bold", "brave". The name is particularly popular in Scotland.

Arden
Pronunciation: ARD-en
The name Arden is of Latin origin. The name means "great forest". It is the name of the magical forest in Shakespeare's "As You Like It". Arden is also the surname of Shakespeare's mother.

Ariel
Pronunciation: AR-ee-el
Ariel is of Hebrew origin. The meaning of Ariel is "lion of God". A biblical place name; used in Isaiah 29 to refer to Jerusalem. Ariel is also the scriptural name for a place in Sumeria. The name is used in literature to identify various spirits. Shakespeare gave this name to a spirit who can disappear at will in "The Tempest". Ariel is

given to both male and females as a name.

Aries
Pronunciation: A-ries
The name Aries is of Latin origin. The meaning of the name is "ram". Aries is the name of the astrological sign for those born from March 21 to April 19.

Arnold
Pronunciation: AR-nold
Arnold is of Old French and Old German origin. The meaning of the name Arnold is "eagle power". A Puritan adoption, an early saint of this name was a musician at the court of Charlemagne. The name died out during the Middle Ages, and was revived in the 19th Century.

Arthur
Pronunciation: AR-ther
The name Arthur is of Celtic origin. The name could possibly have been derived from the Celtic word "artos", which means "bear". The 6th-century King Arthur and his Round Table of Knights have become renowned figures. The name was first found in the Latin form Artorius, which is of obscure origin.

Ashely
Pronunciation: ASH-lee
Ashley is an adopted surname and place name, of Old English origin. The meaning of the name Ashley is "ash meadow". Initially used as a boy's name, Ashley is now used more commonly for girl's names. Ashley is an English saint's name from the 17h century. The name was first recorded as a given name in the 16th Century. Earl of

Shaftesbury, Anthony Ashley Cooper made the name more popular in the early 19th century. The humanitarian was renowned for the legislation designed to improve conditions among the working classes.

Asher
Pronunciation: ASH-er
The name Asher is of Hebrew origin. The meaning of the name Ashe is "happy". A biblical name; borne as the eighth son of Jacob, was promised a life blessed with an abundance. The Puritans brought the name Asher to England.

Ashton
Pronunciation: ASH-ten
Ashton is an adopted surname of Old English origin. The meaning of the name is "ash tree town". Although the name has been used as a boy's name since the 1600's, the name is commonly given to girls.

Aston
Pronunciation: AS-ton
The name Aston is of Old English origin, and the meaning of the name is "east town", "ash tree settlement". Aston is also a place name.

Atlas
Pronunciation: AT-las
The name Atlas is of Greek origin. The meaning of Atlas is "to carry". The name bears connotations of great strength. Atlas was a mythical Titan who bore the weight of the world on his shoulders.

Auberon
Pronunciation: A(u)-be-ron
Auberon is from an Old French name of Old German origin. The

meaning of the name Auberon is "noble", "royal bear". The name is possibly a variation of Aubrey or *Adalbero*. Auberon is the king of the fairies in Shakespeare's, *A Midsummer Night's Dream* (1605).

August

Pronunciation: AW-gust
August is of Latin origin. The meaning of the name August is "great", "magnificent". The Latin version, Augustus is more commonly used in English-speaking countries.

Augustine

Pronunciation: AW-gus-tin
Augustine is of Latin origin. The meaning of Augustine is "great", "magnificent". Borne by perhaps the greatest of fathers of the Christian church, Saint Augustine of Hippo (354-430). Saint Augustine (sixth century) was the first Archbishop's of Canterbury, recognised for the frank "confessions", in which he speaks, "Oh God, make me chaste – but not yet". Augustine is diminutive of August, the English form of the Latin name *Augustinus*.

Augustus

Pronunciation: AW-gust-us
Augustus is of Latin origin. The meaning of Augustus is "great", "magnificent". It was given by the Senate to the Roman emperor Octavian in 27BC. Subsequently the name Augustus was used by his successors. The name was popular in the 18th century after German princely families brought the name to Britain.

Austin

Pronunciation: AW-sten

The name Austin is of French and Latin origin. The name is a variation of Augustine. The meaning of the name is "great", "magnificent". The name was popular in England during the 17th Century. Saint Augustine (seventh century) was occasionally called Austin.

Axel

Pronunciation: AX-el

Axel is of Hebrew origin. The meaning of the name Axel is "father is peace". Scandinavian variant of Absalom.

Aydan

Pronunciation: AY-dan

Aydan is a variant of the Gaelic name, Aidan, an anglicised form of the ancient Gaelic name Aedan. The meaning of the name Aydan is "fire".

B

Barnabas
Pronunciation: BAR-na-bus
The name Barnabas is of Greek and Aramaic origin. The meaning of Barnabas is "son of consolation". A biblical name; borne in the New Testament by Apostle who accompanied St Paul on his missionary journeys. Saint Barnabas's feast day is 11th June.

Barnaby
Pronunciation: BAR-naby
Barnaby is a medieval dialect form of the Greek, Aramaic name Barnabas. Charles Dickens popularized the name during the mid-19th century with his novel, *'Barnaby Rudge'* (1841).

Baron
Pronunciation: BARE-an
The name Baron is of Old German and Old English Origin. The meaning of the name Baron is "young warrior". It is an adopted surname which was first used during the post-Conquest period to mean a vassal of a nobel. A baron was the lowest rank of a hereditary peerage that entitles the holder to serve in the House of Lords in England.

Barrett
Pronunciation: BARE-et
The name Barrett is possibly from Middle English *baret*, which means "dispute", "argument", or from the Old French word, *Barrette* meaning *"cap"*. The adopted surname was a given name used mostly in the 19th century.

Barry
Pronunciation: BARE-ee
Barry is of Irish and Gaelic origin, derive from the Old Irish name, Bairre. The

meaning of the name Barry is "fair-haired". Saint *Bairre* (seventh century) founded a monastery that became the city of Cork in Ireland.

Bartholomew
Pronunciation: bar-THAWL-oh-myoo
Bartholomew is of Aramaic origin. The meaning of Bartholomew is "son of Talmai". Talmai being another name for Nathaniel, the apostle. Biblical; by name of one of the twelve apostles, Nathanael, who was known as the patron saint of tanners and vintners. Bartholomew was a common boys name in the Middle Ages.

Basil
Pronunciation: BAZ-el
The name Basil is of Greek origin. The meaning of Basil is "royal", "kingly". From the Greek name Basileios, which is derived from "basileus". Saint Basil (fourth century) of Caesarea was called "Saint Basil the Great", he was regarded as one of the Fathers of the Eastern Church. Basil is also the name of several early saints martyred in the East. The name was common in the eastern Mediterranean and was brought to England by the Crusaders. Basil is also the name of a common herb.

Beau
Pronunciation: boh
The name Beau is of French origin, and the meaning of Beau is "handsome", "sweetheart". The novel "*Beau Geste*"(1924) was a bestseller and a popular movie. Beau is also the name of Ashley and Melanie Wilkes child in Margaret

Mitchell's legendary "Gone with the Wind" (1936).

Benedict
Pronunciation: BEN-a-dikt
Benedict is of Latin origin from the Latin word, B*enedictus*. The meaning of Benedict is "blessed". Saint Benedict founded the Christian monastic order, the Benedictines. The name is popular with Roman Catholics and there have been 16 popes who shared the name Benedict.

Benjamin
Pronunciation: BEN-ja-men
Benjamin is of Hebrew origin, from the Hebrew name Benyamin. The meaning of Benjamin is "son of the right hand", "son of my old age". A biblical name; borne by the youngest and most beloved son of the patriarch Jacob and Rachel, who died giving birth to him. He was originally named Benoni.

Bennett
Pronunciation: BEN-et
Bennett is of French and Latin origin. The adopted surname has been used for both girl's and boy's names. Taken from the medieval vernacular form of Benedict.

Benson
Pronunciation: BEN-son
The adopted surname has been used as a given name since the 19th century. The meaning of the name Benson is "son of Ben". The name is also connected to a place name, Benson (formerly Bensington) in Oxfordshire.

Bentley
Pronunciation: BENT-lee
The name Bentley is of Old English origin. The meaning

of the name Bentley is "bent grass meadow". The adopted surname is used more commonly as a boy's name, however it is also used as a girl's name. Bentley is also a place name for many places in England.

Bernard
Pronunciation: ber-NARD
The name Bernard is of Old French and Old German origin. The meaning of the name is "strong", "brave bear". The name was brought to England by the Norman Conquest.
Three famous medieval saints bore the name. An 11th century Saint Bernard of Menthon is revered as the patron saint of mountaineers. Saint Bernard of Clairvaux (1090-1153), a founder of a monastic order, and a scholastic philosopher.

Blaise
Pronunciation: blayz
The name Blaise is of French and Latin origin. From Latin Blasius, and derived from "*blaesus*". The meaning of the name is "lisping", "stammering". Saint Blaise, a 4th-century Armenian bishop is supposedly endowed with miraculous healing power. He is regarded as the patron of those suffering from sore throats.

Blake
Pronunciation: blayk
Blake is of Old English origin. The meaning of the name Blake is "black", "pale". The adopted surname is used as both a boy's name and a girl's name. Blake was originally used as a nickname for someone with skin or hair that was either very dark

("blaec") or very light ("blac").

Boaz
Pronunciation: boa-Z
Boaz is of Hebrew origin. A biblical name; Boaz is the name of several characters. The name was revived by the Puritans, it was occasionally used in England during the 17th and 18th centuries. The meaning of the name is "swiftness", "strength".

Boris
Pronunciation: BOR-iss
Boris is of Russian and Slavic origin. Originally from the Tartar nickname, *Bogoris*. The meaning of the name is "small", "battle glory". Borne by a 9th-century ruler of Bulgaria who converted his Kingston to Christianity. A 10th-century Russian saint also known as Romanus, Saint Boris is known as the patron saint of Moscow.

Bowen
Pronunciation: BOH-en
The name Bowen is of Welsh origin. The meaning of the name Bowen is "son of Owen", "son of the young one".

Boyd
Pronunciation: boyd
Boyd is of Gaelic and Scottish origin. Boyd is an adopted Irish and Scottish surname. The name was first used as a surname in Scotland in the 13th century, it has been in regular use as a first name since the early 20th century. Scottish Gaelic, from the word *buidhe*, which means "yellow", "blonde".

Braden
Pronunciation: BRAY-den
The name Braden is of Irish and Gaelic origin. The

meaning of the name is "descendant of bradán". Bradán is a personal name that means "salmon". Braden is an adoptive Irish surname.

Bradley
Pronunciation: BRAD-lee
Bradley is of Old English origin. The meaning of Bradley is "broad meadow", "broad wood". Bradley is an adopted surname and also a place name. Bradley has been used as a given first name since the mid-19th century.

Brady
Pronunciation: BRAY-dee
The name Brady is of Irish and Gaelic origin. The meaning of the name is "descendant of Brádach". The name is used as both a boy's name and as a girl's names.

Brandon
Pronunciation: BRAN-den
Brandon is of Old English origin. The meaning of the name Brandon is "broom", "hill". Brandon is an adopted surname and an English Place name.

Braxton
Pronunciation: b-rax-ton
Braxton is of Old English origin. The meaning of Braxton is "Brock's town". Brock is an informal word used for "badger". Braxton is an adopted surname and a place name.

Brendan
Pronunciation: BREN-den
Brendan is of Celtic, Irish and Gaelic origin. The meaning of the name Brandan is "Prince". From an old Irish Gaelic name *Bréanainn*. The name was borne by a legendary 6th-century Irish abbot and

saint. Saint Brendan of Ireland is renowned for his adventurous traveling and scholarship. He was known as "the Voyager" after a seven-year voyage, possibly to North America.

Brennan
Pronunciation: BREN-an
Brennan is of Irish and Gaelic origin. The meaning of the name Brennan is "teardrop". Brennan is used as both a boy's name and as a girl's name. The name is also a variant of Brendan.

Brent
Pronunciation: brent
The name Brent is of Old English and Celtic origin. The meaning of the name is "hill", "mount". The name might also have been used to refer to criminals branded or burned as punishment. Brent is an adopted surname.

Brenton
Pronunciation: BREN-ton
Brenton is of Old English origin. The meaning of Brenton is "Bryni's settlement". Brenton is also an adopted surname and a place name.

Brett
Pronunciation: bret
The name Brett is of Latin origin. The meaning of the name is "from Britany", "from Britain". Brett is an adopted surname which originated in the Middle Ages, as an ethnic name for a native of Brittany.

Brian
Pronunciation: BRY-en
The name Brian is of Celtic, Irish and Gaelic origin. The meaning of the name Brian is "high", "noble". The name was possibly introduced to England by Norman invaders; however

the name was born by a great Irish chieftain, Brian Boroimhe. He was a warrior who became high king of Ireland and one of its greatest national heroes. After he defeated a Viking invasion and liberated the country from the Danes in 1014.

Broderick
Pronunciation: BRAH-der-ik
Broderick is a transferred use of the surname, which is derived from the Welsh personal name Rhydderch. The name could possibly be of Old German and mean, "famous power".

Brody
Pronunciation: BROH-dee
The name Brody is of Irish and Gaelic origin. The meaning of Brody is "ditch". Brody is also a place name, there is a Castle Brodie in Scotland. It could also possibly be related to "brathair" which means, "brother" in Irish.

Brooks
Pronunciation: brux
Brooks is of Old English and Old German origin. The meaning of Brooks is "water", "small stream". Brooks is used as both a boy's name and a girl's name.

Bruce
Pronunciation: brooce
Bruce is of Norman-French origin, introduced to Britain by the Norman Conquest. Adopted Scottish surname, originally a Norman baronial name and place name.

Bruno
Pronunciation: BROO-noh
The name Bruno is of Old German origin. From Old

German *brun*, the meaning of the name Bruno is "brown". Bruno was used as a name in the ruling families of Germany during the Middle Ages. Saint Bruno was a 10th-century German saint who founded an order of Carthusian monks, whom the German town of Brunswicl is named.

Bryn
Pronunciation: br-yn
The name Bryn is of Welsh origin. The meaning of the name Bryn is "hill". The name is also a short form of Brynmor. Bryn is used as both a boy's name and girl's name.

Bryce
Pronunciation: Bryce
The name Bruce is of Scottish origin. The meaning of Bryce is "of Britain". Bryce is a variant of Brice which originated as a transferred use of the Scottish surname, derived from the medieval given name.

Buddy
Pronunciation: bud-DEE
Buddy is a variant of the English word Bud. The meaning of Buddy is "brother", and it has been used as a nickname since the medieval times.

Byron
Pronunciation: BYE-ron
Byron is an adopted surname and English place name derived from *byre*, "barn", "cowshed". The name is of Old English origin. The meaning of Byron is "at the byres". The name was popular in the 19th century. Lord Byron was a poet renowned for his wildness and debauchery.

C

Caddis
Pronunciation: CAD-is
The name Caddis is of Old English origin. The meaning of Caddis is "worsted fabric".

Cade
Pronunciation: kayd
The name Cade is of Old English and Old French origin. The meaning of the name Cade is "round", "gentle cask". The adopted surname was originally used as a nickname. Cade was also the name of a character in Margaret Mitchell's, "Gone with the Wind" (1936).

Caden
Pronunciation: KAY-den
Caden is of Scottish origin, taken from the Scottish surname McCadden. The meaning of the name is "son of Cadán".

Cadogan
Pronunciation: ca-do-gan
Cadogan is of Welsh origin. Anglicised form of Cadwgan or cadwgawn, derived from *cad*, meaning "battle", *gwogann*, meaning "glory". The meaning of the name Cadogan is "battle glory". It is the name of several Welsh princes from the early Middle Ages. Borne by two characters in *Mabinogian*, the collection of Welsh legends.

Caesar
Pronunciation: SEE-zer
The name Caesar is of Latin origin. The meaning of Caesar is "head of hair". A famous bearer of the name was Julius Caesar (104-44BC). Due to his success and power, the name Caesar then became the title of the Roman emperors with the meaning "ruler".

Caius

Pronunciation: keys

The name Caius is of Latin origin. The meaning of Caius is "happy". The name is a common Roman form of the name Gaius.

Caiden

Pronunciation: KAY-den

The name Caiden is of Arabic origin. The name may also refer to an Old English word meaning "round". The name Caiden means "companion". It also a variant of the name Kaden.

Cain

Pronunciation: KA-yn

The name Cain is of Hebrew origin. The meaning of Cain is "acquired, spear". A Biblical name; Cain was Adam and Eve's first born son. He killed his brother in anger and jealousy, and he spent the rest of his life as a wanderer in exile.

Cairo

Pronunciation: KIE-ro

Cairo is of Arabic origin. The meaning of the name is "victorious". Cairo is also a place name, the capital of Egypt.

Caesar

Pronunciation: SEE-zer

The name Caesar is of Latin origin. The meaning of Caesar is "hair". From the family name of the legendary Roman emperor Gaius Julius Caesar, which was traditionally said to be derived from *caesus*, 'cut'. Cut from his dead mother's womb, Caesar was the first baby to have been delivered by Caesarean section.

Caleb

Pronunciation: KAY-leb

Caleb is of Hebrew origin. The meaning of the name Caleb is "faith, wholehearted". A biblical name; a companion of Moses and Joshua. Caleb was noted for his fearlessness and his devotion to God. The name was popular among the Puritans.

Callan
Pronunciation: KAL-an
The name Callan is of Gaelic and Scottish origin. The meaning of Callan is "battle, rock". Callan is originally a surname.

Callum
Pronunciation: KAL-um
Callum is of Scottish Gaelic origin. The name is a variant of Calum. Derived from the Latin first name Columba, meaning 'dove'. Borne by an early Celtic saint (521-597).

Calvin
Pronunciation: KAL-vin
The name Calvin is of French origin. The meaning of Calvin is "little bald one". An adopted French surname, from Old French *chauve*, 'bald'. Given at first in honor of the French theologian Jean Calvin (1509-1564).

Camden
Pronunciation: KAM-den
The name Camden is of Scottish and Gaelic origin. The meaning of the name Camden is "winding valley." Camden is also a place name.

Cameron
Pronunciation: KAM-er-en
Cameron is of Scottish and Gaelic origin. The meaning of Cameron is "crooked nose, crooked stream". Cameron is used as both a boy's name and a girl's name. The adopted Scottish surname was borne by a prominent Highland clan. The name was rarely used outside of Scotland before

the 1950's.

Camilo

Pronunciation: ka-MEE-loh

Camilo is of Latin origin. The meaning of the name Camilo is "helper to the priest". The name is a masculine variation of the name Camilla.

Campbell

Pronunciation: CAM-bel

Campbell is of Scottish and Gaelic origin. An adopted Scottish surname, from *cam beaul*. The meaning of the name Campbell is "crooked mouth". A family name of the Dukes of Argyll. The name has been in use since the mid-20th century.

Carl

Pronunciation: karl

The name Carl is of Old German origin. The name Carl is an old fashioned variation of Karl, the German form of Charles.

Carlos

Pronunciation: KAR-lohs

Carlos is of Spanish origin. The meaning of the name Carlos is "free man". The name is a variant of the name Charles.

Carlton

Pronunciation: KARL-ten

The name Carlton is of Old English origin. The meaning of Carlton is "free peasant settlement". Adopted surname and common English place name, from Old English carl.

Carson

Pronunciation: KAR-sen

Carson is of Scottish and Old English origin. The meaning of the name Cason is "son of the marsh dwellers". Carson is an adopted Scottish surname, possibly taken from the medieval name de Carsan. The first known bearer was Robert de Carsan in the 13th century.

75

Carter

Pronunciation: KAR-ter

Carter is of Old English origin. The meaning of the name Carter is "one who transports goods". Originally a surname and a given occupational name.

Casey

Pronunciation: KAY-see

The name Casey is of Irish and Gaelic origin. The meaning of Casey is "alert, watchful". The name Casey is used as both a boy's name, and as a girl's name. Casey is from the male Gaelic name *Cathasaigh*.

Cassius

Pronunciation: KASH-us

Cassius is of Latin origin. The meaning of the name Cassius is "empty, hollow". The name is an old Roman family clan name.

Cecil

Pronunciation: SESS-ul

The name Cecil is of Latin origin. The meaning of Cecil is "blind". An adopted surname from the Roman family name Caecilius, derived from Latin Caecus, 'blind'. The name was popular during the late 19th century.

Cedric

Pronunciation: SED-rik

The name Cedric is of Old English origin. The meaning of Cedric is "kind, loved". Possibly an altered form of the name Cerdic, a 6th-century king of Wessex. The name Cedric was invented by Sir Walter Scott for the character Cedric of Rotherwood for his book, *Ivanhoe* (1819).

Cesar

Pronunciation: sez-ZAR

Cesar is of Latin origin. The meaning of the name Cesar is "head of hair".

Chance

Pronunciation: chans

The name Chance is of Middle English origin. The meaning of Chance is "good fortune". Originally a surname. Chance is also a variant of the name Chauncey.

Chandler

Pronunciation: CHAND-ler

Chandler is of Middle English and Old French origin. The meaning of the name Chandler is "candle maker". The adopted surname was also an occupational name from 'chandele' meaning 'candle'. Chandler is used as both a boy's name and as a girl's name.

Charles

Pronunciation: charlz

Charles is of Old German origin. The meaning of the name Charles is "free man". Charles the Great (742-814) was also known as Charlemagne, was a powerful German leader who created a more ordered society out of the chaos that followed the fall of Rome. Charles became king of the Franks in 771, he was the first Holy Roman Emperor in 800. He united France and much of central Europe. He was said to have been eight feet tall and extremely strong. His widespread fame gave rise to many forms of his name. Charles and its variant forms have been favored by royalty of several different countries. Diminutives: Charley, Charlie, Chas, Chay, Chuck.

Chester

Pronunciation: CHES-ter

Chester if of Old English and Latin origin. The meaning of the name Chester is "camp of soldiers". Chester is an adopted surname and English place name that is derived from Latin castra, 'camp'.

77

Chris

Pronunciation: kris

The name Chris is of Greek origin. The meaning of Chris is "bearing Christ". Chris is a short form of the names Christopher and Christian.

Christian

Pronunciation: KRIS-chen

Christian is of Latin origin. The meaning of the name Christian is "follower of Christ". According to the Bible the term was first used at Antioch (Acts 11:26); 'And when he had found him, he brought him unto Antioch. And the disciples were called Christians first in Antioch'. The name Christian comes from the Latin girls name, Christianus. It may have become a popular male name due to the success of John Bunyan's 'Pilgrim's Progress' (1678), whose hero is called Christian.
Diminutives: Chris, Christie, Christy.

Christopher

Pronunciation: KRIS-toh-fer

Christopher is of Greek origin. The meaning of the name Christopher is "bearing Christ". From the Greek name Khristophoros, from Khristos. The name was popular among early Christians. The symbolic legend of giant Saint Christopher, 'the bearer of Christ', carried the Christ child safely across a river. Saint Christopher is considered the patron saint of travelers. The name has been in constant use since the 15th century.
Diminutives: Chris, Kris, Christie, Kester, Christy.

Cian

Pronunciation: KEE-an

The name Cian is of Irish and Gaelic origin. The meaning of Cian is "ancient". Borne by the name of Brian Boru's son in law, who played a major role in the battle of Clontarf in the 11th century.

Clarence
Pronunciation: KLARE-ence

Clarence is of Latin origin. The meaning of Clarence is "one who lives near the river Clare". Clarence was first used as a given name since the mid-19th century.

Clark
Pronunciation: klark

The name Clark is of Latin origin. The meaning of Clark is "clerk, cleric". An adopted surname, originally an occupational name for a clerk or cleric. The name was popularized in the 20th century by the actor Clark Gable (1901-1960). The name was also made famous by the fictional character Clark Kent, otherwise known as Superman.

Clay
Pronunciation: KLAY

Clay is of Old English origin. Originally an occupational or place name which involved clay. Clay was a valued natural resource in earlier times. Clay can be used as a short form of the name Clayton.

Clayton
Pronunciation: KLAYT-en

The name Clayton is of Old English origin. The meaning of Clayton is "clay settlement". The name is an adopted surname and English place name derived from Clay. Its use as a first name dates back to the beginning of the 19th century.

Clement
Pronunciation: KLEM-ent

Clement is of Latin origin. The meaning of the name Clement is "merciful". Borne by several early saints, including Clement of Alexandria (c.150-c215). A disciple of St Paul who became the first of thirteen popes bearing the name. The name was popular during the Middle Ages.

Clifford

Pronunciation: KLIF-erd

The name Clifford is of Old English origin. The meaning of Clifford is "cliff-side ford". Originally a surname used as given name from the seventh-century.
Diminutive; Cliff.

Clifton

Pronunciation: KLIF-ten

The name Clifton is of Old English Origin. The meaning of Clifton is "town by the cliff". Originally a surname used as given name.

Clinton

Pronunciation: KLIN-ten

Clinton is of Old English origin. The meaning of Clinton is "fenced settlement". Clinton is both a surname and a place name from *Glympton*, in Oxfordshire.

Clive

Pronunciation: kleeve

The name Clive is of Old English origin. The meaning of Clive is "cliff, slope". Clive is an adopted surname and place name from Old English Clif. The name was made popular in honour of Robert Clive, a famous English soldier known as Clive of India.

Clyde

Pronunciation: klyd

The name Clyde is of Scottish origin. Clyde is also a place name, the River Clyde in Scotland. Clyde Barrow was a notorious outlaw, who made the name well known during The Great Depression with his partner Bonnie.

Cody

Pronunciation: KO-dee

The name Cody is of Irish and Gaelic origin. The meaning of the name Cody is "helper". Cody is used as both a boy's name, and as a girl's name.

Cole

Pronunciation: kohl

Cole is of Middle English and Old French origin. The meaning of Cole is "charcoal". Originally a surname that was derived from a medieval given name. Cole is used as both a boy's name and as a girl's name.

Colin

Pronunciation: KOH-lin

Colin is of Irish and Scottish Gaelic origin. The meaning of the name is "young creature". The name has been used as an Anglicized form of Cailean. Collin is a diminutive form of the medieval name Colle, which is a short form of the Greek name Nicholas.

Conan

Pronunciation: KOH-nan

Conan is of English, Irish and Scottish Gaelic origin. The meaning of Conan is "hound, high". The name was taken to Ireland after the Norman Conquest. Borne in Irish legend, Conan was a warrior who fought under Finn mac Fumhail (Finn McCool). Also the name of a seventh-century saint who was an Irish missionary on the Isle of Man.

Connor

Pronunciation: KAH-ner

Connor is of Irish and Gaelic origin. Anglicised form of the Irish Gaelic name Conchobhar, Borne in Irish legend by the son of Nessa, who became a legendary king of Ulster. As an old man, he lusted after the young Deirdre and forced her to marry him. The meaning of Connor is "hound lover".

Conrad
Pronunciation: KAHN-rad

Conrad is of Old German origin. The meaning of Conrad is "brave, counsel". The name of 10th-century bishop of Constance, it was reintroduced to the English-speaking world in the 19th century. Conrad is also the name of nine saints and several German kings during the Middle Ages.

Constantine
Pronunciation: KAHN-stan-teen

Constantine is of Latin origin. The meaning of Constantine is "constant". Constantine the Great (c. 288-337) was the first Cristian emperor, who left Rome to found Constantinople. The name was popular among the Puritans as virtue name. Constantine was also the name of 11 Byzantine emperors and a royal name in Greece. Borne by three Scottish kings.

Cooper
Pronunciation: KOO-per

The name Cooper is of Old English origin. The meaning of Cooper is "barrel maker". The name may also be the English form of a German surname which means "coppersmith".

Corey
Pronunciation: KOR-ee

The name Corey is an English surname derived from an Old Norse personal name Kori. Corey is used as both a boy's name, and as a girl's name. The meaning of the name may mean "God, peace".

Cornelius
Pronunciation: kor-NEEL-yus

The name Cornelius is of Latin origin. The Roman family name may be derived from cornu. The meaning of Cornelius is "horn".

Cornelius is a famous Latin clan name. A biblical name: borne by a Roman centurion converted by St Peter. Cornelius is also the name of a third-century pope who is venerated as a saint.

Cortez

Pronunciation: kor-TEZ

Cortez is of Spanish origin. The meaning of the name Cortez is "courteous". The name is also a variant of Curtis. Cortez was the surname of the 16th-century Spanish explorer Hernando Cortes. His small expeditionary force conquered the Aztec civilization of Mexico.

Courtney

Pronunciation: COURT-ney

Courtney is of Old French origin. The meaning of Courtney is "domain of Curtis". The name is both a surname and a place name. Courtney is a Norman baronial name from places in Northern France called Courtenay. Courtney is used as both a boy's name and a girl's name.

Craig

Pronunciation: krayg

Craig is of Scottish and Gaelic origin. The meaning of Craig is "rocky". The name is derived from the word "crag". Originally Craig was used as a Scottish surname.

Cruz

Pronunciation: Krooz

Cruz is of Spanish and Portuguese origin. The meaning of the name Cruz is "cross."

Curtis

Pronunciation: KERT-iss

The name Curtis is of English and Old French origin. The meaning of Curtis is "Courteous, polite". Originally used as a nickname in the Middle Ages, for courteous person.

83

Curtis is also used as a surname. Curtis was originally used as a first name in the 19th century.

Cyrus

Pronunciation: SY-russ

Cyrus is of Greek origin. The meaning of Cyrus is "lord". Derived from Kyros of the name of several kings of Persia. A biblical name; Cyrus is named in the book of Isaiah, as the one who would overthrow Babylon and liberate the Israelites. In the fifth century BC, Cyrus the Great conquered Babylon at the height of its powers and founded the Persian Empire.

D

Dace
Pronunciation: dayce
The name Dace is of French origin. The meaning of Dace is "of the nobility". The name may also be used as a form of Dasius and Datius.

Dacey
Pronunciation: DAY-cee
Dacey is of Irish, Gaelic and Latin origin. The meaning of Dacey is "from the South". The name is used as both a boy's name and as a girl's name.

Dag
Pronunciation: dag
Dag is of Scandinavian origin. The meaning of the name Dag is "daylight". Borne in mythology; Dag was the son of Night who brought the daylight as he rode his horse around the earth.

Dagan
Pronunciation: DAY-gan
The name Dagan is of Hebrew origin. The meaning of Dagan is "the earth".

Dagobert
Pronunciation: DAG-o-bert
The name Dagobert is of Old German origin. The meaning of Dagobert is "bright day".

Dahy
Pronunciation: DA-hy
Dahy is of Irish and Gaelic origin. The meaning of the name of Dahy is "quick footed".

Dailey
Pronunciation: DAY-lee
The name Dailey is of Irish and Gaelic origin. The meaning of Dailey is "assembly".

Dainard
Pronunciation: DAYN-ard
Dainard is of Old English origin. The meaning of Dainard is "bold Dane".

Dakota
Pronunciation: da-KOH-tah
Dakota is of Native American Indian origin. The meaning of the name Dakota is "friend". Originally a tribal and place name.

Dale
Pronunciation: dayl
The name Dale is of Old English origin. The meaning of Dale is "Valley". Originally a surname, Dale is also a place name.

Dalton
Pronunciation: DOLL-ton
The name Dalton is of Old English origin. The meaning of Dalton is "from the valley town". Dalton is also a place name.

Damian
Pronunciation: DAY-mee-en
Damian is of Greek origin. The meaning of the name Damian is "to tame". Anglicised from the Greek name Damianos, from *daman*, 'to tame'. Saint Damian, a 4th-century Greek martyr is known as the patron saint of doctors. The Belgian priest Father Damien is honored for giving his life to the lepers of Molokai in Hawaii.

Damon
Pronunciation: DAY-mon
The name Damon is of Greek origin. The meaning of Damon is "one who Tames". From Greek demos, 'land' or 'people'.

The name is a variant of Damian.

Dane
Pronunciation: dayn
Dane is of English origin. The meaning of the name Dane is "from Denmark". Originally a surname that indicated Danish ancestry.

Daniel
Pronunciation: DAN-yel
The name Daniel is of Hebrew origin. The meaning of Daniel is "God has judged". A biblical name; borne in the Old Testament by a prophet and writer, his story is told in the book of Daniel. He is probably most known for being thrown into a den of lions and surviving (Daniel 6:16). Diminutives: Dan, Dannie, Danny

Danny
Pronunciation: DANN-ee
Danny is of Hebrew origin. The meaning of the name Danny is "God has judged". Danny is a variant of the name Daniel.

Dante
Pronunciation: DAHN-tay
Dante is of Spanish, Latin and Italian origin. The meaning of the name Dante is "lasting, enduring". Poet, Dante Alighieri was best known for Dante's Inferno, his graphic description of the medieval version of Hell.

Danyal
Pronunciation: DAN-yal
The name Danyal is of Hebrew origin. The meaning of Danyal is "God has judged". Danyal is a variant of the name Daniel.

Darcy
Pronunciation: DAR-cee

The name Darcy is of Irish and Gaelic origin. The meaning of Darcy is "dark". An adopted Norman baronial surname (D'Arcy). The name was introduced to Britain during the Norman Conquest. Darcy is used as both a boy's name, and as a girl's name. Darcy is also a Norman place name.

Dargan
Pronunciation: DAR-gan
The name Dargan is of Irish origin. The meaning of Dargan is "black haired". The name is a variant of Deegan.

Darius
Pronunciation: DARE-ee-us
The name Darius is of Greek and Persian origin. The meaning of Darius is "maintains possessions well". From the Greek name Dareios, derived from Old Persian *darayavush*, from *daraya*, 'posses', and *vahu*, 'well'. A biblical name; born in the Old Testament by Darius the Great. He was the governor of Persia, who became king in 521BC (Ezra 4:5). Darius is also the name of a saint, who was martyred at Nicaea.

Darrell
Pronunciation: DARR-ell
The name Darrell is of Old English and Old French origin. The meaning of Darrell is "open". An adopted surname and originally a French place name, Arielle in the northern region of Calvados. Darrell is also a variant of the name Darryl.

Darren
Pronunciation: DAR-en
Darren is of Irish and Gaelic origin. The meaning of the

89

name Darren is "great". Originally an adopted Irish surname, first used as a given name in the 20th century. The name became popular during the 1960's.

Dave
Pronunciation: DAY-ve
The name Dave is of Hebrew origin. The meaning of Dave is "beloved; son of David". Dave is a variant of the name David.

David
Pronunciation: DAY-vid
The name David is of Hebrew origin. The meaning of David is "beloved". From Hebrew *dawid*, which means 'beloved'. A biblical name; borne in the Old Testament by the youngest son of Jesse. David was a shepherd, poet, musician, soldier, king and a prophet. He slew the giant Goliath and found favor with Saul with his talented harp playing. He is the only David mentioned in the Bible. The 6th-century saint, St David is regarded as patron saint of Wales. Diminutives: Dave, Davey, Davy.

Dawson
Pronunciation: DAW-sun
The name Dawson is of Old English origin. The meaning of Dawson is "son of David". Originally a form of the medieval surname.

Deacon
Pronunciation: DEE-ken
Deacon is of Greek origin. The meaning of the name Deacon is "dusty one; messenger". A deacon is a ministerial assistant in a Christian congregation.

Dean
Pronunciation: deen

Dean if of Old English origin. The meaning of the name Dean is "Valley". An adopted surname, derived from the Old English *denu*, meaning 'valley'. Dean is also a place name.

Declan
Pronunciation: DECK-lan
The name Declan is of Irish origin. The meaning of Declan is unknown. Anglicised form of the Irish Gaelic name Deaglán. Borne by a 5th century Irish bishop of Ardmore.

Dennis
Pronunciation: DEN-iss
Dennis is of English and Greek origin. The meaning of the name Dennis is "follower of Dionysius". The name is a variant of Dionysius. A biblical name; borne by a judge of Athens who was converted to Christianity by the apostle Paul. A 3rd-century evangelist missionary to Gaul and a traditional patron saint of France was said to have been beheaded in Paris in 272. He was then supposed to have walked for two miles carrying his own head, before placing it down on the site which is now where the Cathedral of Saint Denis stands. Diminutives: Dennie, Denny.

Denzil
Pronunciation: DEN-zil
The name Denzil is of Old English origin. The meaning of Denzil is unknown. An adopted surname, from Denzell, in Cornwall. It was first adopted by the Holles family, when it became connected to them by marriage.

Derek

Pronunciation: DARE-ik

The name Derek is of Old German origin. The meaning of Derek is "people's ruler". The name is German form of Theodoric. Derek was introduced to Britain in the late Middle Ages by immigrant Flemish weavers and merchants.

Desmond

Pronunciation: DEZ-mund

The name Desmond is of Gaelic and Irish origin. The meaning of Desmond is "from South Munster". Originally an adopted surname and Irish place name referring to Munster which is one of the five regions of ancient Ireland. From Irish Gaelic Deas Mumhain, which means 'South Munster'. The name was first used in Ireland in the mid-19th century.

Devon

Pronunciation: DEV-en

Devon is of English origin. The meaning of the name Devon is uncertain. Devon is originally an adopted surname, English county name, and the name of several towns in America. The name is used as both a boy's name and as a girl's name.

Dexter

Pronunciation: DEKS-ter

The name Dexter is of Old English and Latin origin. The meaning of Dexter is "right handed, fortunate". Originally derived from Greek *dexi*, meaning ' worship'. Dexter is an Old English occupational name.

Diego

Pronunciation: dee-AY-go

Diego is of Spanish origin. The meaning of the name Diego is "he who supplants". Borne by a Mexican peasant to whom the Virgin of Guadalupe appeared was called Juan Diego.

Digby

Pronunciation: DIG-bee
The name Digby is of Old Norse origin. The meaning of Digby is "town by the ditch". Digby is also a place name.

Dillan

Pronunciation: DILL-an
The name Dillan is of Irish and Gaelic origin. The meaning of Dillan is "like a lion, loyal". The name is a variant of Dillon. Dillan is used as both a boy's name and as a girl's name.

Dion

Pronunciation: DEE-on
Dion is of Greek origin. The meaning of the name Dion is unknown. Dion is a short form of the Dionysius.

Dirk

Pronunciation: derk
The name Dirk is of Dutch origin. The meaning of the Dirk is "the people's ruler". The name is a variation of Derek. The name was made popular by a Scottish born actor and writer, Dirk Bogarde. Dirk is also a Scottish term for a small, sharp knife.

Dominic

Pronunciation: DAH-ma-nik
Dominic is of Latin origin. The meaning of the name Dominic is "Lord". From Latin *Dominicus*, which means 'of the Lord'. St Dominic (1170-1221) founded the Dominican order of the monks. The name became popular

93

throughout the Christian world. Diminutive: Dom.

Donald
Pronunciation: DAHN-ald
Donald is of Gaelic and Scottish origin. The meaning of Donald is "great chief". Anglicised form of the Scottish Gaelic name Domhall (*doe-nall*). From Old Celtic *dubno*, meaning 'world', and *val*, 'rule'. Donald is one of the clan names of Scotland. Borne by several early kings of Scotland. Diminutives: Don, Donny.

Donovan
Pronunciation: DAH-na-vun
The name Donovan is of Irish and Gaelic origin. The meaning of Donovan is "dark haired chieftain".

Doran
Pronunciation: DOR-an
The name Doran is of Irish and Gaelic origin. The meaning of Doan is "stranger, exile".

Dorian
Pronunciation: DOR-ee-en
The name Dorian is of Greek origin. The meaning of Dorian is "Descendant of Dorus". Borne by an ancient Greek people and meaning 'from Doris' (an area of northern Greece). The name was popularised by Oscar Wilde's novel, *The Picture of Dorian Gray* (1891).

Dougal
Pronunciation: DOO-gal
The name Dougal is of Celtic origin. The meaning of Dougal is "dark stranger". Anglicised of the Irish Gaelic name Dubhghall, meaning 'dark stranger'. The name was given by the Irish to

invading Vikings in the 9th century. Diminutives: Dough, Dougie.

Douglas
Pronunciation: DUG-las
The name Douglas is of Gaelic and Scottish origin. The meaning of Douglas is "black river". Initially derived from the River Douglas, the name is also a place name. The name was adopted by a powerful clan and used as a first name in the 16th century. The river name and surname is also found in Ireland, Scotland and in the Isle of Man. Diminutives: Doug, Dougie.

Dudley
Pronunciation: DUD-lee
Dudley is of Old English origin. The meaning of the name Dudley is "people's field". Dudley is an adopted surname and English place name. An aristocratic family name of the Earls of Leicester. Dudley has been used as a given name since the 19th century.

Duncan
Pronunciation: DUN-kin
The name Duncan is of Gaelic and Scottish origin. The meaning of Duncan is "dark warrior". Borne by a 7th-century abbot of Iona and two medieval kings of Scotland, including Duncan I who was murdered by Macbeth in 1040. Shakespeare immortalised him in his play, *Macbeth* (1606).

Dunstan
Pronunciation: DUN-sten
Dunstan is of Old English origin. The meaning of Dunstan is "brown hill". From Old English *dun*, 'hill', and *stan* meaning, 'stone'. St Dunstan was a

renowned 10th century Archbishop of Canterbury, who restored the monastery system in England. Dunstan is also a place name.

Dylan
Pronunciation: DIL-an
The name Dylan is of Welsh origin. The meaning of Dylan is "son of the sea". Borne in a Welsh legend by the son of a sea god. Welsh poet Dylan Thomas (1914-1953), and American singer Bob Dylan (1941) popularised the name.

E

Eamon
Pronunciation: AY-mon
Eamon is of Irish and Gaelic origin. The meaning of the name Eamon is "wealthy protector". The name is a variant of Edmund.

Earl
Pronunciation: erl
The name Earl is of Old English origin. The meaning of Earl is "nobleman, warrior". From Old English *eorl*. The name was originally based on the English title, and used as a nickname for people who worked for the aristocratic household of Earl.

Earland
Pronunciation: erl-AND
The name Earland is of Old English origin. The meaning of Earland is "earl's land". Earland is also a place name.

Earlston
Pronunciation: erl-ST-on
The name Earlston is of Old English origin. The meaning of Earlston is "earl's settlement".

Early
Pronunciation: erl-EE
Early is of Old English origin. The meaning of the name Early is "eagle wood". Possibly derived from the Old English term *eorlic*, or from the English word 'early'.

Earvin
Pronunciation: EAR-vin
The name Earvin is of Gaelic origin. The meaning of Earvin is "green, freshwater". The name is a variant of Irvin. The name was made famous by American basketball legend Earvin 'Magic' Johnson.

Eastman
Pronunciation: EES-tman
The name Eastman is of Old English origin. The meaning of Eastman is "man from the East".

Easton
Pronunciation: EES-tun
Easton is of Old English origin. The meaning of the name Easton is "East settlement". The name may possibly have been derived from an Old English phrase meaning, 'island of stones'.

Eben
Pronunciation: EBB-an
The name Eben is of Hebrew origin. The meaning of Eben is "stone". The name is also used as a nickname for Ebenezer.

Ebenezer
Pronunciation: EBB-an-ee-zer
The name Ebenezer is of Hebrew origin. The meaning of Ebenezer is "stone of help". A biblical name; Ebenezer was the name of a memorial stone set up by the prophet Samuel in order to mark a critical battle and victory in Jewish history. The name was first used as a given first name in the 17th century by the Puritans. Charles Dicken's popularised the name in his novel, *A Christmas Carol* (1843).

Edan
Pronunciation: EE-dan
The name Edan is of Irish, Gaelic and Scottish origin. The meaning of Edan is "fire". The name is a variant of Aidan. Edan is also a saint's name.

Edbert
Pronunciation: ED-bert

The name Edbert is of Old English origin. The meaning of Edbert is "bright".

Eddie

Pronunciation: ED-ee
Eddie is of English origin. The meaning of the name Eddie is unknown. The name is used as a nickname for Edgar, Edmund, Edward and Edwin. Eddie is used as both a boy's name and as a girl's name.

Edel

Pronunciation: ED-el
Edel is of Old German origin. The meaning of the name Edel is "noble".

Edgar

Pronunciation: ED-gar
Edgar is of Old English origin. The meaning of the name Edgar is "spear". From the Old English name Eadgar, from *ead*, 'riches' or 'prosperous', and *gar*, 'spear'. A royal name in Anglo-Saxon England. Borne by a 10th-century king of England. Edgar is one of few early Anglo-Saxon names to have survived the Norman Conquest. Shakespeare used the name for the son of the Duke of Gloucester in *King Lear* (1605). Diminutives: Ed, Eddy, Eddie

Edmund

Pronunciation: ED-mund
The name Edmund is of Old English origin. The meaning of Edmund is "wealthy protector". From the Old English name Eadmund, from *ead*, 'rich', and *mund*, 'protection'. Edmund is the name of several early royal and saintly figures. The name was one of few early Anglo-Saxon names to have survived the Norman Conquest. Diminutives: Ed,

Eddy, Eddie, Ned, Neddie, Neddy, Ted, Teddy, Teddie.

Edward
Pronunciation: ED-werd
Edward is of Old English origin. The meaning of the name Edward is "wealthy guard". From the Old English name Eadweard, from *ead*, 'rich', and *weard*, 'guardian'. Edward is one of the few Anglo-Saxon names to have survived the Norman Conquest. Borne by three Anglo-Saxon kings and eight kings of England since the Norman Conquest. King Edward the Confessor, 1042-1066 was also a saint. Edward is a consistently popular name. Diminutives: Ed, Eddie, Eddy, Ned, Neddy, Neddie, Ted, Teddy, Teddie.

Edwin
Pronunciation: ED-win
The name Edwin is of Old English origin. The meaning of Edwin is "wealthy friend". From the Old English name Eadwine, from *ead*, 'rich', and *wine*, 'friend'. Borne by a 7th-century king of Northumberland who converted to Christianity. Edwin is one of the few Anglo-Saxon names to have survived the Norman Conquest. The name was revived in the 19th century. Diminutives: Ed, Eddie.

Eli
Pronunciation: EE-lye
The name Eli is of Hebrew origin. The meaning of Eli is "high". The Hebrew meaning is, "height, elevation". A biblical name; borne in the Old Testament by a high priest who brought up the prophet Samuel. The holy name was

101

popular among Puritans in the 17th century.

Elias

Pronunciation: ee-LYE-us

Elias is of Greek and Hebrew origin. The meaning of the name Elias is "Jehovah is God". A biblical name; borne in the New Testament, from the Greek form of Elijah.

Eliot

Pronunciation: EL-i-ot

The name Eliot is of Greek and Hebrew origin. The meaning of Eliot is "Jehovah is God". The name is a variant of the biblical name, Elias. An adopted surname, diminutive of Elie. Also the Old French form of Elias.

Elroy

Pronunciation: EL-roy

Elroy is of French origin. The meaning of the name Elroy is "the king". The name is a variation of Leroy. Possibly influenced by the Spanish *el*, 'the'.

Elwin

Pronunciation: EL-win

The name Elwin is of Old English origin. The meaning of Elwin is "elf, fair brow". From Old English *aethel*, 'nobel', and *wine*, 'friend'. Variant of Elvin.

Elwyn

Pronunciation: EL-win

Elwyn is of Gaelic and Welsh origin. The meaning of the name Elwyn is, "white, blessed, holy". Influenced by Welsh *(g)wyn*. A variant of the name Alan. Elwyn is also a form of the name of a 6th-century Irish saint.

Emil

Pronunciation: AY-mul

The name Emil is of Latin origin. The meaning of Emil is "rival, eager". The German name is derived from the Latin *Aemilius*, meaning 'eager'.

Emile
Pronunciation: AY-mile
Emile is of Latin origin. The meaning of the name Emile is "rival, eager". The name is a variant of Emil. From the Roman surname *Aesmilius*. The name was made popular by the French writer Emile Zola (1840-1902).

Emanuel
Pronunciation: ee-MAN-yo-el
Emanuel is of Hebrew origin. The meaning of the name Emanuel is "God is with us". A biblical name; borne in the Old Testament to the child whose birth Isaiah foretold. The name was applied to the New Testament, to the coming Messiah. Diminutive: Manny.

Emmanuel
Pronunciation: ee-MAN-yoo-el
Emmanual is of Hebrew origin. The meaning of the name Emmanuel is "God is with us". The Hebrew for of Immanuel. A biblical name; borne in the Old Testament. The name was applied to the New Testament, a name title for the coming Messiah. Diminutive: Manny.

Eric
Pronunciation: AIR-ik
The name Eric is of Old Norse origin. The meaning of Eric is "complete ruler". Old Norse, from *ei*, 'always', and *ric*, 'ruler'. The name was introduced to Britain during the 9th century by Scandinavian settlers. The original form is Erik, borne by nine Danish kings. The name was revived in the 19th century. Eric is also used as

a nickname for Frederic. Diminutives: Rick, Ricky.

Ernest
Pronunciation: ERN-ist
Ernest is of Old German origin. The meaning of the name Ernest is "seriousness". From the Old German name Ernst, meaning 'earnestness', or 'seriousness'. The Hanoverians introduced the name to Britain during the 18th century. The name became more popular due to Oscar Wilde's play, *The Importance of Being Ernest* (1899). Diminutives: Ern, Ernie, Erny.

Esmond
Pronunciation: EZ-mund
Esmund is of Old English origin. The meaning of Esmond is "ease of protection". From an Old English name, Eastmund, from *east*, 'grace', and *mund*, 'protection'. The name is an adopted surname in modern times, due to the success of Thackeray's *History of Henry Esmond* (1852).

Ethan
Pronunciation: EE-than
Ethan is of Hebrew origin. The meaning of the name Ethan is "firmness". A biblical name; Ethan the Ezrahite was mentioned in the Old Testament. Known for his wisdom, Solomon was superior in wisdom. Ethan Allen (1738-1789) made the name more popular in America after he played an important role in the American War of Independence.

Eugene
Pronunciation: you-JEEN
The name Eugene is of Greek origin. The meaning of Eugene is "noble

aristocrat". From the Old French form of a Greek name, derived from *eugenios*. 'noble'. Borne by several saints, two bishops and four popes. Variations: Eoan, Euan, Ewan, Ewen.

Evan
Pronunciation: EV-an
The name Evan is of Hebrew, Scottish and Welsh origin. The meaning of Evan is "God is gracious". Anglicisation of Ieuan, Evan is the Welsh form of John. Scotland also uses Evan as an anglicised form of Eoghan. The Hebrew meaning of Evan means "rock".

Evelyn
Pronunciation: EV-e-lyn
Evelyn is of Norman origin. Anglicised form of the Norman French feminine name Aveline. Evelyn is used as both a boy's name, and as a girl's name. The named was adopted as a boy's name in the 17th century. Originally a surname and used as a given name.

Everard
Pronunciation: EV-er-ard
Everard is of Old English and Old German origin. The meaning of the name Everard is " brave, boar". Taken from an Old English name, from *eofor*, 'boar', and *heard*, 'strong'. The Norman invaders used an Old German version. The Norman name has been used as a given name since the 19th century.

Ezra
Pronunciation: AIRZ-rah
The name Ezra is of Hebrew origin. The meaning of Ezra is "help". A biblical name;

105

borne by prophet and author of the fifteenth book of the Bible. Ezra is one of the Old Testament names used by the Puritans.

F

Fabian
Pronunciation: FAY-bee-en
Fabian is of Latin origin. The meaning of the name Fabian is "bean". From the Roman family name Fabius. Borne of 16 saints and a 3rd-century pope. The socialist Fabian Society, founded in 1884, was named after a Roman general who resisted Hannibal's 3rd-century advance on Rome.

Farran
Pronunciation: FA-rran
The name Farran is of Old English and Old French origin. The meaning of Farran is "handsome servant". The name is a variant of the Old English name, Farren.

Felix
Pronunciation: FEEL-iks
The name Felix is of Latin origin. The meaning of Felix is "happy, lucky". From Felicitas, Roman goddess of good fortune and happiness. The name was borne by several saints and three popes. Felix was a popular name for early Christians.

Fergus
Pronunciation: FER-gus
Fergus is of Irish, Gaelic and Scottish origin. The meaning of the name Fergus is "vigorous man". Irish, anglicised form of Gaelic name Fearghas, from *fear*, 'man', and *gus*, 'vigour'. The name was borne in Irish legend by Fergus mac Roich. Saint Fergus (8th century) was a missionary to Scotland.
Diminutive: Fergie

Fenton
Pronunciation: FEN-ton
The name Fenton is of Old English origin. The meaning of Fenton is "marsh settlement". Fenton is also a

108

place name from *fenn tûn*.

Finbar
Pronunciation: FIN-bar
Finbar is of Gaelic and Irish origin. The meaning of the name Finbar is "white, fair head". Irish, anglicised form of the Gaelic name Fionnbharr, from *fionn*, 'white, fair', and *barr*, 'head'. Finbar is a fairy king in Irish mythology. Finbar was a 6th-century bishop of Cork, said to have crossed the Irish Sea on horseback. Diminutives: Finn, Bairre, Barry.

Fingal
Pronunciation: FIN-gal
The name Fingal is of Gaelic and Scottish origin. The meaning of Fingal is "fair, white stranger". Borne in Gaelic legend by the heroic father of Ossian. The name was originally used by the Irish for Norse settlers in Ireland. James Macpherson's poem Fingal (1762).

Finlay
Pronunciation: FIN-lay
Finlay is of Scottish and Gaelic origin. The meaning of the name Finlay is "fair, white warrior". Scottish, anglicised form of the Gaelic name Fionnlagh, from *fionn*, 'white, fair' and *laogh*, 'Warrior'.

Finn
Pronunciation: FIN
The name Finn of Irish, Gaelic and Old German origin. The meaning of Finn is "white, fair". Irish, anglicised form of *fionn*, 'fair, white'. Finn mac Cumhaill is a legendary hero of Irish mythology.

Fletcher
Pronunciation: FLECH-er

Fletcher is of Old French origin. The meaning of the name Fletcher is "arrow maker". The adopted surname is originally an occupational name for an arrow maker. From Old French *fleche*, 'arrow'. Fletcher Christian was the famous leader of the mutiny on the Bounty in 1789.

Florian
Pronunciation: FLOR-ee-an
The name Florian is of Latin origin. The meaning of Florian is "Flower". Derived from the Latin word flos, 'flower'. From a Roman clan name. Saint Florian was a 3rd century Roman soldier.

Floyd
Pronunciation: F-lo-yd
The name Floyd is of Welsh origin. The meaning of Floyd is "grey haired". The adopted Welsh surname, is a derivative of Lloyd, from the Welsh *llwyd*, 'grey'.

Flyn
Pronunciation: FL-yn
Flyn is of Irish and Gaelic origin. The meaning of the name Flyn is "descendant of Flann". The name is a variant of Flynn.

Francesco
Pronunciation: FRAN-ches-co
Francesco is of Latin origin. The meaning of the name Francesco is "Frenchman". Francesco is a variant of the Latin name, Francis.

Francis
Pronunciation: FRAN-sis
The name Francis is of Latin origin. The meaning of Francis if "Frenchman". Anglicised form of the Italian name Francisco, derived from the Latin Franciscus which means

'French'. France was originally the kingdom of the Franks. The name was assumed by Saint Francis of Assisi (1181-1226), he is known as the gentle giant and associated with nature after preaching birds. Frances is the feminine form. Diminutives: Frank, Frankie

Franklin
Pronunciation: FRANK-lin
The name Franklin is of Old English origin. The meaning of Franklin is "freeman". The adopted surname is taken from Old English *francoleyn,* which means 'a freeman', specifically a landowner, not of noble birth, typically a prosperous farmer. Diminutives: Frank, Frankie.

Frederick
Pronunciation: FRED-er-ik
The name Frederick is of Old French and Old German origin. The meaning of Frederick is "peaceful ruler". The Old English name Freodhoric was superceded by the Old German, Frithuric, derived from *frithu*, 'peace', and *ric*, 'ruler'. The Hanoverians brought the name to Britain in the 18th century.

G

Gabriel

Pronunciation: GAY-bree-el

The name Gabriel is of Hebrew origin. The meaning of Gabriel is "Hero of God". A biblical name; borne by the name Archangel Gabriel, one of God's chief messengers, and sometimes regarded as the angel of death. In the New Testament, he appeared to Mary and told her that she was to be the mother of Christ. Diminutive: Gabe.

Gareth

Pronunciation: GARE-eth

Gareth is of Welsh origin. The meaning of the name Gareth is "gentle". The name first appeared in Sir Thomas Malory's 15th-century account of the legendary Round Table, *Morte D'Arthur*. Sir Gareth was well known for his modesty and bravery. Diminutives: Garth, Gary, Garry.

Garfield

Pronunciation: GARF-ield

The name Garfield is of Old English origin. The meaning of Garfield is "spear field". The adopted surname was most likely used as a first name in honour of J A Garfield (1831-1881), a 20th-century president of the U.S,

Garry

Pronunciation: GAR-ee

The name Garry is of Old English origin. The meaning of Garry is "spear". The name is a diminutive of Gareth. Gary Cooper popularised the name during the 1930's, he had taken the name from his hometown Gary, Indiana.

Gavin

Pronunciation: GAV-en

113

Gavin is of Welsh origin. The meaning of the name Gavin is "white falcon". The name is a variation of the medieval name Gawain.

Gawain
Pronunciation: GA-wain
The name Gawain is of Welsh and Scottish origin. The meaning of Gawain is "white falcon". The name is a variant of Gavin.

Geoffrey
Pronunciation: JEF-ree
Geoffrey is of Old German origin. The meaning of the name Geoffrey is "peace". The name was introduced to Britain during the Norman Conquest. Geoffrey was a popular name during the medieval era.

George
Pronunciation: JORJ
The name George is of Greek origin. The meaning of George is "farmer". From Greek *georgos*, meaning 'farmer'. The name was influenced by Old Latin and Old French. Borne by several early saints, including St George, a knight who became the patron saint of England. He achieved legendary status through the medieval story of him slaying a fire breathing dragon. The legend is a symbolic tale of good triumphing evil, with the dragon being the devil. The name is a royal name, borne by six kings of England.

Gerald
Pronunciation: JARE-ald
The name Gerald is of Old German origin. The meaning of Gerald is "spear ruler". The name was popular during the medieval era and was later revived in the 19th century.

Diminutives: Ged, Der, Gerry. Jed, Jerry,

Gerrard
Pronunciation: JARE-ard
The name Gerrard is of Old German origin. The meaning of Gerrard is "spear ruler". The name is a variant of Gerald. The name was popular during the medieval era, and later revived during the 19th century. Diminutives: Gerry, Jerry.

Gilbert
Pronunciation: GIL-bert
Gilbert is of Old French origin. The meaning of the name Gilbert is "bright promise". It was a Norman introduction to Britain. Diminutives: Gil, Gilly, Gillie.

Giles
Pronunciation: jiles
The name Giles if of Greek origin. The meaning of Giles is "small goat". The name is an altered version of the Latin name Aegidius, from the Greek name Aigidios. The name refers to the goat skin that ancient shields were made of. St Giles is regarded as the patron saint of cripples, beggars, and blacksmiths. Churches that are dedicated to him are typically located outside of city centers, where cripples were condemned to live.

Glen
Pronunciation: glen
Glen is of Irish and Gaelic origin. The meaning of Glen is "glen". The adopted surname is from Gaelic *gleann*, meaning 'valley'. A Glen is a narrow valley between hills. The name is also a place name.

Glyn
Pronunciation: glin
The name Glyn is of Irish and Gaelic origin. The meaning of Glyn is "valley of water". Glyn is a place name. The name is also a variant of Glen. Glyn is used as both a boy's name and as girl's name.

Goldwin
Pronunciation: GOLD-win
The name Goldwin is of Old English origin. The meaning of Goldwin is "golden friend". From the Old English name Goldwine.

Gordon
Pronunciation: GORD-en
Gordon is of Old English and Gaelic origin. The meaning of the name Gordon is "large fortification". An adopted Scottish surname, derived from a place name. The name was first adopted as a first name in honour of Charles Gordon (1833-1885), a British general who was killed at Khartoum.

Graham
Pronunciation: GRAY-em
The name Graham is of Old English origin. The meaning of Graham is "gravel area". The name was derived from the Lincolnshire town of Grantham. The adopted surname, was taken to Scotland in the 12th century by Sir William de Graham.

Grant
Pronunciation: GRAN-t
The name Grant is of English and Gaelic origin. The meaning of Grant is "tall, big". An adopted surname derived from French *le grand* and given to tall men. The name first became popular as a first name in Scotland and America.

Granville

Pronunciation: GRAN-vill

The name Granville of Old French origin. The meaning of Granville is "big town". Originally a place name. Granville is also an adopted French surname, derived from *grande ville*, which means 'large town'.

Gregory

Pronunciation: GREG-er-ee

Gregory is of Greek origin. The meaning of the name Gregory is "watchful, vigilant". Gregory the great (c. 540-604) was the first of sixteen popes of that name and one of the eleven Doctors of the Western Church. He founded monasteries and remodeled the church liturgy, and developed the Gregorian chants.

Greville

Pronunciation: GREV-vill

The name Greville is of Old French origin. The meaning of Greville is unknown. As adopted surname, from the French name for one from Greville.

Griffin

Pronunciation: GRIF-en

Griffin is of Latin origin. The meaning of Griffin is "hooked nose". Borne in Greek mythology and medieval legend; the Gryphon was a fierce creature with foreparts of an eagle and the hindquarters of a lion.

Guy

Pronunciation: gye

The name Guy is of Old German origin. The meaning of Guy is "wood". From the Old French name Guido, derived from the Old

German name Wildo, from *witu*, meaning 'wood'. Guy was the French name of the early Christian martyr St Vitus. Guy Warwick, a medieval figure of romance and a hero of the Crusades, popularised the name. The name remained popular until it became associated with the leader of the Gunpowder Plot (1605), Guy Fawkes.

Gwyn
Pronunciation: GW-in
The name Gwyn is of Welsh origin. The meaning of Gwyn is "fair, blessed, holy, white". The name is used as both a boy's name, and as a girl's name.

H

Hadrian
Pronunciation: HAY-dree-en
Hadrian is of Latin origin. The meaning of the name Hadrian is "from Hadria". The name is a variation of Adrian. Hadria was a north Italian city.

Haydn
Pronunciation: HAY-den
The name Hayden is of Old English origin. The meaning of Hayden is "hedged valley". The name is conjectured to be a Welsh variant of Aidan.

Hamish
Pronunciation: HA-mish
The name Hamish is of Scottish origin. The meaning of Hamish is "he who supplants". The name is a Scottish form of James.

Harald
Pronunciation: HA-ra-ld
Harald is of Old Norse origin. The meaning of Harald is "army ruler". From Haraldr, an Old Norse form of Harold. The name is a variant of Harold.

Hardy
Pronunciation: HAR-dee
Hardy is of Old German origin. The meaning of Hardy is "bold, brave". Originally from the surname meaning, 'bold'.

Harley
Pronunciation: HAR-lee
The name Harley is of Old English origin. The meaning of Harley is "hare meadow, harewood".

Harold
Pronunciation: HARE-uld
The name Harold is Old English origin. The meaning of Harold is "army ruler". Old English from *here*, meaning 'army', and *weald*,

120

'power'. The name was influenced by the Old Norse name Haraldr. Diminutive: Harry

Harrison
Pronunciation: HARE-ee-sun
The name Harrison is of Old English origin. The meaning of Harrison is "son of Harry". Harrison is an adopted surname.

Harry
Pronunciation: HARE-ee
The name Harry is of Old German origin. The meaning of Harry is "home leader". The name is a diminutive of Henry or Harold.

Hartley
Pronunciation: HART-lee
Hartley is of Old English origin. The meaning of the name Hartley is "stag meadow". Hartley is an adopted surname from Old English place name.

Harvey
Pronunciation: HAR-vee
The name Harvey is of Old English and Old French origin. The meaning of Harvey is "eager for battle". The name is a variant of the French name Herve.

Hasan
Pronunciation: HAS-an
The name Hasan if of Arabic origin. The meaning of Hasan is "beautiful, good-looking". The name is a variant of Hassan. Al Hasan was the Prophets grandson, the son of Fatima and Haidar. Hasan and his brother, Husayn are regarded as the rightful successors of Muhammad by the Shiites.

121

Hector
Pronunciation: HEK-tor
The name Hector is of Greek origin. The meaning of Hector is "to restrain". Greek meaning, 'holding fast'. Borne as the Prince of Troy, Hector was the Trojan hero who was killed by being lashed to his chariot and dragged around the walls of Troy, by Achilles. Diminutives: Heck, Heckie.

Hedley
Pronunciation: HED-lee
The name Hedley is of Old English origin. The meaning of Hedley is "heathered meadow". The name is an adopted surname, derived from an English place name.

Henry
Pronunciation: HEN-ree
Henry is of Old German origin. The meaning of the name Henry is "home ruler". From Old German *haim*, meaning 'home', and *ric*, 'ruler'. The name was adopted by the Normans and brought to Britain. The name is borne by eight English Kings. Diminutives: Hal, Hank, Harry, Hen.

Herbert
Pronunciation: HER-bert
The name Herbert is of Old German origin. The meaning of Herbert is "illustrious warrior". The name was brought to Britain by the Normans and died out by the Middle Ages. The name was later revived in the 19th century. Herbert is most notably the family name of the Earls of Pembroke.

Herman
Pronunciation: HER-man
Herman is of Old German origin. The meaning of Herman is "soldier". From the Old German name

Hariman, from *here*, meaning 'army'. The Normans brought the name to Britain, where it died out in the Middle Ages. The name was later revived in the 19th-century. St Herman from the 11th-century, wrote hymn "Salve Regina".

Horace
Pronunciation: HOR-ess
The name Horace is of Latin origin. The meaning of Horace is unknown. From the Roman family name Horatius. Borne by Roman lyrical poet, Quintus Horatius Flaccus (65-8BC).

Howard
Pronunciation: HOW-erd
The name Howard is of Old English origin. The meaning of Howard is "noble watchman". An adopted aristocratic and occupational surname. Howard is the family name of the Dukes of Norfolk. The name was used as a given first name during the 19th century.

Howell
Pronunciation: HOWE-ll
The name Howell is of Welsh origin. The meaning of Howell is "eminent, remarkable". Anglicised form of the Welsh name Hywel. Howell is also an adopted surname.

Hugh
Pronunciation: HEW
Hugh is of Old German origin. The meaning of Hugh is "soul, heart, intellect". The name was introduced to Britain by the Normans and became popular during the Middle Ages. St Hugh of Lincoln was a 14th-century bishop of Lincoln.

123

Humbert

Pronunciation: HUM-bert

The name Humbert is of Old German origin. The meaning of Humbert is "famous warrior". Old French name from Old German *hun*, meaning 'warrior' and *berht*, 'bright'. The name was introduced to Britain by the Normans.

Humphrey

Pronunciation: HUM-free

Humphrey is of Old German origin. The meaning of Humphrey is "peaceful warrior". The name was made popular by Hollywood actor, Humphrey Bogart (1899-1957). Diminutive: Humph

I

Iago
Pronunciation: I-ago
The name Iago is of Spanish and Welsh origin. The meaning of Iago is "he who supplants". The name is a variation of the name Jacob. Iago is also a Hebrew variant of the name James. Shakespeare gave the name to his villain in *Othello* (1604).

Ian
Pronunciation: EE-an
Ian is of Gaelic and Scottish origin. The meaning of the name Ian is "God is gracious". Ian is a Scottish variant of the name John. The name was anglicised to Ian. Iain is the Gaelic spelling.

Ibrahim
Pronunciation: ee-bra-HEEM
The name Ibrahim is of Arabic origin. The meaning of Ibrahim is "father of many". The name is variant of the Hebrew name Abraham.

Idan
Pronunciation: EE-dan
Idan is of Hebrew origin. The meaning of the name Idan is "era, time".

Idris
Pronunciation: E-dris
The name Idris is of Arabic and Welsh origin. The meaning of Idris is "fiery leader, Prophet". Borne in Welsh legend by a giant magician, astronomer and prince whose observatory was on Cader Idris. Described in the Koran, the Arabic name was borne by a man described as 'a true man' and 'a prophet', he was also the founder of the first Shiite dynasty (788-974). The name is used as

both a boy's name and as a girl's name.

Ignatius
Pronunciation: eeg-NAH-see-ers
Ignatius is of Latin origin. The meaning of Ignatius is "fire, burning". From a Roman family name, Egnatius. Borne by several saints, including the Spanish-born Saint Ignatius. Loyola (1491-1556). He founded the Society of Jesus, the Jesuits.

Igor
Pronunciation: EE-gor
The name Igor is of Russian origin. The meaning of Igor is "watchfulness of Ing". The name is a Russian form of the Scandinavian name Ingvarr.

Immanuel
Pronunciation: ih-Man-yoo-el
The name Immanuel is of Hebrew origin. The meaning of Immanuel is "God is with us". The name is a variant of Emmanuel.

Ingram
Pronunciation: IN-gram
The name Ingram is of Old English and Scandinavian origin. The meaning of Ingram is "raven of peace".

Inigo
Pronunciation: I-ni-go
The name Inigo is of Spanish origin. Inigo is a Medieval Spanish variation of Ignatius. St Ignatius Loyola was born Inigo Lopez de Recalde. The name is often associated with the great English architect, Inigo Jones.

Ira
Pronunciation: EYE-rah
Ira is of Hebrew origin. The meaning of the name Ira is "full grown, watchful". From Hebrew, meaning, 'watchful'. A biblical name; borne in the Old Testament, the name of a priest of King David.

Irvine
Pronunciation: EYE-van
Irvine is of Gaelic and Scottish origin. The meaning of the name Irvine is "fresh water". Originally a Scottish surname that derived from a Celtic river. Irvin is a variation of Irvine or Irving. Irvine is also a place name of a town in Ayrshire.

Isaac
Pronunciation: EYE-zik
The name Isaac is of Hebrew origin. The meaning of Isaac is "laughter". Hebrew derived from the verb 'to laugh'. A biblical name; borne in the Old Testament he was the only son of Abraham and Sarah. God tested Abraham's faith when Isaac was a young boy, he asked him to sacrifice his own son. God relented and provided him with a Ram as a substitute, whilst Abraham prepared to kill his son. The name was introduced to Britain by the Normans. Izaak is a variation of the name. Diminutives: Ike, Zak, Zack.

Isaiah
Pronunciation: eye-ZY-ah
Isaiah is of Hebrew origin. The meaning of the name Isaiah is "God is salvation". Hebrew, meaning 'the Lord is generous'. A biblical name; borne by one of the major prophets in the Old Testament. He wrote the

book of Isaiah and was best known for foretelling the coming of the Messiah. The name was popular in the 17th century with the Puritans.

Ivan

Pronunciation: EYE-van

The name Ivan is of Hebrew and Russia origin. The meaning of Ivan is "God is gracious". Ivan is the Russin form of the name John. Ivan IV of Russia was famously known as Ivan the Terrible (1533-1584).

Ivor

Pronunciation: EYE-vor

Ivor if of Old Norse and Scandinavian origin. The meaning of the name Ivor is "yew, army". Scandinavian, from Old Norse *yr*, 'yew' and *herr*, 'army'. In Welsh, the name is used as a form of *Ifor*, meaning 'lord'. The name is also used as an anglicised form of the Scottish Gaelic name Lomhar.

J

Jabez
Pronunciation: j(a)-bez
The name Jabez is of Hebrew origin. The meaning of Jabez is "borne in pain". A biblical name; borne in the Old Testament, Jabez is well-respected man whose prayer to God for blessing was answered (4:9-11).

Jabin
Pronunciation: j(a)-bin
Jabin is of Hebrew origin. The meaning of the name Jabin is "God had built". A biblical name; meaning 'discerner', or 'the wise'.

Jabir
Pronunciation: j(a)bir
The name Jabir is of Arabic origin. The meaning of Jabir is "consolation".

Jacan
Pronunciation: JA-can
The name Jacan is of Hebrew origin. The meaning of Jacan is "trouble". A biblical name; he is mentioned as a family leader of the tribe of Gad (5:13).

Jace
Pronunciation: jayce
Jace is of English origin. The meaning of the name Jayce is "the Lord is my salvation". The name is a short form of the Hebrew name Jason.

Jachin
Pronunciation: j(a)-chin
The name Jachin is of Hebrew origin. The meaning of Jachin is "he establishes". A biblical name; Jachin and Boaz were the names given by their craftsman to two large cast bronze pillars, that stood on either side of the entrance to the Temple in Jerusalem.

Built by King Solomon according to God's instructions.

Jacinto
Pronunciation: ha-CEEN-toh
Jacinto is of Spanish and Greek origin. The meaning of Jacinto is unknown. Jacinto is a masculine form of the Greek flower name, Hyacinth.

Jack
Pronunciation: jak
Jack is of Old English origin. The meaning of the name Jack is "God is gracious". Jack is a diminutive of John. The name was popular during the Middle Ages and has recently undergone a new surge in popularity.

Jacob
Pronunciation: JAY-kub
The name Jacob is of Hebrew origin. The meaning of Jacob is "he who supplants". An anglicised form of the Hebrew name Yaakov. A biblical name; borne by the greatest patriarch of the Old Testament, the son of Isaac and Rebekah. He was the father of the twelve tribes of Israel. After wrestling with an angel, he was given the name Israel and became the ancestors of the nation of Israel.

Jamil
Pronunciation: JA-mil
The name Jamil if of Arabic origin. The meaning of Jamil is "handsome, graceful". The name is a variant of Jamal.

James
Pronunciation: jayms
The name James is of Hebrew origin. The meaning of James is "he who supplants". The name

is a variation of Jacob, derived from the Latin form, Jacomus. A biblical name; borne in the New Testament by one of the twelve apostles of Jesus. He was a relative of Jesus, possibly a brother or a cousin. The name spread to Britain and became popular during the 13th century. The name became associated with the royal house Stuart. Diminutives: Jamie, Jem, Jim, Jimmy, Jemmy.

Jared
Pronunciation: JARE-ed
The name Jared is of Hebrew origin. The meaning Jared is "descending, rose". A biblical name; borne in the Old Testament by the father of Enoch. Jared was a pre-Flood ancestor of Jesus. The Puritan adoption underwent a revival in the 1960's. This was possibly due to the TV Western *Big Valley* (1965-1969), with its character Jarrod.

Jason
Pronunciation: JAY-sun
The name Jason is of Greek and Hebrew origin. The meaning of Jason is "healer; the Lord is salvation". The name is a variant of Joshua. A biblical name; borne by an early Christian associate of Paul. Jason is an anglicised form of a Greek name, borne in Greek mythology. Jason was the leader of Argonauts who sailed his ship to *Argos* in search of the Golden Fleece.

Jasper
Pronunciation: JAS-per
Jasper is of Greek origin. The meaning of the name Jasper is "treasure holder". English form of the French

name, Gasper, and the German name, Caspar. In medieval tradition, the name was given to one of the three Magi. Jasper is also the name of a gemstone.

Jeremiah
Pronunciation: jare-ah-MYE-ah
The name Jeremiah is of Hebrew origin. The meaning of Jeremiah is "appointed by God". A biblical name; borne by one of the major 7th century BC Hebrew Prophets. The scholar was the author of the Book of Lamentations and the Book of Jeremiah. The name was popular among the Puritans. Diminutive: Jerry.

Jerome
Pronunciation: jer-OME
The name Jerome is of Greek origin. The meaning of Jerome is "sacred name". From Greek, meaning 'holy name'. Saint Jeroma (c. 342-420), was a biblical scholar who translated the Vulgate Bible into Latin, for the Western Church. He is often portrayed with a lion beside him, whilst he is writing or studying in cardinal's dress. His feast day is 30th September. Diminutive: Jerry.

Jesse
Pronunciation: JESS-ee
Jesse is of Hebrew origin. The meaning of the name Jesse is "God exists". A biblical name; borne in the Old Testament by the shepherd father of King David, from whom the ancestry of Christ can be traced. Jesse was adopted by the Puritans. The name was revived in the 20th century.

Jethro
Pronunciation: JETH-roh

The name Jethro is of Hebrew origin. The meaning of Jethro is "pre-eminence, eminent". A biblical name; borne by in the Old Testament by Moses's father in law. The name was common among Puritans.

Jocelyn

Pronunciation: JOS-e-lyn
The name Jocelyn is of Old German origin. The meaning of Jocelyn is "one of the Goths". The name was introduced to Britain by the Normans. Jocelyn is used as both a boy's name, and as a girl's name. Diminutive: Joss.

Joel

Pronunciation: JOH-ul
The name Joel is of Hebrew origin. The meaning of Joel is "Jehovah is the Lord". A biblical name: borne by a prophet of the 8th century BC, he was also the author of the Old Testament Book of Joel.

John

Pronunciation: JO-hn
John is of Hebrew origin. The meaning of the name John is "God is gracious". A biblical name; borne by several figures, including the longest-lived of the twelve apostles. St John the Baptist, who was the relative and forerunner of Christ. He was sent 'to prepare the way of the Lord', and baptized Christ in the Jordan River. The name is possibly the most popular name in history, borne by numerous saints, popes and kings. Diminutives: Hank, Jack, Jock, Johnnie, Johnny.

Johnathan
Pronunciation: JOHN-a-thun
The name Johnathan is of Hebrew origin. The meaning of Johnathan is "gift of God. The name is a variant of Jonathan. Diminutives: Johnnie, Johnny, John, Jon.

Jonathan
Pronunciation: JAHN-a-thun
Jonathan is of Hebrew origin. The meaning of the name Jonathan is "gift of God, God has given". A biblical name; borne in the Old Testament by son of King Saul, Jonathan was renowned for his manliness and generosity. He was also a great friend of King David, he later saved his life from Saul. Jonathan was eventually killed in battle. The name was adopted by the Puritans. Diminutives: Johnnie, Johnny, Jon.

Jordan
Pronunciation: JOR-dan
Jordan is of Hebrew origin. The meaning of the name Jordan is "down-flowing". From the name of the river in the Middle East where Christ was baptized by John the Baptist. The name has been used as a first name since the Crusades. The name underwent a popular revival in the 1980's. Jordan is used as both a boy's name, and as a girl's name.

Joseph
Pronunciation: JOH-sef
The name Joseph is of Hebrew origin. The meaning of Joseph is "Jehovah increases, God will add". A biblical name; borne by three major figures. The son of Jacob and Rachel, Joseph was sold

into slavery by his jealous brothers. He later became an important advisor to the Pharaoh and a supreme power in Egypt. St Joseph the husband of Virgin Mary and the earthly father of Jesus. He is the patron saint of carpenters, and his feast day is 19th March. St Joseph of Arimathea was a rich Jew who would not declare his faith publicly. He was the one who brought Christ down from the cross and buried him in a private tomb. Diminutives: Jo, Joe.

Joshua
Pronunciation: JOSH-yoo-ah
Joshua is of Hebrew origin. The meaning of the name Joshua is "God is salvation". A biblical name; Joshua was an attendant to Moses, and later succeeded him as the leader of the Israelites. Joshua is also known for leading the defeat of the city of Jericho by the blowing of trumpets. Diminutive: Josh.

Jude
Pronunciation: JU-de
The name Jude is of Greek origin. The meaning of Jude is "praised". The name is a variation of Judas. A biblical name; the apostle St Jude was the author of the New Testament epistle of Jude. He is regarded as the patron saint of hopeless causes. Thomas Hardy popularised the name during the 19th century with his novel, *Jude the Obscure* (1895).

Julian
Pronunciation: JOO-lee-en
The name Julian is of Greek origin. The meaning of Julian is "Jove's child". From the Roman family name Julius. Julian is borne

by several saints. The name was brought to Britain during the Middle Ages.

Julius

Pronunciation: JU-li-us
Julius is of Greek origin. The meaning of the name Julius is "Jove's child". A Roman family name of several of the most powerful Roman emperors, including Emperor Gaius Julius Caesar.

Justin

Pronunciation: JUS-tin
The name Justin of Latin origin. The meaning of Justin is "just, righteous". From the Latin name Justinius, derived from j*ustus*, meaning 'just'. Borne by four saints, St Justin (2nd century) was a Greek philosopher who wrote of the moral values of Christianity. The name was also borne by Byzantine emperors. Justin was revived in the 20th century.

K

Kacey
Pronunciation: KAY-see
The name Kacey is a variant of Casey. Kacey is used as both a boy's name, and as a girl's name

Kade
Pronunciation: kayd
Kade if of Scottish origin. The meaning of the name Kade is "from the wetlands". The name is also a variant of Cade.

Kaden
Pronunciation: KAYD-en
The name Kaden is of Arabic origin. The meaning of Kaden is "Companion". Kaden is also an Old German place name.

Kamal
Pronunciation: KA-mal
Kamal is of Arabic origin. The meaning of Kamal is "perfection". The name is also found in India, where its origin is from Sanskrit.

Kane
Pronunciation: KAYN
The name Kane is of Gaelic and Irish origin. The meaning of Kane is "battle". Anglicised form of the Irish Gaelic name *Cathán,* derived from *cath,* 'battle'.

Kareem
Pronunciation: kah-REEM
Kareem is of Arabic origin. The meaning of the name Kareem is "generous, noble".

Karl
Pronunciation: karl
The name Karl is of Old German origin. The meaning of Karl is "free man". Karl is the German form of Charles.

Kavanagh
Pronunciation: KAV-a-nagh
The name Kavanagh is of Irish and Gaelic origin. The meaning of Kavanagh is "follower of Kevin". Originally an Irish surname.

Kay
Pronunciation: KAY
The name Kay is of Latin and Old Welsh origin. The meaning of Kay is "happy". An ancient name borne in the legend by a knight of the Round Table. Kay is used as both a boy's name and as a girl's name.

Keanu
Pronunciation: kee-AH-noo
Keanu is of Hawaiian origin. The meaning of the name Keanu is "cool breeze from the mountains".

Keegan
Pronunciation: KEE-gan
The name Keegan is of Irish and Gaelic origin. The meaning of Keegan is "little fiery one".

Keir
Pronunciation: KEE-er
The name Keir is of Gaelic origin. The meaning of Keir is "dusky, dark haired". The name may have been adopted in honour of the first Labour MP, James Keir Hardie (1856-1915). Actor Keir Dullea also made the name popular during the 1970's.

Kelvin
Pronunciation: KEL-vin
The name Kelvin is of English origin. The meaning of Kelvin is "friend of ships". Kelvin is also a place name referring to a Scottish river.

Kendall
Pronunciation: KEN-dal

The name Kendall is of Old English origin. The meaning of the Kendall is "the Kent River Valley". An adopted surname, from a Cumbrian place name, Kendal. The name is used as both a boy's name, and as a girl's name. Kendal has been used as a given name since the 19th century.

Kendrick
Pronunciation: KEN-drik
Kendrick if of Welsh origin. The meaning of the name Kendrick is "greatest champion". An adopted Welsh surname, derived from an early first name, Cywrig. The name is also possibly from Old Welsh *cyne*, 'royal', and *ric*, 'ruler'.

Kenneth
Pronunciation: KEN-eth
Kenneth is of Irish and Gaelic origin. The meaning of the name Kenneth is "handsome". Anglicisation of the Gaelic name Cainnech, which means 'handsome'. Diminutives: Ken, Kenny.

Kent
Pronunciation: KENT
Kent is of Old English origin. The meaning of the name Kent is "edge". The adopted surname is also a place name derived from the English county.

Kenton
Pronunciation: KENT-on
The name Kenton is of Old English origin. The meaning of Kenton is "the royal settlement". An adopted surname and English place name.

Kester
Pronunciation: KES-ter
Kester is of Greek and Gaelic origin. The meaning of the name Kester is

"bearing Christ". Kester is a Medieval diminutive of Christopher.

Kevin
Pronunciation: KEV-in
The name Kevin is of Irish and Gaelic origin. The meaning of Kevin is "handsome beloved". Anglicization of the Irish Gaelic name Caoimnin, from *caomh*, 'handsome'. Borne by an Irish hermit saint of the 7th century, he was the patron saint of Dublin. The name was rarely used outside of Ireland until the 20th century, when it became hugely popular. Diminutive: Kev.

Kieran
Pronunciation: KEER-en
Kieran is of Irish and Gaelic origin. The meaning of the name Kieran is "black". Anglicization of the Irish Gaelic name Ciaran, which means 'dark'. Borne by two Celtic saints of the 5th and 6th century. The name was revived and became popular during the 20th century.

Kim
Pronunciation: KIM
The name Kim is of English origin. The meaning of Kim is "gold". Originally a diminutive of Kimball or Kimberley. The name is used as both a boy's name and as a girl's name.

Kingsley
Pronunciation: KINGS-lee
The name Kingsley is of Old English origin. The meaning of Kingsley is "king's meadow". The adopted surname is also a place name, from the Old English name Cyningesleah, which means 'king's wood'. Writer Charles Kingsley (1817-1875) made the name

more popular in the 19th century.

Kingston
Pronunciation: KING-ston
The name Kingston is of Old English origin. The meaning of Kingston is "King's settlement". Kingston is also a place name.

Konrad
Pronunciation: KAHN-rad
The name Konrad is of Polish and German origin. The meaning of Konrad is "bold advisor". The name is a variant of the Old German name Conrad. From German *rad* 'counsel' and *conja*, meaning 'bold'.

Kumar
Pronunciation: KU-mar
The name Kumar is of Hindi and Sanskrit origin. The meaning of Kumar is "male child".

Kurt
Pronunciation: KURT
Kurt is of German origin. The meaning of the name Kurt is "courageous advice". The name is a variant of the Old German name Conrad.

Kyle
Pronunciation: KYL
The name Kyle is of Gaelic origin. The meaning of Kyle is "straight". An adopted Scottish place name, from the Scottish term *kyle*, which means 'straight', or 'channel'. Derived from the Gaelic *caol*, 'narrow'. Kyle is the name of the central district of Ayrshire in western Strathclyde.

L

Lachlan
Pronunciation: LOCH-lan
The name Lachlan is of Irish and Gaelic origin. The meaning of Lachlan is "from the land of lakes". From the Scottish name Lachlann, the Gaelic word for Norway. Diminutive: Lockie.

Lambert
Pronunciation: LAMB-bert
Lambert is of Scandinavian origin. The meaning of the name Lambert is "land brilliant". Old German from *landa*. St Lambert popularised the name in medieval Belgium and Netherlands. He was a 7th-century bishop of Maastricht. The name spread to Britain in the Middle Ages.

Lance
Pronunciation: LANCE
The name Lance is of French origin. The meaning of Lance is "land". French from the Old German name Lanzo. Diminutives: Lancelot, Launcelot.

Lancelot
Pronunciation: LANS-e-lot
The name Lancelot is of Old French origin. The meaning of Lancelot is "servant". Borne in Arthurian legend by the most famous knight of the Round Table, Lancelot du Lac. His seduction of Queen Guinevere, started a war that resulted in the destruction of the Round Table, and the death of King Author.

Laurence
Pronunciation: LAUR-ence
The name Laurence is of French origin. The meaning of Laurence is "from Laurentium", an ancient

Italian town of olive groves. Laurence is a variant of the Latin name Lawrence. Borne by a 3rd-century deacon of Roman, he was martyred in 258 by being roasted on a gridiron. He is considered the patron saint of curriers and his feast day is 10th August. Diminutives: Lanty, Larry, Laurie, Lawri.

Lee
Pronunciation: LEE
Lee is of Old English origin. The meaning of the name Lee is "wood, meadow, clearing". An adopted surname and place name. Lee was first used as a first name in the 19th century, probably in honour of the Confederate general Robert E. Lee (1807-1870). The name is used as both a boy's name and as a girl's name.

Leighton
Pronunciation: LAY-ton
The name Leighton is of Old English origin. The meaning of Leighton is "meadow settlement". The adopted surname was derived from the place name, from Old England *leac*. Leighton has been used as a first name since the 19th century.

Lennox
Pronunciation: LEN-iks
The name Lennox is of Gaelic and Scottish origin. The meaning of Lennox is "with many elm trees". An adopted Scottish surname, from the Levenach. The name also appears in Shakespeare's *Macbeth* (1606).

Leo
Pronunciation: LEE-oh

The name Leo is of Latin origin. The meaning of Leo is "Lion". From Latin *leo*. The name was popular in Roman times. Leo is the fifth sign of the zodiac. The name was borne by thirteen popes, including Leo the Great (5th century) and four saints.

Leon
Pronunciation: LEE-ahn
Leon is of Greek origin. The meaning of the name Leon is "Lion". Lion is a variant of Leo.

Leonard
Pronunciation: LEN-ard
The name Leonard is of Old German origin. The meaning of Leonard is "lion strength". From the Old German name Leonhard. The name was popularised in the 6th century by St Leonard, he was a Frank at the court of Clovis. He is the patron saint of prisoners, and his feast day is 6th November. Diminutives: Len, Lennie, Lenny, Leo.

Leslie
Pronunciation: LEZ-lee
The name Leslie is of Gaelic and Scottish origin. The meaning of Leslie is "Holly garden". An adopted Scottish surname, derived from the place name Lesslyn. It was used as a first name in the 19th century. Diminutive: Les.

Lester
Pronunciation: LES-ter
The name Lester is of Old English origin. The meaning of Lester is "from Leicester". The adopted surname was adopted in the 19th century.

Lewis
Pronunciation: LOO-iss

The name Lewis is of Old German origin. The meaning of Lewis is "famous warrior". An anglicised form of the name Louis.

Liam
Pronunciation: LEE-am
Liam is of Old German origin. The meaning of the name Liam is "determined protector". The name is originally a diminutive of Uilliam, an Irish variation of William. The name became popular in its own right.

Lincoln
Pronunciation: LINK-en
The name Lincoln is of Old English origin. The meaning of Lincoln is "lake colony". An adopted surname and English place name, originally used to indicate 'the Roman colony at the lake'. Abraham Lincoln (1809-1865) popularised the name as a first name. He was the 16th president of the US whose presidency won the Civil War, and abolished slavery.

Lindsay
Pronunciation: LIN-d-say
Lindsay is of Old English origin. The meaning of the name Lindsay is "Lincoln's marsh". Sir Walter de Lindesay brought the name to Scotland from Lindsey, Lincolnshire. The name is used as both a boy's name and as a girl's name.

Linford
Pronunciation: LIN-ford
The name Linford is of Old English origin. The meaning of Linford is "linden tree ford". An adopted surname and English place name.

Linus

Pronunciation: LYE-nus
The name Linus is of Greek origin. The meaning of Linus is "flax". The name is a Latin form of the Greek name Linos. A biblical name; borne by a Christian companion to Paul in Rome. In Greek mythology, Linus is the name of Hercules's music tutor.

Lionel

Pronunciation: LYE-a-nel
The name Lionel is of Latin origin. The meaning of Lionel is "Lion". The name is originally a medieval diminutive of Leon. The name was borne by a knight of King Author's Round Table.

Llewellyn, Llewelyn

Pronunciation: loo-ELL-en
The name Llewellyn is of Welsh origin. The meaning of Llewellyn is "like a lion, leader". Borne by two 13[t]-century Welsh princes, Llewelyn ap Iorwerth and Llywelyn ap Gruffydd.

Lloyd

Pronunciation: loyd
The name Lloyd is of Welsh origin. The meaning of Lloyd is "gray haired". An anglicised form of the Wlesh name Llwyd.

Louis

Pronunciation: LOO-iss
The name Louis is of French and Old German origin. The meaning of Louis is "famous warrior". From the Old German name Chlodovech. The name was borne by nineteen kings of France and numerous saints. Diminutive: Lou.

Lucas

Pronunciation: LOO-kas
Lucas is of Greek origin. The meaning of the name

Lucas is "man of Lucania", in southern Italy. The name is a variation of Loukas. The name was introduced to Britain in the 12th century.

Lucian
Pronunciation: LOO-shun
The name Lucian is of Latin origin. The meaning of Lucian is "light". From the Roma clan name Lucianus. St Lucian of Antioch was a 4th-century scholar.

Lucius
Pronunciation: LOU-cius
The name Lucius is of Latin origin. The meaning of Lucius is "light". From Latin *lux*. Lucius was a popular name in Ancient Rome. The name was borne by three popes.

Luke
Pronunciation: LOO-k
The name Luke is of Greek origin. The meaning of Luke is "man of Lucania", a region in southern Italy. A biblical name; St Luke the Evangelist, apparently wrote the third gospel and the Acts of the Apostles. He is a patron saint of doctors and artists, and is described in the Bible as a physician (Colossians 4:14).

Lyall
Pronunciation: LYE-al
The name Lyall is of Old Norse origin. The meaning of Lyall is "Wolf". From an Old Norse name, Liulfr.

Lyle
Pronunciation: LYE-el
The name Lyle is of Old French origin. The meaning of Lyle is "the island". An adopted Scottish surname, from Old French *de lisle*, which means 'of the island'.

Lyndon

Pronunciation: LIN-dan

The name Lyndon is of Old English origin. The meaning of Lyndon is "linden tree hill". Lyndon is an adopted surname and place name. The name became popular in America after Lyndon Baines Johnson (1908-1978), who was the 36th president.

M

Mackenzie
Pronunciation: ma-KEN-zee
The name Mackenzie if of Gaelic and Irish origin. The meaning of Mackenzie is "son of the wise ruler". An adopted Scottish surname, from Gaelic Mac Coinnich. Mackenzie is used as both a boy's name, and as a girl's name.

Magnus
Pronunciation: MAG-ness
The name Magnus is of Latin origin. The meaning of Magnus is "great". The name was adopted by St Olaf of Norway, an admirer of Charlemagne. The name is borne by several Norwegian Kings and several Scandinavian saints. The name was introduced from Scandinavia to Scotland by one of the Saints, who visited the Scottish islands of Orkney and Shetland.

Malachi
Pronunciation: MAL-a-kye
Malachi is of Hebrew origin. The meaning of the name Malachi is "messenger of God". A biblical name; borne by the author of the last book of the Old Testament, and a prophet. His prophesies are focus mainly on the coming of Judgment Day. The name is believed to have come from the text itself: 'Behold, I will send my messenger, and he shall prepare the way before me' (Malachi 3:1).

Malachy
Pronunciation: MAL-a-key
The name Malachy is of Hebrew origin. The meaning of Malachy is "messenger of God". The name is a variant of Malachi. The name was first

154

adopted in reference to an early Irish King, Maoileachlainn. The name was popularized in the 12th century by St Malachy (1095-1148), he was a bishop of Armagh.

Malcolm

Pronunciation: MAL-cum
Malcolm is of Gaelic and Scottish origin. The meaning of the name Malcolm is "devotee of Saint Columba". Anglicised from the Gaelic name Mael Coluim. The name was borne by four medieval Scottish kings. Malcolm is also the name of the prince of Scotland who became King of Scotland, after Macbeth murdered his father. Shakespeare immortalised the true story in his play, *Macbeth* (1606).

Mallory

Pronunciation: MALL-or-ee
The name Mallory is of Old French origin. The meaning of Mallory is "unfortunate". The name is used as both a boy's name and as a girl's name.

Manfred

Pronunciation: MAN-fred
The name Manfred is of Old German origin. The meaning of Manfred is "man of peace". From Old German *man*, meaning 'man', and *fred*, 'peace'. The name was introduced to Britain by the Normans and fell out of use after the Middle Ages. Manfred was later revived in the 19th century. Lord Byron used the name for his epic poem *Manfred* (1817).

Manley

Pronunciation: MAN-lee

The name Manley is of Old English origin. The meaning of Manley is "shared land, wood". Manley is also a place name.

Marius
Pronunciation: MAR-ee-us
Marius of Latin origin. The meaning of the name Marius is "dedicated to Mars". The name is an adoption of the Roman family name Marius, from Mars, Roman god of war. The name is also a variant of Mario.

Mark
Pronunciation: MAR-k
The name Mark is of Latin origin. The meaning of Mark is "dedicated to Mars". The name is an anglicised form of the Latin name, Marcus. A biblical name; borne in the New Testament by St Mark, author of the second Gospel who died in c. 68. His feast day is 25th April.

Marshall
Pronunciation: MAR-shal
The name Marshal is of Old French origin. The meaning of Marshall is "caretaker of horses". An adopted surname, originally derived from a Norman French occupational name for a groom, *mareshcal*. Marshall is also a law enforcement title and a military title. The name has been used as a first name since the early 19th century.

Martin
Pronunciation: MART-en
Martin is of Latin origin. The meaning of the name Martin is "dedicated to Mars". Martin is an anglicised form of the Latin name Martinus. The name originates with the Roman war god, Mars. St Martin of

Tours (c. 316-97) popularised the name throughout medieval Europe. He was converted to Christianity while a soldier in Rome and later became bishop of Tours. He is best known for cutting his cloak in two and sharing it with a beggar. His feast day is 11th November. Civil rights activist Martin Luther King popularised the name in the 20th century.

Matthew

Pronunciation: MATH-yoo
The name Matthew is of Hebrew origin. The meaning of Matthew is "gift of God". A biblical name; borne in the New Testament by one of Christ's twelve apostles. Also known as Levi, he wrote the first Gospel account of the life of Jesus. His feast day is 21st September. Matthew is the form of the Hebrew name, Mattathia. The name was introduced to Britain by the Norman's. Diminutives: Mat, Matt, Mattie.

Matthias

Pronunciation: ma-THYE-us
The name Mattias is of Greek, Hebrew and German origin. The meaning of Mattias is "gift of God". New Testament Greek form of the Hebrew name Mattathia. A biblical name; borne in the New Testament by the disciple who was selected to replace Judas as an apostle, 'the thirteenth apostle' (Acts 1:23-26).

Maurice

Pronunciation: maw-REESE
Maurice is of Latin origin. The meaning of the name Maurice is "Moorish".

From the Latin name Mauricius. Borne by a 3rd-century saint who was martyred in Switzerland. The Roman name was introduced to Britain by the Normans.

Maxim
Pronunciation: MAX-im
Maxim is of Latin origin. The meaning of the name Maxim is "greatest". The name is a variation of Maximus. The name was used by Daphne du Maurier in his novel, *Rebecca* (1940). Maxim is also the name of three Roman emperors and several early saints.

Maximilian
Pronunciation: MAX-i-mi-lian
The name Maximilian is of Latin origin. The meaning of Maximilian is "greatest". From the Latin name Maximilianus. Borne by a 3rd-century martyr. The name of three Roman emperors and several early saints.

Maxwell
Pronunciation: MAKS-wel
The name Maxwell is of Old English origin. The meaning of Maxwell is "Mack's stream". An adopted Scottish surname and place name. The name has been used in Scotland since the mid-19th century

Maynard
Pronunciation: MAY-nerd
The name Maynard is of Old German origin. The meaning of Maynard is "brave, strength". Maynard is an adopted surname, originally from Norman French *magin*, meaning 'strength'. The name was introduced to Britain by the Normans.

Melville

Pronunciation: MEL-ville

The name Melville is of Old French origin. The meaning of Melville is "bad settlement". Originally a Norman French baronial name derived from Malleville. The surname was adopted by those fleeing to Scotland from a poor settlement in northern France. Herman Melville (author of *Moby Dick*), popularised the name during the 19th century. Diminutive: Mel.

Melvin

Pronunciation: MEL-vin

The name Melvin in of uncertain origins. Possibly a variation of Melville or a masculine form of Malvina. Diminutive: Mel.

Merlin

Pronunciation: MER-lin

Merlin is of Welsh origin. The meaning of the name Melvin is "sea fortress". From Latinate form, Merlinus, of the Old Welsh name Myrddin. Borne in Arthurian legend by magician Merlin Ambrosius. The name is used as both a boy's name and as a girl's name.

Merton

Pronunciation: MERT-on

Merton is of Old English origin. The meaning of the name Merton is "town by the lake". Merton is an adopted surname and English place name, from Old English *mere*, meaning 'lake', and *tun*, 'settlement'.

Michael

Pronunciation: MYE-kal

The name Michael is of Hebrew origin. The meaning of Michael is "who is like God?" A biblical name; borne by St Michael the Archangel who defeated the dragon. He was the leader of the seven archangels and leader of the celestial armies. Angels, Michael and Gabriel are given personal name in the canonical Bible. Several saints, Emperors and Kings have borne the name. Michael has been popular in the English-speaking world since the Middle Ages. Diminutives: Mick, Mickey, Micky, Mike, Mikey, Mischa, Misha, Mitch.

Miles
Pronunciation: myls
The name Miles if of Latin origin. The meaning of Miles is "soldier". Derived from Latin *miles*, meaning 'solider', owing to the military association of St Michael the Archangel.

Montgomery
Pronunciation: mon-GOH-mer-ree
The name Montgomery is of Old French origin. The meaning of Montgomery is "mountain of the powerful one". Montgomery is an adopted surname, and originally a Norman baronial name and place name, from Calvados. The Welsh county of Montgomeryshire was named after a Norman settler. Montgomery is the surname of English and Scottish earls.

Mordecai
Pronunciation: MOR-de-cai
Mordecai is of Hebrew origin. The meaning of the name Mordecai is "little man, follower of Marduk (a god of the Babylonians)". A biblical name; borne in the Old Testament by a cousin and guardian of Esther.

Mordecai warned Esther of Haman's plans to massacre all Jews (Esther 4-7). The name was popular in the 17th and 18th century.

Morley
Pronunciation: MOOR-lee
The name Morley is of Old English origin. The meaning of Morley is "meadow on the moor". An adopted surname and English place name.

Mortimer
Pronunciation: MORT-im-er
Mortimer is of Old French origin. The meaning of the name Mortimer is "dead sea". Mortimer is an adopted aristocratic surname, itself derived from a Norman baronial name and place name, Mortimer in Normandy. The name has been used as a first name since the 19th century.

Morton
Pronunciation: MORT-on
The name Morton is of Old English origin. The meaning of Morton is "moor town, settlement on the moor". An adopted surname and English place name. Morton has been used as a first name since the 19th century.

Moses
Pronunciation: MOH-ziz
Moses is of Hebrew and possibly Egyptian origin. The meaning of Moses is "saviour". Anglicised form of the Hebrew name Moshe. A biblical name; borne by the Hebrew baby who was found floating on the River Nile and adopted by an Egyptian Pharaoh's daughter. Moses was a

patriarch who led the Israelites out of Egypt for the Promised Land. The name was popular in medieval Britain and was later revived by the Puritans after the Reformation.

Mostyn
Pronunciation: MOS-tyn
The name Mostyn is of Welsh origin. The meaning of Mostyn is "mossy settlement". An adopted Welsh surname and place name in Clywd, North Wales.

Muhammad
Pronunciation: mo-HAM-med
The name Muhammad is of Arabic origin. The meaning of Muhammad is "praiseworthy". Borne by the Prophet and founder of Islam, Abu al-Qasim Muhammad. He was borne at Mecca in c.570 and died at Medina in 632. Mohammad is one of the most popular Islamic boy's names.

Murray
Pronunciation: MUR-ee
The name Murray is of Gaelic origin. The meaning of Murray is "sea". Murray is an adopted Scottish surname, from Scottish Gaelic *muir*. Murray is the surname of an ancient Scottish clan. The name was adopted as a first name in the 19th century.

Myron
Pronunciation: MYE-an
The name Myron is of Greek origin. The meaning of Myron is "myrrh, fragrant oil". Borne by a Greek sculptor of the 5th century BC, he was renowned for his realistic statues of athletes, animals, and gods.

N

Naim
Pronunciation: NA-im
The name Naim is of Arabic origin. The meaning of Naim is "comfortable, tranquil". Variations: Naeem.

Nairn
Pronunciation: NA-ir-n
The name Nairn is of Scottish and Gaelic origin. The meaning of Nairn is "river with alder trees". Celtic dweller by the alder tree. Nairn is also a place name.

Nathan
Pronunciation: NAY-than
Nathan is of Hebrew origin. The meaning of the name Nathan is "God has given". Hebrew, meaning 'gift'. A biblical name: borne in the Old Testament, Nathan was God's prophet who advised King David to build the temple during the reigns of David and Solomon.

Nathaniel
Pronunciation: na-THAN-yel
The name Nathaniel is of Hebrew origin. The meaning of Nathaniel is "God has given". Hebrew, meaning 'gift of God'. A biblical name; borne in the New Testament by one of Christ's twelve apostles. He was also known as Bartholomew. Shakespeare used the name Nathaniel in *Love's Labour's Lost* (1594). Diminutives: Nat, Nath, Nathan.

Ned
Pronunciation: ned
The name Ned is of English origin. The meaning of Ned is "wealthy guard". Ned is used as a nickname for Edward.

Neil

Pronunciation: neel

Neil is of Irish and Gaelic origin. The meaning of Neil is "Champion". The name is a Scottish variation of Niall which dates back to the Middle Ages.

Nelson

Pronunciation: NEL-sun

The name Nelson is of Irish and Gaelic origin. The meaning of Nelson is unknown. The adopted surname was first used as a first name in the 19th century. Naval hero of Trafalgar, Admiral Lord Horatio Nelson (1758-1805) popularised the name.

Neville

Pronunciation: NEV-il

The name Neville is of Old French origin. The meaning of Neville is "new village". Neville is an adopted aristocratic surname and Old French place name. From Old French, *neuve*, meaning 'new', and *ville*, 'town'. It was introduced to Britain during the Norman Conquest.

Niall

Pronunciation: NYE-al

Niall is of Irish and Gaelic origin. The meaning of Niall is "Champion". Borne by a 5th-century Irish king, Niall of the Nine Hostages.

Nicholas

Pronunciation: NIK-oh-lus

Nicholas is of Greek origin. The meaning of the name Nicholas is "people of victory". Anglicised from the Greek name Nikolaos, from *nike*, meaning 'victory', and *laos*, 'people'. A biblical name: borne by one of seven qualified men in the first-century

Christian congregation. The name is also borne by a 4th-century bishop of Myra who is now considered patron saint of Greece and Russia, as well as children, scholars, sailors and pawnbrokers. St Nicholas in his Dutch incarnation of Santa Claus is well known throughout the Christian world for bringing Christmas presents.

Nigel
Pronunciation: NYE-jel
The name Nigel if of Gaelic and Irish origin. The meaning of Nigel is "Champion". The name was revived in the 19th century, during the craze for medieval names.

Noel
Pronunciation: NOH-el
Noel is of French origin. The meaning of the name Noel is "Christmas". An Old French, from *noel*, which was derived from the Latin *dies natalis*, meaning birthday. Referring directly to the birthday of Christ. The name is used as both a boy's name and as a girl's name.

Norman
Pronunciation: NOR-mahn
The name Norman is of Old German origin. The meaning of Norman is "northerner". Derived from Old German *nord*, 'north', and *man*, 'man'. The name was already in use in Britain before the Norman Conquest, however it was then reinforced and used to describe the Norman invaders and their descendants. The name was revived in the 19th century. Diminutive: Norm.

O

Odysseus

Pronunciation: OD-ys-seus
Odysseus is of Greek origin. The meaning of the name Odysseus is "angry man". Original Greek form of the hero of Homer's epic, the *Odyssey*.

Olaf

Pronunciation: OH-loff
The name Olaf is of Old Norse origin. The meaning of Olaf is "ancestor's relic". From the Old Norse name Anleifr, meaning 'relic of his ancestor's'. A royal name in Norway. It was borne by several Scandinavian kings, including St Olaf, patron saint of Norway.

Oliver

Pronunciation: AH-lih-ver
Oliver is of Latin origin. The meaning of the name Oliver is "olive tree". The name may be a variation of the Olaf. The name fell from favor after the death of Oliver Cromwell (1599-1658) but became popular again in the 19th century. Possibly due to the influence of Charles Dickens's novel Oliver Twist (1838). Diminutives: Noll, Ol, Ollie,

Omar

Pronunciation: OH-mar
The name Omar is of Arabic and Hebrew origin. The meaning of Omar is "speaker, long-lived". The name is a variation of Umar, or from Hebrew meaning 'eloquent'. A biblical name: the son of Esau, a sheik of Edom. Omar Khayyam (12th century) was an astronomer, a mathematician and also a poet.

Orlando

Pronunciation: or-LAHN-doh

Orlando is of Spanish origin. The name is an Italian form of Roland (Old German). The name means "renowned land".

Orson

Pronunciation: OR-sun

The name Orson is of Latin origin. The meaning of Orson is "bear". Old French *ourson*, meaning 'little bear'. A French medieval legend, the name was borne by the twin brother of Valentine. The children were sons of an exiled Byzantine Princess. Orson was carried off by a bear as a baby and reared by bears in the forest. Director and Actor Orson Welles (1915-1985) made the name popular.

Oscar

Pronunciation: OS-ker

Oscar is of Old English origin. The meaning of the name Oscar is "spear of the gods". The name was used by Scottish writer, James Macpherson (1736-17-96) for the son of Ossian In his Ossian poems. Napoleon Bonaparte, was a great admirer of Macpherson's work, and later gave the name to his godson. He ascended the throne of Sweden as Oscar I.

Oswald

Pronunciation: OZ-wild

The name Oswald is of Old German origin. The meaning of Oswald is "God's power". From an Old English name, from *os*, 'god', and *weald*, 'rule'. The Shropshire town of Oswestry is said to have been named after a 7th-

century saint and king of Northumbria borne with the name. The name Oswald was popular during the Middle Ages. Diminutives: Oz, Ozzie, Ozzy.

Otto
Pronunciation: AW-toh
Otto is of Old German origin. The meaning of the name Otto is "wealth". A modification of a common element of Old German names, *od*, meaning 'prosperity'. Borne by four Holy Roman Emperors. The name became less popular in Britain after the Middle Ages.

Owen
Pronunciation: OH-en
The name Owen is of Scottish and Greek origin. The meaning of Own is "born of youth". The name is a variant of the Latin name Euenuis. Borne in Welsh legend by several important figures. One being, Owen Glendower (1359-1416). He fought unsuccessfully for Welsh independence from England. The name has huge popularity in Wales.

P

Pablo
Pronunciation: PAB-low
The name Pablo is of Spanish origin. The meaning of Pablo is "little". The name is a variant of Paul. Borne by artist Pablo Picasso (1881-1973).

Pacifico
Pronunciation: PAS-if-i-co
The name Pacifico is of Spanish and Latin origin. The meaning of Pacifico is "calm, tranquil".

Palmer
Pronunciation: PAHL-mer
The name Palmer is of Old English origin. The meaning of Palmer is "Pilgrim". Originally a surname used to refer to the palm branch carried by a Christian pilgrim, whilst they travelled to a holy shrine.

Paris
Pronunciation: PARE-iss
The name Paris is of Greek origin. In Greek mythology, Paris was the name of the young prince of Troy, whose love affair with Helen caused the Trojan war. Paris is used as both a boy's name and as a girl's name. The name was also an English given surname for immigrants from the capital of France.

Parker
Pronunciation: PAR-ker
Parker is of Old English origin. The meaning of Parker is "park keeper". Originally an occupational name, that was used as a surname. Parker became a popular given name in the 19th century.

Parry
Pronunciation: PAR-ry
The name Parry is of Old Welsh origin. The meaning

172

of Parry is "son of Harry". The name is also an English variant of Perry.

Patrick
Pronunciation: PAT-rik
The name Patrick is of Latin origin. The meaning of Patrick is "patrician". St. Patrick (c. 389-461) was a Briton and a Roman citizen who travelled as a missionary to Ireland. After he arrived in Wicklow in 432, he is credited with converting almost the entire country to Christianity. St Patrick is also renowned for ridding Ireland of snakes and vermin. He is the patron saint of Ireland, his feast day is 17th March. The name spread outside of Ireland in the 18th century.

Paul
Pronunciation: pahl
Paul is of Latin origin. The meaning of the name Paul is "small". From the Roman family name Paulus, originally from *paulus*, 'small'. Borne by Saul of Tarsus (Acts 13:9), he was a Roman citizen and persecutor of Christians until his conversion. As St Paul, he is considered to be the co-founder of the Christian Church with St Peter.

Perceval
Pronunciation: PER-ce-val
The name Perceval is of Old French origin. The meaning of Perceval is "pierce the vale". From Old French *perce*, 'pierce', and *val*, 'valley'. Invented by a medieval poet, Chretien de Troyes in his 12th century accounts of Arthurian legend.

Percy

Pronunciation: PER-see

Percy is of Latin origin. The meaning of the name Percy is "to penetrate the hedge". Percy is an adopted aristocratic surname, born by the Duke of Northumberland. Derived from the Old French *perce*, 'piece', and *haie*, 'hedge'.

Peter

Pronunciation: PEE-tar

The name Peter is of Greek origin. The meaning of Peter is "rock". A biblical name: borne as one of the twelve apostles. The name was given to his apostle Simon by Jesus. Peter the fisherman was impulsive and had a strong faith. "Thou art Peter, and upon this rock I will build my church" (Matthew 16:18). St Peter is considered to be one of the co-founders of the Christian Church with St Paul. In the Catholic tradition the first Bishop of Rome and the first pope. Peter is considered the patron saint of fisherman, his feast day is 29th June. J M Barrie's play Peter Pan (1904) revived the name and made it more popular.

Philip

Pronunciation: FIL-ip

The name Philip is of Greek origin. The meaning of Philip is "horse lover". The Greek name *Philipos*, which means 'lover of horses'. A biblical name; borne by one of Christ's twelve apostles and several early saints. Philip has been in regular use since the early Christian times. St Philip the Apostle's feast day is 1st May.

Piers

Pronunciation: PEE-ers

The name Piers if of Greek origin. The meaning of Piers is "rock". French medieval vernacular form of the name Peter. The name was introduced to Britain by the Normans in the Middle Ages.

Plantagenet
Pronunciation: P-lanta-genet
Plantagenet is of Old French origin. The meaning of the name Plantagenet is "shoot of broom". The name was commonly given to the English royal line from Henry II to Richard III. Broom is an English flower.

Porter
Pronunciation: PORT-er
The name Porter is of English origin. The meaning of Porter is "gatekeeper". Originally an English occupational name and given surname. Porter is also a French name given to people who made their living carrying loads. The French meaning of Porter is "to carry".

Presley
Pronunciation: PRES-ley
Presley is of Old English origin. The meaning of the name Presley is "priest's meadow". The name has been used since the Middle Ages. Presley is also a place name. The name was made famous by the single Elvis Presley.

Preston
Pronunciation: PRES-ten
The name Preston is of Old English origin. The meaning of Preston is "priest's settlement". Preston is also a place name.

Price

Pronunciation: PRI-ce

The name Price is of Old French origin. The meaning of Price is "prize".

Purvis

Pronunciation: PUR-vis

The name Purvis if of English and French origin. The meaning of Purvis is "purveyor". Originally a term for someone who provides food and provisions.

Q

Qasim
Pronunciation: KA-sim
The name Qasim is of Arabic origin. The meaning of Qasim is "charitable, generous".

Quade
Pronunciation: kwayde
The name Quade is of Gaelic origin. The meaning of Quade is unknown. The name is derived from a Scottish clan name McQuade.

Quanah
Pronunciation: KWAH-ne
The name Quanah is of Native American Indian origin. The meaning of Quanah is "sweet smelling". The name was borne by a 19th-century chief of the Comanche.

Quennell
Pronunciation: KWEN-el
The name Quennell is of Old French origin. The meaning of Quennell is "small oak". Originally a place name.

Quentin
Pronunciation: KWEN-tin
The name Quentin is of Latin origin. The meaning of Quentin is "fifth". Old French form of the Latin name Quintius, from *quintus*, 'fifth'. It was the name of a 3rd-century saint and missionary to Gaul.

Quigley
Pronunciation: KWIG-lee
The name Quigley is of Irish and Gaelic origin. The meaning of Quigley is "one with messy hair".

Quillan
Pronunciation: KWIL-an
The name Quillan is of Irish and Gaelic origin. The

meaning of Quillan is "cub".

Quimby
Pronunciation: KWIM-bee
Quimby is of Old Norse origin. The meaning of Quimby is "estate of the woman". Quimby is also a place name.

Quincey
Pronunciation: KWIN-cey
Quincey is of Old French origin. The meaning of the name Quincey is "Estate of the fifth son". Adopted surname, originally a baronial name from Cuinchy in northern France. Quincey can be used as a both a boy's name, and as a girl's name.

Quinn
Pronunciation: KWIN
The name Quinn is of Irish and Gaelic origin. The meaning of Quinn is "counsel". An adopted Irish surname, from the Gaelic name O Cuinn, meaning 'decedent of Conn'. Quinn has been used a given name from very ancient times.

Quintin
Pronunciation: KWIN-tin
Quintin is of Old English origin. The meaning of the name Quintin is "fifth". The name is a variant of Quentin. Quintin is an adopted surname and a place name, from Old English cwen, 'queen' and tun, 'settlement'.
Diminutive: Quent, Quint.

Quinton
Pronunciation: KWIN-ton
The name Quinton is od Old English origin. The meaning of Quinton is "queens settlement". Originally a place name.

Quintus

Pronunciation: KWIN-tus

The name Quintus is of Latin origin. The meaning of Quintus is "fifth". The Roman name was often given to the fifth born son, in the days of large families. Quintus is a variant of Quentin. Diminutive: Quent, Quint.

Quintrell

Pronunciation: kwin-TREL

The name Quintrell is of English origin. The meaning of Quintrell is "dashing, elegant".

R

Ralph
Pronunciation: RAL-f
The name Ralph is of French origin. The meaning of Ralph is "counsel". From the Norman French name Raulf.

Ramsey
Pronunciation: RAM-see
Ramsey is of Old English origin. The meaning of the name Ramsey is "raven island". An adopted Scottish surname, which was originally derived from the Huntingdonshire town of Ramsey. Earl of Huntington brought the name to Scotland in the 12th century.

Ranald
Pronunciation: RAN-ald
The name Ranald is of Scottish origin. The meaning of Ranald is unknown. The name is an anglicised form of Raghnall.

Randall
Pronunciation: RAN-dall
The name Randall is of Old English origin. The meaning of Randall is unknown. The name is a medieval form of Randolf. Diminutives: Ran, Randy.

Randolf
Pronunciation: RAN-dolf
The name Randolf is of Old Norse origin. The meaning of Randolf is "shield, wolf". From the Old Norse name Rannulfr. Diminutives: Ran, Randy.

Raoul
Pronunciation: RA-oul
The name Raoul is of French origin. The meaning of Raoul is "wolf counsel". The name is a French form of Ralph. The name was popular in medieval Britain.

Ravi
Pronunciation: RAV-ee

The name Ravi is of Indian origin. The meaning of Ravi is "sun". Ravi was the name of the sun god.

Raymond
Pronunciation: RAY-mund
The name Raymond is of Old German origin. The meaning of Raymond is "protecting hand". From the Old French name Raimund. The name was borne by a 11th-century Count who was a Crusader leader of the First Crusade. The name was introduced to Britain by the Normans. Diminutive: Ray.

Rayner
Pronunciation: RAY-ner
The name Rayner is of Old German origin. The meaning of Rayner is "judgment warrior". The name was introduced to Britain by the Normans.

Reuben
Pronunciation: ROO-ben
The name Reuben is of Hebrew origin. The meaning of Reuben is "Behold, a son". A biblical name: borne by the firstborn of Jacob's twelve sons.

Rex
Pronunciation: reks
The name Res is of Latin origin. The meaning of Res is "king". The name is also considered a diminutive of Reginald.

Rhys
Pronunciation: rees
Rhys is of Welsh origin. The meaning of the name Rhys is "passion, enthusiasm". Rhys is a native Welsh form of Reece. The name was

borne by two medieval Welsh lords.

Richard
Pronunciation: RICH-erd
The name Richard is of Old German origin. The meaning of Richard is "powerful leader". From an Old German name Ricohard. Diminutives: Rick, Dickie, Dickon, Dicky, Rich, Richie, Rick, Ricky.

Ridley
Pronunciation: RID-lee
The name Ridley is of Old English origin. The meaning of Ridley is "reed meadow". Originally an adopted surname and place name, from Old English elements hreod.

River
Pronunciation: RIV-er
The name River is of English origin. The name was popular during the 1960's when people took names from nature. Hollywood actor, River Phoenix (1970-1993) popularised name.

Roald
Pronunciation: ROH-al
The name Roald is of Old Norse origin. The meaning of Roald is "famous ruler, famed power".

Robert
Pronunciation: RAH-bert
Robert is of Old German origin. The meaning of the name Robert is "bright fame". From the Old German name Hrodebert. The name was introduced to Britain by the Normans. Robert has been a popular boys name since the Middle Ages. King Robert the Bruce (1274-1329) popularised the name in Scotland. Diminutives: Bob,

Bobbie, Bobby, Hob, Rab, Rabbie, Rob, Robbie, Robby.

Robin
Pronunciation: RAH-bin
The name Robin is of English origin. The meaning of Robin is unknown. Robyn is originally a diminutive of Robert. The name has been popular since the medieval days of Robin Hood.

Roderick
Pronunciation: RAH-der-ik
The name Roderick is of Old German origin. The meaning of Roderick is "famous power". The name was first introduced to Britain by the Norman invaders. The name was revived by Sir Walter Scott in his poem *The Vision of Don Roderigo* (1811). Diminutives: Rod, Rody.

Rodney
Pronunciation: RAHD-nee
Rodney is of Old English and Old German origin. The meaning of the name Rodney is "Roda's island". An adopted surname and place name. It was originally adopted in honour of Admiral Lord Rodney (1719-1792), who led the French Navy to defeat in 1759. Diminutives: Rod, Roddy.

Roger
Pronunciation: ROH-jer
The name Roger is of Old German origin. The meaning of Roger is "famous spearman". From from the Old French name Rogier, which is derived from Old German *hrod*. The name was introduced to Britain by the Normans. Roger was a popular name throughout the Middle Ages

185

and in the 19th and 20th centuries.

Roland
Pronunciation: ROH-land
The name Roland is of Old German origin. The meaning of Roland is "renowned land". Roland is rejoiced in the 12th century French poetic sagas, *Chanson de Roland*, as a hero in the service of Charlemagne. He was the most famous of Charlemagne's soldiers, who died c. 778. Roland is also known as the Christian Theseus and the Achilles of the West. Roland is an anglicised form of the name Rowland. The name was introduced to Britain by the Normans. Diminutive: Roly.

Rollo
Pronunciation: ROH-llo
The name Rollo is of Latin origin. The meaning of Rollo is unknown. Rollo is Latin from of the name Roul. The name was borne by an ancestor of William the Conqueror and a Norman pirate (c. 860-932).

Roman
Pronunciation: roh-MAHN
The name Roman is of Latin origin. The meaning of Roman is "citizen of Rome". Roman is an anglicised form of the name Romeo. The name is also a variant of Romanus, the name of several saints and a pope.

Romeo
Pronunciation: ROAM-ee-ohh
Romeo is of Latin origin. The meaning of the name Romeo is "citizen of Rome". The name was made famous by Shakespeare's *Romeo and Juliet* (1595).

Ronald
Pronunciation: RAH-nald
The name Ronald is of Old Norse origin. The meaning of Ronald is "ruler's counselor". The name was revived in the 19th century. Diminutives: Ron, Ronnie.

Rory
Pronunciation: ROR-ee
The name Rory is of Irish and Gaelic origin. The meaning of Rory is "red king". The name is an anglicised form of the Irish Gaelic names *Ruaidhrí, Ruarí*, and Scottish Gaelic names, *Ruairidh, Ruaraidh*.

Ross
Pronunciation: ros
Ross is of Scottish and Gaelic origin. The meaning of the name Ross is "headland, cape". Derived from Scottish Gaelic *ros*, meaning 'headland'. Ross is an adopted surname and place name.

Rowan
Pronunciation: RO-wan
The name Rowan is of Gaelic origin. The meaning of Rowan is "little red-haired one". An adopted Irish surname. Borne by a 6th-century saint who founded the monastery of Lothar.

Roy
Pronunciation: roy
The name Roy is of Irish and Gaelic origin. The meaning of Roy is "red". From Scottish Gaelic, *ruadh*. The name was also influenced by the Old French term *roi*, which means 'king'.

Rudolf

Pronunciation: ROO-dol-f
The name Rudolf is of Latin origin. The meaning of Rudolf is "famous wolf". From Rudolphus, the Latinate form of Hrodwulf. Diminutives: Rudi, Rudy.

Rufus

Pronunciation: ROO-fuss
The name Rufus is of Latin origin. The meaning of Rufus is "red-haired". Rufus was first used a first name during the 19th century. A biblical name; borne by the name of two 1st century Christians.

Rupert

Pronunciation: ROO-pert
The name Rupert is of Old German origin. The meaning of Rupert is unknown. From Rupprecht, a German form of Robert. The name was popularised throughout Britain by Prince Rupert of the Rhine (1618-1692). He was the nephew of Charles I. St Rupert of Salzburg of the 8th century was involved in the founding of Salzburg.

Russell

Pronunciation: RUSS-el
Russell is of Old French origin. The meaning of the name Russell is "little red". Russell is an adopted surname from Old French *roux*. The name was first used as a first name in the 19th century. Diminutives: Russ.

Ryan

Pronunciation: RYE-an
The name Ryan is of Gaelic origin. The meaning of Ryan is "king". From the Irish Gaelic surname O'Riain, which means 'a descendant of Rian'.

S

Saahdia
Pronunciation: sa(ah)-dia
The name Saahdia is of Aramaic origin. The meaning of Saahdia is "the Lord's help".

Saarik
Pronunciation: sa(a)-rik
The name Saarik is of Hindi origin. The meaning of Saarik is unknown. Saarik is also the name of a small songbird.

Saber
Pronunciation: S-(a)-ber
The name Saber is of French origin. The meaning of Saber is "sword". Saber is the name of a curved sword.

Sabino
Pronunciation: sa-BEE-noh
Sabino is of Latin origin. The meaning of the name Sabino is "Sabine". The Sabines were a tribe from Italy. Romulus arranged for the Sabine women to be kidnapped, and provided as wives for the citizens of Rome. Sabino is also a saint's name.

Sacha
Pronunciation: S(a)-cha
The name Sacha is of Greek and Russian origin. The meaning of Sacha is "man's defender". The name is used as both a boy's name and as a girl's name. Sacha is a diminutive of Alexander.

Sadiki
Pronunciation: S(a)-dee-kee
The name Sadiki is of Swahili origin. The meaning of Sadiki is "faithful, loyal".

Sadler
Pronunciation: SAD-ler
Sadler is of Old English origin. The meaning of the name Sadler is "harness maker". Originally a surname and occupational

name. The name was first used as a first name in the 19th century.

Safford
Pronunciation: SAFF-ord
Safford is of Old English origin. The meaning of the name Safford is "willow river crossing". Originally a place name.

Saffron
Pronunciation: SAFF-ron
Saffron is the name of a plant. Saffron is used as bright orange/yellow spice. The name is used as both a boy's name and as a girl's name.

Sage
Pronunciation: sage
The name Sage is of Latin origin. The meaning of Sage is "healing herb". Sage is also the name of a plant. The name is used as both a boy's name and as a girl's name.

Sahil
Pronunciation: SA-hill
The name Sahil is of Hindi origin. The meaning of Sahil is "leader".

Salvador
Pronunciation: SAL-va-dor
The name Salvador is of Latin origin. The meaning of Salvador is "savior". The name is a Spanish form of Salvator. Salvador is a place name in Latin America.

Samuel
Pronunciation: SAM-yoo-el
The name Samuel is of Hebrew origin. The meaning of Samuel is "God has heard". A biblical name; borne in the Old Testament as the prophet and judge who anointed Saul and David as kings of

Israel (1 and 2 Samuel). The name was used by the Puritans. Samuel was a popular name throughout the 17th, 18th, and 19th centuries. The diminutive, Sam is one of the most popular boy's names in the English speaking world.
Diminutives: Sam, Sammie, Sammy.

Scott
Pronunciation: skaht
Scott is of Old English origin. The meaning of the name Scott is "from Scotland, a Scotsman". An adopted Scottish surname, the name has been in regular use since the early 20th century. American writer, F Scott Fitzgerald (1896-1940) popularised the name.

Sean
Pronunciation: shon
The name Sean is of Irish and Hebrew origin. The meaning of Sean is "God is gracious". The name is an Irish form of John, derived from the French form Jean. The name spread outside of Ireland in the 20th century.

Sebastian
Pronunciation: se-BASS-tian
Sebastian is of Greek origin. The meaning of the name Sebastian is "man of Sebastia". From the Latin name Sebastianus. The original form of the name referred to those from a particular city or region of Asia Minor. Borne by an early Roman soldier who converted to Christianity, his fellow officers tried to kill him with arrows. St Sebastian was a 3rd century martyred centurion who became the patron saint of soldiers. Shakespeare used

the name for the twin brother of Viola in *Twelfth Night* (1601). Diminutives: Bastian, Bastien, Seb.

Seth
Pronunciation: seth
The name Seth is of Hebrew origin. The meaning of Seth is "set, appointed". A biblical name: borne in the Old Testament by the third son of Adam and Eve as a replacement for their dead son. Eve said Seth had been appointed to take the place of Abel, who had been killed by Cain. The name was popular with the Puritans of the 17th century.

Seymour
Pronunciation: SEE-mor
The name Seymour is of English origin. The meaning of Seymour is "Saint Maur". An adopted aristocratic surname and French place name from St Maur in France. The Norman French name Maur is derived from the Latin name Mauricius. The name has been in use as a first name since the 19th century.

Shane
Pronunciation: shayn
The name Shane is of Irish and Hebrew origin. The meaning of Shane is "God is gracious". The name is a variation of Sean. The name became more popular during the 1950's and 1960's due to the classic western film *Shane* (1953).

Sheldon
Pronunciation: SHEL-den
The name Sheldon is of Old English origin. The meaning of Sheldon is "steep valley". The adopted surname is derived from various

English place names, including 'flat-topped hill'.

Sheridan
Pronunciation: SHARE-a-den
The name Sheridan is of Irish and Gaelic origin. The meaning of Sheridan is "seeker". An adopted Irish surname, from O Sirideain. The name was popularised by Irish playwright Richard Brinsley Sheridan (1751-1861). The name is used as both a boy's name and as a girl's name.

Sidney, Sydney
Pronunciation: SID-nee
Sidney is of Old English origin. The meaning of the name Sidney is "wide meadow". Sidney is an adopted surname and place name. The name has been used as a first name since the 17th century. Charles Dickens boosted the popularity of the name when he used it for his hero in *A Tale Of Two Cities* (1859). Australian city of Sydney was named in honour of Thomas Townshend. The name is used as both a boy's name and as a girl's name.

Silvester
Pronunciation: SIL-vest-er
The name Silvester is of Latin origin. The meaning of Silvester is "of the woods". The name was borne by an early Christian martyr and three popes.

Simon
Pronunciation: SYE-mun
The name Simon is of Hebrew origin. The meaning of Simon is "to hear, to be heard". The name is a variation of Simeon. A biblical name; borne in the New Testament by several characters. Simon

was the name of two of the apostles, Simon Peter and Simon the Zealot. The name was popular from the Middle Ages through to the 18th century.

Sinclair
Pronunciation: sin-KLARE
Sinclair is of English origin. The meaning of the name Sinclair is "from Saint Clair". The name is an adopted Scottish surname, derived from a French baronial name and place name.

Sky
Pronunciation: SKY
The name Sky is of English origin. The meaning of Sky is unknown. The name is a variant of Skye. Sky is also used as a nickname for the Skyler variant. The name was popular during the 1960's when people took names from nature.

Solomon
Pronunciation: SAH-lah-mun
Solomon is of Hebrew origin. The meaning of the name Solomon is "peace". A biblical name; borne in the Old Testament by a king of Israel, the son of David and Bathsheba. He was known for his wisdom and justice, and wrote the Book of Proverbs. Solomon was a popular name during the Middle Ages, the name was revived in the 17th century.

Spencer
Pronunciation: SPEN-ser
The name Spencer is of Middle English origin. The meaning of Spencer is "dispenser of provisions". The adopted aristocratic

surname, was originally an occupational name for a steward or butler. The name has been associated with the Churchill family, Dukes of Marlborough since the 18th century.

Stafford
Pronunciation: STAFF-ord
The name Stafford is of Old English origin. The meaning of Stafford is "Ford by a landing place". An adopted aristocratic surname and English place name. Stafford has been in occasional use as a first name since the mid-19th century.

Stanford
Pronunciation: STAN-ford
Stanford is of Old English origin. The meaning of the name Stanford is "stoney ford". Stanford is also a place name.

Stanley
Pronunciation: STAN-lee
The name Stanley is of Old English origin. The meaning of Stanley is "stony meadow". Stanley is an adopted surname and place name. The name was first used as a first name in the 19th century. Diminutive: Stan.

Stephen
Pronunciation: STEE-ven
The name Stephen is of Greek origin. The meaning of Stephen is "garland, crown". From Greek stephanos, which means 'crown'. St Stephen was the first person to be martyred for his Christian faith. Accused of blasphemy, he was stoned to death by the Jews (Acts 6-8). The name was borne by several saints and ten popes. The name was introduced to Britain by

the Normans. Diminutives: Steve, Stevie.

Stewart
Pronunciation: STOO-ert
The name Stewart is of Old English origin. The meaning of Stewart is "steward". The name is an early variant of Stuart. Stewart was the family name of the royal house of Scotland from 1371 to 1714, and of England from 1603. Originally an occupational name, a medieval steward was charged with the care of the castle and estate affairs. Diminutives: Stew, Stu.

Stuart
Pronunciation: STU-art
Stuart is of Old English origin. The meaning of the name Stuart is "steward". Originally an occupational name, the steward administers a large feudal household. The name was introduced by Mary Queen of Scots. Stuart and Steward are clan names of the royal house of Scotland. Diminutives: Stew, Stu.

Sullivan
Pronunciation: SIL-IH-VUN
The name Sullivan is of Gaelic origin. The meaning of Sullivan is "dark eyes".

T

Tabor
Pronunciation: TAY-bor
The name Tabor is of Hebrew and Hungarian origin. The meaning of Tabor is "misfortune, bad luck". A biblical name; Mount Tabor a landmark mountain near Nazareth.

Tad
Pronunciation: tad
The name Tad is of English origin. The meaning of Tad is "heart". The name is a diminutive of Tadhg or Thaddeus. Tad is also used in American slang meaning, 'small'.

Tadhg
Pronunciation: teig
The name Tadhg is of Irish, Gaelic and Scottish origin. The meaning of Tadhg is "poet, philosopher".

Talfryn
Pronunciation: tal-(f)-ryn
The name Talfryn is of Welsh origin. The meaning of Talfryn is "high high".

Taliesin
Pronunciation: TAL-ie-sin
The name Taliesin is of Welsh origin. The meaning of Taliesin is "shining forehead". Borne by a 6th century Welsh poet.

Tam
Pronunciation: TAM
Tam is of Aramaic origin. The meaning of the name Tam is "twin". The name is a variant of Thomas. A biblical name: borne by one of the twelve apostles, he is also known as 'doubting Thomas'.

Tancred
Pronunciation: TAN-cred
The name Tancred is of Old German origin. The meaning of Tancred is "counsel, advice". Tancred

was an 11th century Norman knight and Crusader, he was the son of Otho the Good and Emma Guiscard. He appears as one of the leading characters in the Italian Torquato Tasso's poem, *Jerusalem Delivered* (1581). He also inspired Rossini's opera *Tancredi* (1813) and Disraeli's novel *Tancred (1847)*. The name was introduced to Britain by the Normans.

Terence
Pronunciation: TARE-ence
The name Terence is of Latin origin. The meaning of Terence is "one who initiates an idea". Latin from the Roman family name, Terentius. diminutives: Tel, Terry.

Theobald
Pronunciation: THEE-o-bald
The name Theobald is of Old German origin. The meaning of Theobald is "brave people". Diminutive: Theo.

Theodore
Pronunciation: THEE-a-dor
Theodore is of Greek origin. The meaning of name Theodore is "God's gift". Theodore is an early Christian name and a saint's name. The name became popular after a stuffed toy bead was named Teddy in hour of the US president, Theodore Roosevelt (1858-1919). Diminutives: Ted, Teddie, Teddy, Theo.

Theodoric
Pronunciation: THEE-o-dor-ic
The name Theodoric is of Old German origin. The meaning of Theodoric is "people's ruler, leader of the people". The name was

borne by a king of the Ostrogoths (c. 454-526) who invade Italy.
Diminutives: Derek, Derrick, Theo.

Thomas
Pronunciation: TAH-mas
Thomas is of Aramaic origin. The meaning of Thomas is "twin". A biblical name; borne by one of the twelve apostle also known as 'doubting Thomas'. The Apocrypha's Acts of Thomas tells of the apostle's missionary work in India. His feast day in 3rd July.
Diminutives: Tom, Tommie, Tommy, Tam.

Thorley
Pronunciation: THOR-lee
The name Thorley is of Old English origin. The meaning of Thorley is "Thor's meadow, Thor's wood".
Thorley is also a place name.

Thurston
Pronunciation: THER-sten
The name Thurston is of Old English origin. The meaning of Thurston is "Thor's stone".

Tierney
Pronunciation: TIE-r-ney
The name Tierney is of Irish and Gaelic origin. The meaning of Tierney is "Lord". An adopted surname from the Irish Galic name Ó Tighearnaigh.

Timothy
Pronunciation: TIM-oh-thee
Timothy is of Greek origin. The meaning of the name Timothy is "God's honor". A biblical name; born by a young Christian who was a companion of St Paul.

Timothy is derived from the Greek name Timotheos. Charles Dickens popularised the name in the 19th century with his novel, *A Christmas Carol* (1843). Diminutives: Tim, Timmie, Timmy.

Tobias
Pronunciation: TOB-ias
The name Tobias is of Hebrew origin. The meaning of Tobias is "God is good". A biblical name; borne in the Old Testament Apocrypha's Book of Tobit, Tibias, was accompanied on a journey to Ecbatana by the Archangel Raphael. The name was used by the Puritans and later revived in the 19th century.

Todd
Pronunciation: tahd
The name Todd is of Middle English origin. The meaning of Todd is "Fox". The name possibly used to refer to a fox hunter, or to indicate colouring, or cunning. Todd is an adopted surname.

Torquil
Pronunciation: TOR-quil
The name Torquil is of Gaelic and Scottish origin. The meaning of Torquil is "Thor's helmet". Scottish Gaelic, from *porketil*, por being a contraction of Thor (the Norse god of thunder). *Ketil* meaning, 'cauldron'. Thor's cauldron was an instrument used for sacrifices. The name was introduced to Britain by the Vikings.

Traherne
Pronunciation: TRA-herne
The name Traherne is of Welsh origin. The meaning of Traherne is "strength of iron, greatly akin to iron". The name is a variant form of Welsh Trahaearn.

Travers
Pronunciation: TRAV-ers
The name Travers is of Old French origin. The meaning of Travers is "to cross over". An adopted surname from Old French *travers*, meaning 'crossing'. Originally an occupational surname given to gatekeepers and others who collected tolls at bridges.

Travis
Pronunciation: TRAV-iss. Travis is of Old French origin. The meaning of the name Travis is "to cross over". An adopted surname from Old French *travers*, meaning 'crossing'. Travis was an occupational surname given to gatekeepers and others who collected tolls at bridges.

Tremaine
Pronunciation: TRE-maine Tremaine is of English origin. The meaning of Tremaine is "town built with stone". The name is a variant of Tremain. Tremaine is an adopted Cornish surname.

Trevor
Pronunciation: TREV-or
The name Trevor is of Welsh origin. The meaning of Trevor is "great settlement". Trevor is an adopted Welsh surname.

Tristan
Pronunciation: TRISS-tan
The name Tristan is of Celtic origin. The name is influenced by Old French *triste*, from Latin *tristis*, meaning 'sad'. Borne in Arthurian legend as a Knight of the Round Table and the tragic hero of the medieval tale, *Tristan and Isolde*. Tristan was a hero of

Celtic legend and medieval romance.

Troy
Pronunciation: TR-oy
The name Troy is of Irish and Gaelic origin. The meaning of Troy is "descendant of the footsoldier". An adopted surname which was given to those who migrated to England from Troyes in France, after the Norman conquest of 1066. Troy is also associated with the ancient city In Asia Minor where the Trojan wars were fought. The name is used as both a boy's name and as a girl's name.

Tyrone
Pronunciation: TY-rohn
The name Tyrone is of Gaelic origin. The meaning of Tyrone is "land of Eoghan". An adopted surname, derived from the Northern Ireland county of Tyrone. Diminutive: Ty.

U

Ulises

Pronunciation: u-li-ses

Ulises is a variant of the Latin name Ulysses, a variant of the Greek name Odysseus, which means "wrathful".

Ulick

Pronunciation: u-li-ck

The name Ulick is of Irish and Gaelic origin. The meaning of the name Ulick is "little William".

Ulysses

Pronunciation: you-LISS-ees

Ulysses is of Latin origin, a variant of the Greek name Odysseus, which means "wrathful".
Ulysses was an intelligent and resourceful hero of Homer's epic Odyssey.

Umar

Pronunciation: u-mar

The name Umar is of Arabic origin. The meaning of the name is "flourishing". Borne by a lifelong companion of the Prophet Muhammad.

Umberto

Pronunciation: um-ber-to

Umberto is of Italian origin. The name is a variant of the Old German name, Humbert which means "renowned hun". Umerto is a royal name in Italy.

Upton

Pronunciation: Up-ton

Upton is an adopted surname and a place name. The name is of Old English origin, from *up*, "higher" and *tun*, "settlement". The meaning of the name Upton is "upper settlement".

Urban

Pronunciation: ur-ban

Urban is of Latin origin, from urbanus which means, "citizen". The meaning of Urban is "from the city". A biblical name; borne by a character in the New Testament. Urban is also the name of eight popes.

Uriah
Pronunciation: yer-RY-ah
The name Uriah is of Hebrew origin. The meaning of the name Uriah is "my light is Jehovah". A biblical name; borne in the Old Testament one of King David's warriors. He was the husband of Bathsheba, who was sent to certain death in battle by David.

Uriel
Pronunciation: OOR-ee-el
Uriel is of Hebrew origin. The meaning of the name is "angel of light", "flame of God". In the Apocrypha, Uriel is one of the seven archangels.

Urijah
Pronunciation: u-ri-jah
Urijah is a variant of the Hebrew name Uriah. The meaning of the name Urijah is "my light is Jehovah". A biblical name; borne of one of King David's warriors, and the husband of Bathsheba.

Uziel
Pronunciation: u-ziel
The name Uziel is of Hebrew origin. The meaning of the name is "strength", "power".

V

Vachel

Pronunciation: VAY-chel
The name Vachel is of Old French origin. The meaning of Vachel is "small cow".

Vail

Pronunciation: VAY-el
The name Vail is of Old English origin. The meaning of Vail is "Valley". Originally a place name.

Valen

Pronunciation: VA-len
Valen is a variant of the Latin name Valentine. The meaning of the name is "strong", "healthy". Valen is used as a both a boy's name and a girl's name.

Valentine

Pronunciation: VAL-en-tyne
Valentine is of Latin origin. The meaning of Valentine is "strong", "healthy".
Valentine is also a variant of Valentinus, which was the name of more than 50 saints and three Roman emperors.

Van

Pronunciation: van
The name Van is of Danish origin. The name is diminutive of Ewan and Ivan. It is also a nickname for Evan. The adopted surname was introduced as a given name by early immigrants in America.

Vance

Pronunciation: vance
The name Vance is of Old English origin. The meaning of the name Vance is "marshland".

Varun

Pronunciation: va-run
The name Varun is of Hindi origin. The meaning of Varun is "water god".

Vaughn

Pronunciation: von

The name Vaughn is of Welsh origin. The adopted surname was first used as a given first name in early 20th century. The meaning of the name Vaughn is "little" taken from *fychan*, meaning "small".

Vere
Pronunciation: v (e)-re
Vere is of French origin. Vere is an adopted surname and French Baronial name. It is also an upper-class surname in England. Derived from Old French *vern* which means, "alder".

Vernon
Pronunciation: VER-non
Vernon is of Old French origin. Derived from Old French *vern* which means, "alder". The meaning of the name is "alder grove". The aristocratic surname was brought to England the Norman conquest. Richard de Vernon arrived in Britain with William the Conqueror in 1066. Vernon is also a place name.

Vicente
Pronunciation: VICE-nte
Vicente is a variant of the Latin name Vincent. The meaning of the Vicente is "prevailing".

Victor
Pronunciation: VIK-tor
The name Victor is of Latin origin. The meaning of the name Victor is "Champion". Victor is a very popular saint's name, common in Christian Rome.

Vincent
Pronunciation: VIN-sent
Vincent is of Latin origin. The meaning of Vincent is "prevailing". Derived from Latin *vincens*, meaning " conquering". Borne by

several early saints and steadily used since the early Christian days. Saint Vincent of Saragossa was a 4th-century Spanish martyr. Saint Vincent de Paul, a 17th-century priest. The name was popular during the Middle Ages and revived during the 19th century.

Virgil

Pronunciation: VER-jil

Virgil is of Latin origin from *vergilius*. Anglicized form of the name of the Roman poet and philosopher, Publius Vergilius Maro. Regarded as one of the greatest poets of ancient Rome, he was considered to have had magical powers and many medieval romances the poems tell of his exploits. His work has been used to study Roman history and the Latin language for the past two-thousand years.

Vitus

Pronunciation: VI-tus

Vitus is a variant of the Latin name Vito. The meaning of the name is "life-giving".

Vivian

Pronunciation: VIV-ian

The name Vivian is of Latin origin. Old French form of the Latin name Vivianus, from *vivus* which means "alive", "lively". The meaning of the name Vivian is "full of life" Vivian is used as both a boy's name and as a girl's name.

W

Wade
Pronunciation: wayde
Wade is of Old English and Scandinavian origin. The meaning of the name Wade is "river ford". Wade is also a medieval given name taken from Scandinavian mythology.

Wadham
Pronunciation: WAD-ham
The name Wadham is of Old English origin. The meaning of Wadham is "Ford village". Wadham is also a place name.

Wadley
Pronunciation: WAD-lee
The name Wadley is of Old English origin. The meaning of Wadley is "Ford meadow". Wadley is also a place name.

Wadsworth
Pronunciation: WADS-worth
The name Wadsworth is of Old English origin. The meaning of Wadsworth is "village near the ford". Wadsworth is also a place name.

Wagner
Pronunciation: WAG-ner
The name Wagner is of German origin. The meaning of Wagner is "wagon builder". Originally an occupational name.

Wahib
Pronunciation: WA-hib
The name Wahib is of Arabic origin. The meaning of Wahib is "donor". The name is one of Allah's 99 attributes.

Wainwright
Pronunciation: WAYN-right
The name Wainwright is of Old English origin. The

meaning of Wainwright is "wagon builder".

Waite
Pronunciation: WAY-te
The name Waite is of Middle English origin. The meaning of Waite is "guard, watchman". Originally an occupational name. Christmas carolers were known as 'waits'.

Wakeley
Pronunciation: VIV-ian
Wakeley is of Old English origin. The meaning of the name Wakeley is "damp meadow". Wakeley is also a place name.

Walcott
Pronunciation: WALL-cot
The name Walcott is of Old English origin. The meaning of Walcott is "cottage by the wall".

Waldemar
Pronunciation: WALD-e-mar
Waldemar is of Old German origin. The meaning of the name Waldemar is "renowned ruler".

Walden
Pronunciation: WALD-en
The name Walden is of Old English origin. The meaning of Walden is "wooden valley". Walden is also a place name.

Waldo
Pronunciation: WAL-DOH
The name Waldo is of Old German origin. The meaning of the name Waldo is "rule". Derived from a Latinized form of the Old German *wald*, which means "to rule". Waldo is a short form and diminutive of several Old German names such as Oswald.

Walker

Pronunciation: WAHL-ker

The name Walker is Old English origin. The meaning of the name is "cloth washer", "walker". Walker is an occupational name from the medieval era, were workers trod on fabric to cleanse of any impurities.

Wallace

Pronunciation: WAL-iss

The name Wallace is of Old French origin. The meaning of the name is "Welshman". Wallace is originally a Scottish surname which refers to foreigners. Use as a first name probably began in honor of a 13th-century Scottish hero, William Wallace. He was a Scottish patriot who struggled against King Edward 1.

Walter

Pronunciation: WAL-ter

Walter is of Old German origin. The meaning of the name Walter is "commander of the army". From the Old German *wald*, which means "power". It was introduced to Britain by the Normans.

Warren

Pronunciation: war-ren

The name Warren is of Old English origin. The meaning of Warren is "watchman". The name is also possibly from the Norman French *warrene*, which means "stockyard".

Wayne

Pronunciation: wayne

Wayne is an adopted surname of Old English origin. The name was originally given to cart makers or drivers. The meaning of the name Wayne is "wagon builder", "driver". The name was made famous by actor John Wayne (1907-1979).

Wentworth

Pronunciation: WEN-two-rth

The name Wentworth is an adopted surname that is of Old English origin. Wentworth is also a place name from Old English winter, "Winter" and the word, "enclosure". Used as a reference to settlements that was used only during the cold winter months. The meaning of the name is "pale man's settlement".

Wes

Pronunciation: wes

The name Wes is variant of the Old English name Wesley. It is also a variant of the English surname Westley. The meaning of the name Wes is "western meadow".

Wesley

Pronunciation: WES-lee

Wesley is of Old English origin. The meaning of Wesley is "western meadow". Wesley is also a place name and a variant of the English surname Westley. The adopted surname was used in honor of 18th-century brothers John and Charles Wesley, founders of the Methodism Church.

West

Pronunciation: we-ST

The name West is a variant of the Old English place name, Westbrook. The place names refers to the location of a person's dwelling. The meaning of the name West is "western stream".

Wilbur

Pronunciation: wil-BUR

Wilbur is an adopted surname from Old English

will, meaning "desire" and burh, "fortress".

Wilder
Pronunciation: WILD-er
The name Wilder is of German origin. Originally an occupational name for someone who captures and kills wild animals. The meaning of the name is "Hunter".

Wiley
Pronunciation: WYE-lee
The name Wiley is of Old English origin. The meaning of the name Wiley is "crafty". The name is also possibly a place name of a village and a river in England, "water meadow".

Willard
Pronunciation: WIL-erd
Willard is of Old English origin. The meaning of the name is "strong desire" It is an adopted surname from *will*, "deserve", and heard, "brave".

William
Pronunciation: WIL-yum
The name William is of Old German origin. From *wil* meaning "desire" and *helm*, "helmet". The meaning of the name William is "desiring of protection", "determined protector". The name was brought to Britain by Norman invader William the Conqueror. Three out of four English boys were given some form of the conquerors name, William. It was probably the first name to enjoy popularity on a mass scale. William became the most popular name in Britain within a century of the Norman Conquest. The name was also borne by four kings of England and has

remained a royal name in Britain for nearly one thousand years.

Willie
Pronunciation: WIL-ee
The name Willie is of English origin. Willie is used as both a boy's name and also as a girl's name.

Wilmer
Pronunciation: WIL-mer
Wilmer is of Old German origin. The meaning of the name Wilmer is "strong desire".

Windsor
Pronunciation: WIND-sor
Windsor is an adopted surname of Old English origin. The meaning of the name is "riverbank with a winch". From the Old English name Windels-ora, meaning "landing place with a winch". Windsor is also a place name of a town and castle in England. Windsor is the surname of the British royal family.

Winston
Pronunciation: WIN-stun
The name Winston is Old English origin. The meaning of the name Winston is "joyful stone". Winston is an adopted surname and English place name. From the Old English name Wynn, and *tun*, "settlement", which means "Wynn's place". Former British prime minister, Sir Winston Churchill was given the name from his families connections to the region.

Wolfgang
Pronunciation: WOLF-gang
Wolfgang is of Old German origin. The meaning of the name is "traveling wolf". Famous composer, Wolfgang Amadeus Mozart

made the name famous in the English-speaking world.

Wyatt
Pronunciation: WY-ut
The name Wyatt is of Old English origin. The meaning of Wyatt is "war strength". Wyatt is an adopted surname from Old English *wig* meaning, "war" and *heard*, "hardy".

Wynne
Pronunciation: WYN-ne
The name Wynne comes from the Welsh word, *Gwen*, which means "fair, holy, blessed, white". The meaning of the name Wynne is "friend". Wynne is also a variant of the name Wynn. Wynne is used as both a boy's name and as a girl's name.

Wyndham
Pronunciation: WYND-ham
Wyndham is of Old English origin. The meaning of the name is "Wyman's hamlet", "hamlet near the winding way". Wyndham is an adopted surname and also a place name, it is a contracted form of the Norfolk town Wymondham.

X

Xavi
Pronunciation: X-avi
Xavi is a variant of the name Xavier. The meaning of the name is "name house".

Xander
Pronunciation: ZAN-der
The name Xander is of Greek origin. The meaning of the name Xander is "man's defender". The name is also a short form of Alexander.

Xavier
Pronunciation: ecks-ZAY-vee-er
Xavier is of Basque origin. The meaning of the name is "new house". Saint Francis Xavier (1506-52) was a Jesuit missionary, who took Christianity to the Japan and the East Indies. The name is especially popular in Roman Catholic families.

Xenophon
Pronunciation: X-(e)-no-phon
The name Xenophon is of Greek origin. The meaning of Xenophon is "foreign voice". The name was borne by a 4th-century Greek historian.

Xenos
Pronunciation: X-(e)-nos
The name Xenos is of Greek origin. The meaning of Xenos is "hospitality".

Xerxes
Pronunciation: ZURK-seez, Z-uh-rk-sihs
The name Xerxes is of Persian origin. The meaning of the name is "King", "monarch". Several Persian rulers bore the name Xerxes. One of the rulers from the fifth century BC started a war on the Greeks.

Xidorn

Pronunciation: X-(i)-do-rn

The name Xenophon is of American origin. The meaning of Xidorn is "truth seeker".

Xiomar

Pronunciation: zhoh-MAR

Xiomar is of Spanish origin. The meaning of the name Xiomar is "famous in battle". The name is a variant of Geomar.

Y

Yael
Pronunciation: yael
The name Yael is variant of the Hebrew name Jael. The meaning of the name Yael is "mountain goat", "fertile moor". The name is also a variant of the Old English name Yale.

Yannick
Pronunciation: ya-nni-CK
Yannick is a variant of Yann(French, Hebrew). The meaning of the name Yannick is "God is gracious". Yannick is used as both a boy's name and as a girl's name.

Yasser
Pronunciation: YAS-ser
Yasser is of Arabic origin. The name is a variant of the Arabic name Yasir. The meaning of the name Yasser is "wealthy", "well to do".

Yehudi
Pronunciation: yehu-di, ye-hudi
Yehudi is of Hebrew origin. The meaning of the name is "Judah", "praise".

Yoel
Pronunciation: yoel
Yoel is a variant of the Hebrew name Joel. The meaning of the name Yoel is "Jehovah is the Lord". A biblical name; borne as a prophet and writer of the Book of Joel.

Yorick
Pronunciation: yo-ri-ck
The name Yorick is a variation of Jorck, a Danish form of George. Yorick is of Old English origin, and the meaning of the name is "farmer". Shakespeare used the name for the court jester in Hamlet (1601).

Yosef
Pronunciation: YO-sef
Yosef is a variant of the name Yusuf. The meaning of the name Yosef is "the Lord increases".

Yousef

Pronunciation: you-sef
Yousef is a variant of the Hebrew name Joseph. A biblical name; borne of the son of Jacob, he was sold by his brothers into slavery, and become a supreme power in Egypt. The meaning of the name Yousef is "Jehovah increases".

Yusuf

Pronunciation: yu-suf
Yusuf is variant of the Hebrew name Joseph. The meaning of the name is "the Lord increases".

Yves

Pronunciation: eve
The name Eve is of French origin. The meaning of the name is "yew". The name is a French variation of Ivo, which is drawn from Old German, *Ivo*. Saint Yves (14th century) was a French lawyer and a priest. The name is also possibly an occupational name.

Z

Zachariah

Pronunciation: zak-a-RYE-ah

Zachariah is of Hebrew origin. The meaning of Zachariah is "the Lord recalled". Zachariah is a variation of the name Zecharaih. A biblical name; Zachariah was an Old Testament king of Israel.

Zachary

Pronunciation: ZAK-a-ree

The name Zachary is of Hebrew origin. The meaning of the name Zachary is "the Lord recalled". Zachary is variation of the name Zachariah. A biblical name; Zachary is one of several names from the Old Testament.

Zach

Pronunciation: ZAK

The name Zack is diminutive of the several forms of Zachariah and Isaac.

Zachary

Pronunciation: ZAK-a-ree

The name Zachary is of Hebrew origin. The meaning of the name is "the Lord recalled". Zachary is a variant of the name Zachariah. A biblical name; Zachary is one of several names from the Old Testament.

Zahir

Pronunciation: ZA-hir

The name Zahir is of Arabic origin. The meaning of the name Zahir is "blossoming", "flourishing".

Zain

Pronunciation: zain

Zain is a variant of the Hebrew name Zane. It is also possibly a variant of the Hebrew name John. The meaning of the name Zain is "God is gracious".

Zander

Pronunciation: ZAN-der
Zander is of Greek and Slavic origin. The meaning of the name Zander is "man's defender". Zander is a short form of the name Alexander.

Zephaniah

Pronunciation: ze-pha-niah
The name Zephaniah is of Hebrew origin. The meaning of the name is "hidden by God". A biblical name; borne as a minor prophet.

Zeus

Pronunciation: ZOO-SE
Zeus is of Greek origin. The meaning of Zeus is "living". Zeus is the name of the chief of the Olympian gods, and father of the gods and goddesses.

Zion

Pronunciation: ZI-on
The name Zion is of Hebrew origin. The meaning of the name is "highest point". In the Christian religion, Zion is the name for heaven.

A-Z Baby Girl Names For 2016

A

Abigail

Pronunciation: AB-ih-gayl
The name Abigail is of Hebrew origin. The meaning of Abigail is "father's rejoicing". A biblical name; borne in the Old Testament by the wife of King David (1 Samuel). Abigail was described as 'good in discretion and beautiful in form'. Abigail referred to herself as David's handmaiden so often that the name became a popular term for a lady's maid. The name was introduced to Britain in the 16th century. Diminutives: Abbey, Abbie, Abby, Abi, Gail, Gale, Gayle.

Ada

Pronunciation: AY-dah
The name Ada is of Old German origin. The meaning of Ada is "noble". The name possibly derives from the Old German Names Eda or Etta. Ada is also used as a short form of the names Adele and Adelaide. The name was borne by a 7th-century abbess of Saint Julien Des Près at Le Mans. The name was introduced to Britain in the 18th century.

Adela

Pronunciation: a-DELL-ah
Adela is of Old German origin. The meaning of the name Adela is "noble". Derived from Old German, athal. The name was introduced to Britain by the Norman invaders. Adela was the name of William the Conqueror's youngest daughter. The name died out during the Middle Ages and was later revived in the 19th century. Diminutives: Addie, Addy, Della.

Adelaide

Pronunciation: AD-a-layd
The name Adelaide is of Old German origin. The meaning of Adelaide is "noble kind". The name is a Norman French version of the Old German name, Adelheid. The name was

borne by the wife of Otto The Great (10th century), Holy Roman Emperor. Queen Adelaide, wife of William IV popularised the name in the 19th century. The city of Adelaide in Australia is named after her. Diminutives; Addie, Addy.

Adrienne
Pronunciation: AY-dree-en
Adrienne is of Latin origin. The meaning of the name Adrienne is "from Hadria". The name is a French feminine form of Adrian.

Africa
Pronunciation: AF-ree-ca
The name Africa is of Irish Gaelic origin. The meaning of Africa is "pleasant". The name is an Irish Gaelic version of Aifric. Africa is also a place name for the continent.

Agatha
Pronunciation: AG-a-thah
The name Agatha is of Greek origin. The meaning of Agatha is "good". The name is a Latin form of the Greek name, Agathe. Borne by a 3rd-century martyr and saint. She was tortured and murdered at Catania in Sicily after she refused to marry a Roman consul. She is the patron saint of bell ringers. Her feast day is 5th February. The name underwent a popular revival in the 19th century. The name was also made famous by renowned writer, Agatha Christie (1890-1976).

Agnes
Pronunciation: AG-ness
Agnes is of Greek origin. The meaning of the name Agnes is "chaste, holy". The name is a Latin form of the Greek *hagnos*. Borne by a young Roman girl who was martyred at the age of thirteen on the orders of Diocletian in c. 304. Agnes had refused several offers of

marriage, as she declared herself to be devoted to Christ. She is now regarded as the patron saint of virgins, Her feast day is 21st January. Diminutives: Aggie, Aggy, Ness, Nessa, Nesta.

Ailsa
Pronunciation: a(i)-LIS-ah
Ailsa is of Old Norse origin. The meaning of the name Ailsa is "island of Alfsigr". Ailsa is also a place name, Ailsa Craig in the estuary of the River Clyde.
Diminutive: Ailie.

Aimee
Pronunciation: ay-MEE
The name Aimee is of Old French and Latin origin. The meaning of Aimee is "to love, beloved". The name has been used as a first name since the Middle Ages.

Aisha
Pronunciation: ah-EE-shah
Aisha is of Arabic origin. The meaning of the name Aisha is "alive, thriving". Borne by the third wife of Prophet Muhammad. H Rider Haggard popularised the name in his novel *She* (1887).

Alannah
Pronunciation: ah-LAH-nah
Alannah is of Irish Gaelic origin. The meaning of the name Alannah is "O my child". From Irish Gaelic, Oleanbh.

Alberta
Pronunciation: al-BER-tah
The name Alberta is of Old English origin. The meaning of Alberta is "noble, bright". The name is a feminine form of the masculine name Albert. Alberta is also the

name of Canadian province, which was named after Princess Louise Alberta.

Alexandra
Pronunciation: al-eks-AHN-dra
The name Alexandra is of Greek origin. The meaning of Alexandra is "man's defender". The name is a feminine form of the masculine name Alexander. The name was popularised in the 19th century when Edward VII married the Danish Princess Alexandra in 1863. Diminutives: Alex, Alexa, Alix, Lex, Lexie, Lexy, Sandie, Sandra, Sandy, Tiggy, Zandra.

Alexis
Pronunciation: a-LEX-iss
Alexis is of Greek origin. The meaning of the name Alexis is "defender". Derived from Greek, *alexios*, which means 'to defend'. The name is often used a shortened variation of the name Alexander. Although Alexis is traditionally a male name, it is now also used for girls in the modern world. Saint Alexis was a popular saint of Edessa, admired as a 'man of God.'

Alice
Pronunciation: AL-iss
The name Alice is of Old German origin. The meaning of Alice is "noble, exalted". Originally a common adaptation of the name Adelaide, Alice became recognized as a first name in its own right. Lewis Carroll popularised the name with his books, *Alice's Adventures in Wonderland* (1865), and *Through the Looking Glass* (1872). The main character was based on his childhood friend Alice Lidell.

Amalia

Pronunciation: a-ma-LIA

Amalia is of Latin and Old German origin. The meaning of the name Amalia is "work". The name is a variation of Amelia.

Amanda

Pronunciation: ah-MAN-dah

The name Amanda is of Latin origin. The meaning of Amanda is "loveable". From Latin *Amanda*, the female form of *amare*. The name first appeared as first name on a 1212 birth record from Warwickshire, England. The name was popularised in the 17th century by the playwright and poet, Colley Cibber (1671-1757). Diminutives: Manda, Mandi, Mandie, Mandy.

Amelia

Pronunciation: a-MEEL-yah

Amelia is of Latin and Old German origin. The meaning of the name Amelia is "eager worker, labour". From Old German *amal*, and influenced by the Latin name Aemelia. Princess Amelia brought the name to Britain in the 18th century. Diminutives: Emily, Millie, Milly.

Amina

Pronunciation: ah-MEEN-ah

The name Amina is of Arabic origin. The meaning of Amina is "honest, peaceful". Amina bint-Wahab was the mother of the Prophet Muhammad.

Amy

Pronunciation: AY-mee

The name Amy is of Old French and Latin origin. The meaning of Amy is "beloved". Amy is an anglicised form of the name Aimèe. Originally used as a nickname for the Latin name Amata. The name was popularised by characters in Louisa M Alcott's *Little Women* (1868).

Anastasia
Pronunciation: ahn-a-STAH-shah
Anastasia is of Greek origin. The meaning of the name Anastasia is "Resurrection". From the Greek word *anastasis*, which means 'rising up'. Borne by a Roman saint and matron, she was said to have buried the bodies of Saint Peter and Saint Paul with Saint Basilissa. The name is popular in Eastern Europe in honour of a 4th century Dalmation martyr.

Anastasia was made famous in the 20th century by the daughter of Tzar Nicholas II, the last Russian czar. In 1920, a woman claiming to be Anastasia said that she had survived the massacre of the royal family in 1917, thus generating worldwide publicity.

Andrea
Pronunciation: AN-dree-ah
The name Andrea is of Greek origin. The meaning of Andrea is "manly, virile". The name is a feminine form of the masculine names Andreas and Andrew. The name is also used as a nickname for Alexandra. The name dates back to the 17th century.

Angela
Pronunciation: AN-je-lah
The name Angela is of Greek origin. The meaning of Angela is "angel,

messenger of God". The name is a feminine form of Angel and Angelus. The name became popular in Britain from the 18th century. Diminutive: Angie.

Angelica
Pronunciation: an-JEL-ih-kah
Angelica is of Latin origin. The meaning of the name Angelica is "angelic". From the Latin *Angelicus*. Borne by the heroine of Matteo Boiardo's *Orlando Innamorato* (1487), Angelica was the beautiful daughter of the king of Cataio. Orlando's passionate love for Angelica ended up driving him mad. Diminutive: Angie.

Angelina, Angeline
Pronunciation: an-JEL-ih-na
The name Angelina is of Italian origin. The meaning of Angelina is "angel, messenger of God".. The name Angeline is of French origin. Both Angelina and Angeline are variations of the Greek name Angela. Diminutive: Angie.

Angharad
Pronunciation: an-HAR-ad
The name Angharad is of Welsh origin. The meaning of Angharad is "beloved, much loved". Angharad is a character in the Welsh folk tales *Mabinogian*.

Anita
Pronunciation: a-NEE-tah
The name Anita is of Spanish origin. The meaning of Anita is unknown. Anita is originally a Spanish diminutive of Ann. The name was made famous by

237

the Swedish film actress, Anita Ekberg.

Ann, Anne
Pronunciation: ANN-e
The name Anne is of English and Latin origin. The meaning of Anne is "God has favoured me". Anne is the English form of the biblical name Hannah.

Anna
Pronunciation: AN-ah
Anna is of Hebrew origin. The meaning of the name Anna is "God has favoured me". Anna is a Latinate variant of the name Hannah. In classical legend, Anna was the sister of Dido, Queen of Carthage. A biblical name; borne in the New Testament by an elderly prophetess (Luke 2:36-38).

Annabel
Pronunciation: AN-a-BELL
The name Annable is of Latin origin. The meaning of Annabel is "loveable". The name is a variation of Amabel. The name has been a popular first name in Scotland since the 12th century.

Anneka
Pronunciation: AN-ee-ka
Anneka is of Swedish origin. The meaning of the name Anneka is "sweet-faced". Anneka is a Swedish form of the name Ann(e).

Anneliese
Pronunciation: AN-ee-lee-se
Anneliese is of German origin. The meaning of the name Anneliese is "graced with God's bounty". Anneliese is a variant of the Latin name Annalisa. The German name is a compound of Anna and Liese (Elizabeth).

Annette
Pronunciation: an-NET
The name Annette is of French origin. The meaning of Annette is unknown. Annette is feminine diminutive form of Antoine. Diminutive: Net, Nettie, Netty, Toinette, Toni.

Antoinette
Pronunciation: ann-twa-NET
The name Antoinette is of French origin. The meaning of Antoinette is unknown. Antoinette is a feminine diminutive form of the name Antoine. The name was made famous by the French Queen Marie Antoinette (1755-1793). Diminutives: Net, Nettie, Netty, Toinette, Toni.

Antonia
Pronunciation: ann-TONE-yah
Antonia is of Latin origin. The meaning of the name Antonia is unknown. Antonia is a feminine form of the masculine name Anthony. The name was a common Roman feminine family name. Diminutive: Toni, Tony, Tonia, Tonya.

Anya
Pronunciation: AN-ya
The meaning of Anya is "resurrection, God had favoured me". Anya is a variant of the Greek name Anastasia. The name is an anglicised spelling of the Spanish form of Ann(e).

Aphra
Pronunciation: AFF-rah
The name Aphra is of Hebrew origin. The meaning of Aphra is "young deer". The name is either derived from Hebrew *aphrah*, which means 'dust'

or possibly a variation of the Latin name Afra.

Aoife
Pronunciation: EE-fra
The name Aoife if of Irish, Gaelic and Scottish origin. The meaning of Aoife is "beautiful". From Irish Gaelic *aoibh*, which means 'beauty'. The name is borne by numerous heroines in ancient Irish legend. Eva is the anglicized form of the name.

April
Pronunciation: AY-prill
The name April is of Latin origin. The meaning of April is "to open". April is also the name of the fourth month of the year. The name may have been influenced by the French equivalent, Avril.

Arabella
Pronunciation: AIR-a-bell-ah
The name Arabella is of Latin origin. The meaning of Arabella is "prayerful". The name might possibly be a variation of the Annabel. The name has been popular in Scotland since the 14th century and spread to England in the 18th century.

Areta
Pronunciation: A-re-ta
The name Areta is of Greek origin. The meaning of Areta is "virtue, excellence". Areta is related to the name Arethusa. The name is also a variant of the Greek name Aretha.

Ariadne
Pronunciation: ar-ee-AHD-nee
The name Ariadne is of Greek origin. The meaning of Ariadne is "most holy".

Borne mythology; Ariadne was the daughter of King Minos of Crete. She helped Theseus to escape by giving him a ball of wool so that he could find his way out of the Labyrinth after he had killed the Minotaur. Saint Ariadne is a 2nd century saint and Christian martyr.

Arianwen
Pronunciation: a-ree-AN-win
The name Arianwen is of Welsh origin. The meaning of Arianwen is "white, holy silver, fair". Borne in the 5th by a daughter of Brychan, a legendary Welsh chieftain.

Artemis
Pronunciation: AR-te-miss
The name Artemis is of Greek origin. The meaning of Artemis is unknown. Borne in Greek mythology; Artemis was a Greek goddess of the moon, hunting, and of chastity, equivalent to the Roman goddess Diana. Artemis is used as both a boy's name and as a girl's name.

Astrid
Pronunciation: AS-trid
The name Astrid is of Old Norse origin. The meaning of Astrid is "beautiful goddess". From Old Norse elements *áss*, which means 'god', and *fríor*, 'beautiful'.

Athene
Pronunciation: a-THEE-nee
The name Athene is of Greek origin. The meaning of Athene is "immortal". Borne in Greek mythology; Athene was the virgin goddess of arts, wisdom and war. She was supposedly born fully armed, from the head of Zeus. Athene was patron of the city of Athens.

Audrey
Pronunciation: AW-dree
The name Audrey is of Old English origin. The meaning of Audrey is "noble strength". Derived from the informal pronunciation of the name of Saint Etheldreda, 7th-century abbess of Ely.

Aurora
Pronunciation: aw-ROHR-ah
The name Aurora is of Latin origin. The meaning of Aurora is "dawn". Borne in mythology; Aurora was the goddess of sunrise. In various versions of the 'Sleeping Beauty' fairytale, the princess's name is Aurora.

Ava
Pronunciation: AY-vah
The name Ava is of uncertain origin. The meaning of Ava is also unknown. The name is possibly a medieval Germanic diminutive for names that begin with AV-. The name may possibly be a variation of Eva. Hollywood actress Ava Gardner (1922-1990) popularised the name.

Aveline
Pronunciation: AY-v-e-line
Aveline is of Norman origin. The meaning of the name Aveline is unknown. The name is a Latinate form of the Norman French name Eveline.

Avril
Pronunciation: AV-ril
The name Avril is of Latin origin. The meaning of Avril is "to open". From French *Avril*, which means 'April'. The name may also be a nickname for Averil.

B

Barbara
Pronunciation: BAR-bra
The name Barbara is of Greek and Latin origin. The meaning of Barbra is "strange, foreign woman". The name was originally an onomatopoeic word describing the babbling sound of an unintelligible foreign tongue. The name was applied to anyone who did not speak Greek. Saint Barbara is invoked as a protector against fire and lighting, she is the patron saint of architects, stonemasons, and fortifications. Her father was about to cut off her head when he was struck by lightning. Her actual existence is disputed.
Diminutives: Bab, Babs, Barbie, Baubie, Bobby.

Bea
Pronunciation: bea
Bea is a diminutive of the names, Beatrice and Beatrix.

Beatrice, Beatrix
Pronunciation: BEE-a-triss
The name Beatrice is of Latin origin. The meaning of Beatrice is "bringer of joy". The name is mentioned in the Domesday book. Shakespeare used the name in Much Ado About Nothing (1598). The name was revived in the 19th century, possibly after Queen Victoria named one of her daughters Beatrice. Beatrice is also the name of the heroine of Dante's, *Divine Comedy* (c. 1309-02).

Belinda
Pronunciation: ba-LIN-dah
The name Belinda is of Old German origin. The meaning of Belinda is "snake". From the Old German name Betlindis.

Diminutives: Bel, Bell, Belle, Linda, Lundy.

Bella
Pronunciation: BELL-ah
Bella is of Italian and Latin origin. The meaning of the name Bella is "beautiful". The name is also a diminutive of names incorporating the element – bella, such as Isabella.

Bennett
Pronunciation: BEN-et
Bennett is of French and Latin origin. The adopted surname has been used for both girl's and boy's names. Taken from the medieval vernacular form of Benedict.

Bentley
Pronunciation: BENT-lee
The name Bentley is of Old English origin. The meaning of the name Bentley is "bent grass meadow". The adopted surname is used more commonly as a boy's name, however it is also used as a girl's name. Bentley is also a place name for many places in England.

Bernadette
Pronunciation: ber-na-DET
The name Bernadette is of French and Old German. The meaning of Bernadette is "strong, brave bear". Bernadette is a French feminine form of the masculine name Bernard. Saint Bernadette Soubirous popularised the name during the 19th century. She was a French peasant girl who had visions of the Virgin Mary and uncovered a spring near Lourdes where miraculous cures are sought. Diminutives: Bernie, Berny.

Berta

Pronunciation: BERT-ah

The name Berta is of Old German origin. The meaning of Berta is "bright". The name was borne by the mother of Charlemagne. The name was introduced to Britain by the Normans.

Beryl

Pronunciation: BEHR-el

The name Beryl is of Greek origin. The meaning of Beryl is "light green semi-precious gemstone". From Old French *beril*, which was derived from Greek *berullos*, denoting a precious pale green stone with light blue, yellow and white lights. The name was popular during the 19th century.

Beth

Pronunciation: beth

The name Beth is of Hebrew origin. The meaning of Beth is "house". Beth is also a diminutive of the name Elizabeth. The name dates back to the 19th century. Louisa M Alcott popularised the name in her novel, *Little Women* (1868).

Bethany

Pronunciation: BETH-a-nee

The name Bethany is of Hebrew origin. The meaning of Bethany is "house of figs". A biblical name, Bethany is the name of the village near Jerusalem. Diminutive: Beth.

Bethia

Pronunciation: BE-thia

The name Bethia is of Hebrew origin. The meaning of Bethia is "daughter of God".

Betsy

Pronunciation: BET-see

The name Betsy is of Hebrew origin. The meaning of Betsy is "God is my oath". Betsy is a diminutive of the name Elizabeth.

Bette

Pronunciation: BET-ee

The name Bette is of Hebrew and French origin. The meaning of Bette is "God is my oath". Bette is a French diminutive of the name Elizabeth. The name was popularised by Hollywood actress Bette Davis (1908-1989).

Betty

Pronunciation: BET-ee

The name Betty is of Hebrew origin. The meaning of Betty is "God is my oath". The name was popular during the 20th century.

Beulah

Pronunciation: bea-u-LAH

The name Beulah is of Hebrew origin. The meaning of Beulah is "married". A biblical name for the land of Israel (Isaiah 62).

Beverly, Beverley

Pronunciation: BEV-er-lee

The name Beverly is of Old English origin. The meaning of Beverly is "beaver". Beverly is an adopted surname and place name, from Old English *beofor*. The name was first used as a masculine name in the 19th century. The name is now given to females.

Bianca

Pronunciation: bee-AHNK-ah

The name Bianca is of Italian origin. The meaning of Bianca is "pure, white". The name was used by Shakespeare in *The Taming of the Shrew* (1593). Bianca was the gentle sister of Katharina, 'the Shrew'. Shakespeare also used the name is Othello (1604).

Billie
Pronunciation: BILL-ee
The name Billie is of Old English origin. The meaning of Billie is unknown. Billie is a diminutive of the names Wilhelmina and William.

Birgit
Pronunciation: ber-GEET
Birgit is of Norwegian origin. The meaning of the name Birgit is "exalted one". Birgit is a variant of the name Bridget.
Diminutives: Birgit, Brita, Britt.

Blake
Pronunciation: blayk
Blake is of Old English origin. The meaning of the name Blake is "black", "pale". The adopted surname is used as both a boy's name and a girl's name. Blake was originally used as a nickname for someone with skin or hair that was either very dark ("blaec") or very light ("blac").

Blanche
Pronunciation: BLAN-che
The name Blanche is of Old French and Old German origin. The meaning of Blanche is "white, pure". Blanche of Lancaster brought the name to Britain in the 14th century.

Blodwen
Pronunciation: B-lod-wen
The name Blodwen is of Welsh origin. The meaning

of Blodwen is "holy flower, white flower". The name was popular in the Middle Ages.

Blossom
Pronunciation: BLOSS-om
Blossom is of Old English origin. The meaning of the name Blossom is "flower-like". The name is a direct adoption of the English vocabulary, denoting a mass of flowers on a fruit tree. Blossom was first used as a first name in the 19th century.

Blythe
Pronunciation: bleeth
The name Blythe is of Old English origin. The meaning of Blythe is "blithe, cheerful". Originally an adopted surname.

Bobbie, Bobby
Pronunciation: BOB-ee
The name Bobbie is of Latin origin. The meaning of Bobbie is "foreign woman". Bobby is a variant of the Latin name Barbara. The name is also a diminutive of the name Roberta.

Bonita
Pronunciation: boh-NEE-tah
The name Bonita is of Spanish origin. The meaning of Bonita is "pretty". Diminutives: Bonni, Bonny.

Brady
Pronunciation: BRAY-dee
The name Brady is of Irish and Gaelic origin. The meaning of the name is "descendant of Brádach". The name is used as both a boy's name and as a girl's names.

Branwen
Pronunciation: BRAN-wen
The name Branwen is of Welsh origin. The meaning of Branwen is "raven, fair". Borne in Welsh legend by the heroine of one of the tales of the *Mabinogian*.

Brenda
Pronunciation: BREN-dah
The name Brenda is of Old Norse origin. The meaning of Brenda is "sword, torch". The name is sometimes considered to be a feminine form of Brendan.

Brennan
Pronunciation: BREN-an
Brennan is of Irish and Gaelic origin. The meaning of the name Brennan is "teardrop". Brennan is used as both a boy's name and as a girl's name. The name is also a variant of Brendan.

Bride
Pronunciation: BRI-de
Bride is of Gaelic origin. The meaning of the name Brid is "exalted one". Bride is a variation of the Gaelic name Bridget.

Bridie
Pronunciation: BRID-ee
Bridie is of Gaelic origin. The meaning of the name Bridie is "exalted one". Bridie is a variation of the Gaelic name Bridget.

Bridget
Pronunciation: BRIH-jet
Bridget is of Gaelic origin. The meaning of the name Bridget is "exalted one". Bridget is an anglicized version of the Irish name Brighid. Borne in mythology; Saint Brigid of Kildare (c. 450-525) is the second patron saint of Ireland, after Saint Patrick.

Her feast day is 1ˢᵗ February. Diminutives: Biddy, Bridie.

Bridgid

Pronunciation: BRID-gid
The name Bridgid is of Gaelic origin. The meaning of Bridgid is "exalted one". Bridgid is a variation of the name Bridget.

Briony, Bryony

Pronunciation: BRI-on-ee
Briony is of Greek origin. The meaning of the name Briony is "luxurious growth". The name was adopted in the 19ᵗʰ century, when botanical names became fashionable.

Brooks

Pronunciation: brux
Brooks is of Old English and Old German origin. The meaning of Brooks is "water", "small stream". Brooks is used as both a boy's name and a girl's name.

Bronwen

Pronunciation: BRON-wen
The name Bronwen is of Welsh origin. The meaning of Bronwen is "white breast, blessed breast". Diminutive: Bron.

Bryn

Pronunciation: br-yn
The name Bryn is of Welsh origin. The meaning of the name Bryn is "hill". The name is also a short form of Brynmor. Bryn is used as both a boy's name and girl's name.

C

Caitlín
Pronunciation: KATE-lin
Caitlín is of Old French and Greek origin. The meaning of the name Caitlín is "pure". Caitlín is the Irish Gaelic form of the name Catherine.

Cameron
Pronunciation: KAM-ren
The name Cameron is of Scottish and Gaelic origin. The meaning of Cameron is "crooked nose". Cameron is a Scottish Highlands clan surname. Cameron is used as both a girl's name and as a boy's name.

Camilla
Pronunciation: ka-MEEL-ah
The name Camilla is of Latin origin. The meaning of Camilla is "helper to the priest". Camilla is a feminine form of the Roman family name Camilus. Fanny Burney popularised the name with her novel, Camilla (1796). Diminutives: Millie, Milly.

Candida
Pronunciation: kan-DEE-dah
The name Candida is of Latin origin. The meaning of Candida is "white". The name is borne by several early saints. Diminutive: Candy.

Carina
Pronunciation: ka-REEN-ah
The name Carina is of Latin origin. The meaning of Carina is "beloved, dear". Carina is a diminutive feminine form deriving from Italian *caro*.

Carla
Pronunciation: kar-LAH
Carla is of Old German origin. The meaning of the name Carla is "free man".

Carla is a feminine form of the masculine name Carl. The name was popular throughout the late 20th century.

Carly
Pronunciation: KAR-lee
The name Carly is of Latin origin. The meaning of Carly is "free man". Carly is a diminutive of the names Carla, Carlotta and Caroline.

Carmel
Pronunciation: kar-MEL
Carmel is of Hebrew origin. The meaning of the name Carmel is "garden, orchard". A biblical name; Mount Carmel was where Elijah summoned Israel to choose between God and Baal (I King 18). In the 12th century, a monastery was founded dedicated to the Virgin Mary.

Carmela
Pronunciation: kar-MEL-ah
The name Carmela is of Italian origin. The meaning of Carmela is "garden, orchard". Carmela is an Italian variant of the name Carmel.

Carmen
Pronunciation: KAR-men
The name Carmen is of Spanish origin. The meaning of Carmen is "song, charm". The name is originally a Spanish form of the name Carmel, influenced by the Latin word, *carmen*. The name was popularised in the 19th century by Bizet's opera, *Carmen* (1875).

Carol
Pronunciation: KARE-ol
The name Carol is of Old German origin. The meaning of Carol is "free man". Carol is a feminine

form of the names Charles, originated from the Latin name Carolus. Originally used as a boy's name, the name is now generally used for girls.

Caroline
Pronunciation: KARE-a-line
The name Caroline is of Old German origin. The meaning of Caroline is "free man". Caroline is a feminine form of the names Charles, originated from the Latin name Carolus. The German-born wife of King George II, Caroline of Ansbach, introduced the name to Britain.
Diminutives: Carly, Caro, Carrie.

Carolyn
Pronunciation: KARE-a-lyn
The name Carolyn is of Old German origin. The meaning of Carolyn is "free man". Carolyn is a variant of the name Caroline, dating back to the 20th century.

Carys
Pronunciation: CHAR-is
Carys is of Welsh origin. The meaning of the name Carys is "love".

Casey
Pronunciation: KAY-see
The name Casey is of Irish and Gaelic origin. The meaning of Casey is "alert, watchful". The name Casey is used as both a boy's name, and as a girl's name. Casey is from the male Gaelic name *Cathasaigh*.

Cassandra
Pronunciation: ka-SAN-dra
Cassandra is of Greek origin. The meaning of Cassandra is "shining upon man". Cassandra is possibly

a variation of the name Alexander. The name is borne in Greek mythology by a Trojan princess. She was blessed with the gitt of prophecy and foretold the fall of Troy. However after turning down Apollo's advances, he was so angry that he arranged for her never to be believed. The name was revived in the 18th century. Diminutives: Cas, Cassie, Sandra.

Catherine
Pronunciation: KATH-rin
The name Catherine is of Greek origin. The meaning of Catherine is "pure". Borne by several early saints, saint Catherine Alexandria was a 4th-century martyr of noble birth. She was condemned to death on a spiked wheel however, the wheel mysteriously broke. This led to her being beheaded. Saint Catherine Alexandria is the patron saint of wheelwrights. Saint Catherine Siena is (1347-1380) is considered the patron saint of Italy. King Henry VIII had three wives names Catherine. Diminutives: Casey, Cate, Cath, Cathie, Cathy, Kate, Kay, Kit, Kitty.

Cathleen
Pronunciation: kath-LEEN
Cathleen is of Greek origin. The meaning of the name Cathleen is "pure". Cathleen is a variation of the name Catherine and was influenced by the Irish Gaelic name Caitlín.

Catrin
Pronunciation: CAT-rin
The name Catrin is of Greek origin. The meaning of Catrin is "pure". Catrin is a Welsh form of the name Catherine.

Catriona

Pronunciation: cat-REE-ona

Catriona is of Scottish Gaelic and Irish origin. The meaning of the name Catriona is "pure". Catriona is a variation of the name Catherine. Robert Louis Stevenson popularised the name during the 19th century, with his novel *Catriona* (1893).

Cecilia

Pronunciation: sess-SEEL-yah

The name Cecilia is of Latin and Old Welsh origin. The meaning of Cecilia is "blind, sixth". Cecilia is a Latinate feminine form of the name Cecil. The name was borne in the 2nd century by a blind Roman martyr and saint. She is regarded as the patron saint of musicians and music. Her feast day is 22nd November. The name was popular during the Middle Ages. The name was later revived in the 18th century. Diminutives: Cis, Ciss, Cissie, Cissy, Sissie, Sissy.

Cecilie

Pronunciation: sess-SEEL-e

The name Cecilie is of Latin and French origin. The meaning of Cecilie is "blind, sixth". Cecilie is a French feminine form of the name Cecil. Cecilie is also a variant of the names Cecilia and Cecily.

Ceinwen

Pronunciation: KAYN-wen

The name Ceinwen is of Welsh origin. The meaning of Ceinwen is "beautiful; gems".

Celeste

Pronunciation: she-LEST

The name Celeste is of Latin origin. The meaning of Celeste is "heavenly". The name was popular among early Christians. Celeste is a masculine form of the name Celestin.

Celine
Pronunciation: SEL-ine
The name Celine is of Latin origin. The meaning of Celine is "heaven". Derived from Latin *caelum*, which means 'sky'. The French name is spelled Cèline. The name was popularised by singer Celine Dion.

Ceridwen
Pronunciation: ke-RID-wen
The name Ceridwen is of Welsh origin. The meaning of Ceridwen is "fair, holy, blessed poetry. Borne in Celtic mythology by the Welsh goddess of poetic inspiration.

Chandler
Pronunciation: CHAND-ler
Chandler is of Middle English and Old French origin. The meaning of the name Chandler is "candle maker". The adopted surname was also an occupational name from 'chandele' meaning 'candle'. Chandler is used as both a boy's name and as a girl's name.

Chandra
Pronunciation: SHAN-drah
Chandra is of Hindi and Sanskrit origin. The meaning of the name Chandra is "moon shining". The greatest Hindu goddess Devi is also known as Chandra.

Chanel
Pronunciation: sha-NELL
Chanel is of Old French origin. The meaning of the name Chanel is "wine, amphora". The name was

influenced by the legendary fashion designer Gabrielle 'Coco' Chanel (1883-1971). Chanel is also the name of the 14th-century French missionary saint.

Chantal
Pronunciation: shanh-TAL
Chantal is of Old French origin. The meaning of Chantal is "stone". An adopted surname and place name, after Chantal in Saóne-et-Loire. The name was originally given in honor of Saint Jeanne-Françoise de Chantal (1572-1641). She lived a strict religious life and founded an order of nuns, the Vistandines.

Charlene
Pronunciation: shar-LEEN
The name Charlene is of Old German origin. The meaning of Charlene is "free man". Charlene is a feminine form of the masculine name Charles.

Charlotte
Pronunciation: SHAR-let
The name Charlotte is of Old German origin. The meaning of Charlotte is "free man". Charlotte is a French feminine diminutive of Charles. The name has been used in England since the 17th century. The name was popularised by King George III's wife, Charlotte Sophia (1744-1817). E.B White also popularised the name in *Charlotte's Web* (1952). Diminutives: Charley, Charlie, Chattie, Chatty, Lottie, Lotty, Totty.

Charmaine
Pronunciation: shar-MAYNE
The name Charmaine is of English origin. The meaning

of Charmaine is "charm". A modern coinage, derived from the name Carminea. The name was first used by Maxwell Anderson and Laurence Stallings in the play, *What Price Glory?* (1924).

Chastity
Pronunciation: CHASS-ti-tee
The name Chastity is of Latin origin. The meaning of Chastity is "pure". The virtue name is from Latin *castus*.

Cherie
Pronunciation: sha-REE
The name Cherie is of French origin. The meaning of Cherie is "darling". From French chère.

Cherry
Pronunciation: CHARE-ee
The name Cherry is of English and Old French origin. The meaning of Cherry is "cherry, tree". Cherry is originally a diminutive of the name Charity. The name later became associated with the sweet fruit. Cherry is also used as a diminutive of Cherie.

Cheryl
Pronunciation: CHER-ell
The name Cheryl is of French and Greek origin. The meaning of Cheryl is "cherry fruit, green gemstone". The name is an early 20th-century variation of the name Cherry.

Chiara
Pronunciation: kee-AH-ra
The name Chiara is of Italian and Latin origin. The meaning of Chiara is "bright, famous". The name is an Italian form of Clara and Claire. The name is

borne by several early Italian saints.

Chloe
Pronunciation: KHLOH-ee
Chloe is of Greek origin. The meaning of the name Chloe is "green shoot". The name is associated with the Greek goddess of agriculture and fertility, Demeter. The name was borne in Longus's Greek romance, *Daphnis and Chloe*. A biblical name; Chloe is briefly mentioned by Saint Paul in the New Testament (1 Corinthians 1:11). The name was popular with the Puritans during the 17th century.

Christabel
Pronunciation: KRIS-ta-bell
The name Christabel is of Latin and French origin. The meaning of Christabel is "beautiful Christian". The name is a medieval coinage from the name Christ with –bel, from Latin *bella*. Samuel Taylor Coleridge popularised the name in his poem Christabel (1816). Christabel Pankhurst (1880-1958) was a pioneer suffragette.

Christiana
Pronunciation: kris-TEEN-iah
Christiana is of Latin origin. The meaning of the name Christiana is "follower of Christ". The name is a medieval Latinate form of Christian. John Bunyan used the name for the wife of Christian in The Pilgrims' Progress (1684). Diminutives: Chris, Christie, Christy.

Christina
Pronunciation: kris-TEEN-ah

Christina is of Latin origin. The meaning of the name Christina is "follower of Christ". Christina is a feminine form derived from the Latin name Christianus. Diminutives: Chris, Chrissie, Chrissy, Tina.

Christine
Pronunciation: kris-TEEN
The name Christine is of French and Latin origin. The meaning of Christine is "follower of Christ". Christine is a French form of the name Christina. The name was introduced to Britain in the 19th century. Diminutives: Chris, Chrissie, Chrissy.

Ciara
Pronunciation: kee-AR-ah
The name Ciara is of Irish and Gaelic origin. The meaning of Ciara is "black". Ciara is a modern Irish feminine form of the name Ciaran.

Cindy
Pronunciation: SIN-dee
The name Cindy is of English and Greek origin. The meaning of Cindy is "from Mount Kynthos". Cindy is a diminutive of the name Lucinda. The name became a popular first name in its own right.

Cissy
Pronunciation: sis-EE
The name Cissy is of Latin and Old Welsh origin. The meaning of Cissy is "blind, sixth". Cissy is a diminutive of the names Cecilia and Cicely.

Claire
Pronunciation: clare
The name Claire is of Latin origin. The meaning of Claire is "bright, famous".

The Norma invaders introduced the name to Britain in the original form of, Clara. The name was revived in the 19th century as the French form of Clare.

Clara
Pronunciation: KLAR-a
Clara is of Latin origin. The meaning of the name Clara is "bright, famous". Clara is a feminine form of the Latin adjective *clarus*. The name has largely been replaced by the names Chiara, Claire and Clare.

Clare
Pronunciation: clare
The name Clare is of Latin origin. The meaning of Clare is "bright, famous". The name was a popular medieval English form of the name Clara.

Clarissa
Pronunciation: kla-RISS-ah
Clarissa is of Latin origin. The meaning of the name Clarissa is "most bright, most famous". Clarissa is a Latinate form of the name Clarice. Samuel Richardson popularised the name in his novel *Clarissa* (1748).

Claudia
Pronunciation: KLAW-dee-ah
The name of Claudia is of Latin origin. The meaning of Claudia is "lame". Claudia is a feminine form derived from the Roman family name Claudius. A biblical name; borne by a Christian woman of Rome greeted by Paul in his second letter to Timothy (2 Timothy 4). The name dates back to the 16th century.

Claudine

Pronunciation: klaw-DEEN

The name Claudine is of French origin. The meaning of Claudine is "lame". Claudine is a French feminine and diminutive form of the name Claude. The name was popular throughout the 20th century.

Cleo

Pronunciation: KLEE-oh

Cleo is of Greek origin. The meaning of the name Cleo is "glory of the father". Cleo is a diminutive of the Greek name Cleopatra. The name became a popular first name in its own right.

Clíodhna

Pronunciation: KOR-ee

The name Clíodhna is of Irish Gaelic origin. The meaning of Clíodhna is unknown. The name is born in Irish legend, Clíodhna was one of the three beautiful daughters of the poet Libra.

Coco

Pronunciation: KO-ko

Coco is of French origin. The meaning of the name Coco is "people of victory". Coco is a diminutive of Nicolette, and also of names starting with CO-. The name was popularised by the famous fashion designer Gabrielle Coco Chanel (1883-1971).

Cody

Pronunciation: KO-dee

The name Cody is of Irish and Gaelic origin. The meaning of the name Cody is "Helper". Cody is used as both a boy's name, and as a girl's name.

Cole

Pronunciation: kohl

Cole is of Middle English and Old French origin. The meaning of Cole is "charcoal". Originally a surname that was derived from a medieval given name. Cole is used as both a boy's name and as a girl's name.

Colette
Pronunciation: ko-LET
The name Colette is of French and Greek origin. The meaning of Colette is "people of victory". Colette is a diminutive of the name Nicolette. The name is borne by a 15th-century French nun and saint, she was renowned for giving her money to the poor. French writer, Sidonie-Gabrielle Colette (1873-1954) popularised the name.

Colleen
Pronunciation: kah-LEEN
The name Colleen is of Gaelic origin. The meaning of Colleen is "girl, wench". Colleen is an Irish vernacular word, which means girl. The name is also used as a feminine of the masculine name Colin.

Concetta
Pronunciation: CON-cetta
The name Concetta is of Italian and Latin origin. The meaning of Concetta is "conceived, conception". Concetta is an Italian form of a Latin name, *concepta*. The name is a reference to the Immaculate Conception.

Constance
Pronunciation: KAHN-stans
The name Constance is of Latin origin. The meaning of Constance is "constant, steadfast". From the Latin *constantia*, which means 'constancy'. The name was introduced to Britain by the Normans. The name was

borne by a virgin saint daughter of Constantine the Great. Diminutive: Connie.

Constantia
Pronunciation: CONST-ant-tia
The name Constantia is of Latin origin. The meaning of Constantia is "constant, steadfast". Constantia is Latin form of Constance. The name was popular with early Christians and also with the Puritans.
Diminutive: Connie.

Corey
Pronunciation: KOR-ee
The name Corey is an English surname derived from an Old Norse personal name Kori. Corey is used as both a boy's name, and as a girl's name. The meaning of the name may mean "God, peace".

Corinna, Corinne
Pronunciation: ko-RINN-nah
The name Corinna is of Greek origin. The meaning of Corinna is "maiden". Corinna was an alternative name for Persephone, and also for a 5th-century poetess. Roman poet Ovid used the name for the woman in his love poetry. The name was later revived in the 16th and 17th centuries.

Cosima
Pronunciation: KOZ-i-ma
The name Cosima is of Greek origin. The meaning of Cosima is "beauty, order". Cosima is a feminine form of Cosmo.

Courtney
Pronunciation: COURT-ney
Courtney is of Old French origin. The meaning of Courtney is "domain of

Curtis". The name is both a surname and a place name. Courtney is a Norman baronial name from places in Northern France called Courtenay. Courtney is used as both a boy's name and a girl's name.

Crystal
Pronunciation: KRISS-tal
The name Crystal is of Greek origin. The meaning of Crystal is "ice". Derived from Greek *krustallos*. Crystal is one of the several stone and mineral names that became fashionable in the late 19th century.

D

Dabney
Pronunciation: DAB-nee
The name Dabney is of Old French origin. The meaning of Dabney is "from Aubigny".

Dacey
Pronunciation: DAY-cee
The name Dacey is of Irish and Gaelic origin. The meaning of Dacey is "from the South".

Dacia
Pronunciation: DAY-sha
Dacia is of Latin origin. The meaning of the name Dacia is unknown. Originally a place name, Dacia was a Roman province.

Dada
Pronunciation: DA-da
The name Dada is of Nigerian origin. The meaning of Dada is "curly haired".

Dagmar
Pronunciation: DAG-mar
The name Dagmar is of Old German and Scandinavian origin. The meaning of Dagmar is "glorious, day's glory". Dagmar is a royal name in Denmark.

Dagny
Pronunciation: DAG-ny
The name Dagny is of Old Norse origin. The meaning of Dagny is "new day". The name possibly relates to the Old German name Dagmar.

Dahlia
Pronunciation: DAL-yah
Dahlia is of Swedish and Scandinavian origin. The meaning of the name Dahlia is "Valley".

Daisy
Pronunciation: DAY-zee
The name Daisy is of Old English origin. The meaning of Daisy is "day's eye". The

name was first used as a diminutive of the French name, Marguerite. Daisy is reference to the flower of the same name that opens during the day. The name was popular during the 19th century when botanical names became fashionable. Henry James also popularised the name in his novel *Daisy Miller* (1878).

Damaris
Pronunciation: DAM-a-ris
The name Damaris is of Greek and Latin origin. The meaning of Damaris is "calf, to tame". A biblical name; borne by an Athenian woman who heard Paul speak at Mar's Hill, she was converted by Saint Paul (Acts 17). The name was adopted by the Puritans.

Dana
Pronunciation: DAY-nah
The name Dana is of Old English origin. The meaning of Dana is "from Denmark". Borne in mythology; Dana was the Celtic goddess of fertility. The name is also used a Scandinavian feminine form of Daniel.

Daniella
Pronunciation: dan-YELL-ah
The name Daniella is of Hebrew and French origin. The meaning of Daniella is "God is my Judge". Daniella is a feminine form of the masculine name Daniel. Daniella is the Latinate form. Diminutives: Dan, Dani.

Danielle
Pronunciation: dan-YELL
The name Danielle is of Hebrew and French origin. The meaning of Danielle is "God is my Judge". Danielle

is a feminine form of the masculine name Daniel. The name has been used as a first name since the 20th century. Daniella is the Latinate form. Diminutives: Dan, Dani.

Daphne
Pronunciation: DAFF-nee
The name Daphne is of Greek origin. The name Daphne is of Greek origin. The meaning of Daphne is "laurel tree". Borne in Greek mythology; by the daughter of the river god Peneus in Thessaly. Daphne has vowed to die a virgin as she fled Apollo's advances. The gods felt sorry for Daphne and turned her into a laurel tree. The name was popular in the 18th and 20th centuries.

Dara
Pronunciation: DAR-ah
The name Dara is of Hebrew origin. The meaning of Dara is "charity, nugget of wisdom".

Darcy
Pronunciation: DAR-cee
The name Darcy is of Irish and Gaelic origin. The meaning of Darcy is "dark". An adopted Norman baronial surname (D'Arcy). The name was introduced to Britain during the Norman Conquest. Darcy is used as both a boy's name, and as a girl's name. Darcy is also a Norman place name.

Daria
Pronunciation: DAR-ee-ah
The name Daria is of Greek and Persian origin. The meaning of Daria is "maintains possessions well". Daria is a feminine form of the masculine name Darius.

Darrell
Pronunciation: DA-rr-ELL
The name Darrell is of French and English origin. The meaning of Darrell is unknown. Originally an adopted surname, derived from a French place name, Arielle (French region of Calvados). The name is used as both a girl's name and as a boy's name.

Davina
Pronunciation: dah-VEE-nah
Davina is of Hebrew and Scottish origin. The meaning of the name Davina is "beloved". Davina is a Scottish feminine form of the name David. The name dates back to the 17th century. Diminutives: Vina, Vinia.

Dawn
Pronunciation: dorn
Dawn is of Old English origin. The meaning of the name Dawn is "the first appearance of light". The name is a direct vocabulary adoption. The name dates back to the 20th century.

Deborah
Pronunciation: DEB-er-ah
The name Deborah is of Hebrew origin. The meaning of Deborah is "Bee". A biblical name; borne by two figures in the Old Testament. One is a prophetess and judge who summoned Barak to battle against an invading army (Judges 4), the other is the nurse of Rebekah (Genesis 35). The name was adopted by the Puritans. Diminutives: Deb, Debbie, Debby, Debs.

Dee
Pronunciation: dee

The name Dee is of Welsh origin. The meaning of Dee is "swarthy". Dee is a diminutive of any name beginning with the letter 'D'.

Delia

Pronunciation: DEEL-yah
The name Delia is of Greek origin. The meaning of Delia is "visible, from Delos". The name derives from Delos, which is the smallest of the Greek islands of the Cyclades. Delia is also used as a diminutive of names ending in –delia.

Delilah

Pronunciation: dee-LYE-lah
Delilah is of Hebrew origin. The meaning of the name Delilah is "amorous, seductive". A biblical name; borne in the Old Testament by the mistress of Samson, she famously persuaded Samson into revealing the secret of his superhuman strength. She then betrayed him by cutting off his hair as he slept (Judges 16). The name was adopted by the Puritans.

Della

Pronunciation: DEL-ah
The name Della is of German origin. The meaning of Della is "noble". Della is a diminutive of Adela. The name has been a popular first name since the late 19th century.

Delora

Pronunciation: del-OR-ah
The name Delora is of Latin origin. The meaning of Delora is "from the seashore".

Delphine

Pronunciation: DEL-fee-ne

The name Delphine is of French origin. The meaning of Delphine is "woman of Delphia, dolphin". Derived from the Latin name Delphina. The name is French form of a name which refers to the Greek town of Delphia, home of Apollo's coracle. The Greeks believed that Delphi was the earth's womb.

Denise
Pronunciation: de-NEES
Denise is of French origin. The meaning of the name Denise is "follower of Dionysius". Denise is a French feminine form of the name Denis. The name was first used in Britain in the 12th century.

Dervla
Pronunciation: DER-vlah
The name Dervla is of Irish and Gaelic origin. The meaning of Dervla is "poet's daughter". From the Irish Gaelic name Deirbhile. The name has undergone a revival in Ireland.

Desdemona
Pronunciation: des-de-mona
The name Desdemona is of Greek origin. The meaning of Desdemona "wretchedness". Desdemona is Latinate form of Greek *dysaimon*, which means, 'ill-starred, miserable'. Shakespeare used the name in *Othello* (1604). Desdemona was the beautiful wife of Othello, wrongly accused of adultery which led to her murder.

Devon
Pronunciation: DEV-en
Devon is of English origin. The meaning of the name Devon is uncertain. Devon is originally an adopted surname, English county

name, and the name of several towns in America. The name is used as both a boy's name and as a girl's name.

Diana
Pronunciation: dy-ANN-ah
The name Diana is of Latin origin. The meaning of the Diana is "divine". Borne in mythology; Diana was an ancient Roman goddess of fertility, hunting and the moon. Her name was possibly derived from Latin *divinus*. The name has been used as a first name since the 16th century. The name was made famous by the Princess of Wales, Diana (1961-1997).

Diane
Pronunciation: DIA-ane
The name Diane is of French and Latin origin. The meaning of Diane is "divine". Diane is French form of Diana, the name dates back to the Renaissance.

Dillan
Pronunciation: DILL-an
The name Dillan is of Irish and Gaelic origin. The meaning of Dillan is "like a lion, loyal". The name is a variant of Dillon. Dillan is used as both a boy's name and as a girl's name.

Dinah
Pronunciation: DYE-nah
Dinah is of Hebrew origin. The meaning of the name Dinah is "judgement". A biblical name: borne by the daughter of Jacob and Leah.

Dolores
Pronunciation: dor-LOR-iss
The name Dolores is of Spanish origin. The meaning of Dolores is "

Maria of the sorrows". From Spanish, 'Maria de los Dolores', which is a reference to the Virgin Mary. Diminutives: Lola, Lolita.

Dominica, Domenica
Pronunciation: dom-ih-NEEk-ah
The name Dominica is of French and Latin origin. The meaning of Dominica is "Lord". Dominica is a feminine form of the masculine name Dominic.

Dominque
Pronunciation: dom-ih-NEEK
The name Dominque is of is of French and Latin origin. The meaning of Dominque is "Lord". Dominque is French form of the masculine name Dominic.

Donna
Pronunciation: DON-nah
Donna is of Italian origin. The meaning of the name Donna is "woman". The name was American coinage of the 1920's.

Dora
Pronunciation: DOR-ah
The name Dora is of Greek origin. The meaning of Dora is "gift". Dora is a diminutive of the names Pandora, Dorothea, Dorothy and Theodora. The name became a popular first name in its own right.

Dorothea
Pronunciation: DOR-o-thee-ah
The name Dorothea is of Greek origin. The meaning of Dorothea is "gift of God". Saint Dorothea was a virgin martyr, she was killed under Diocletian in c. 300. Diminutives: Dora, Thea.

Dulcie

Pronunciation: DUL-cie

The name Dulcie is of Latin origin. The meaning of Dulcis is "sweet". From Latin *dulcis*. The name was revived in the 19th century.

E

Eartha
Pronunciation: ER-thah
The name Eartha is of Old English origin. The meaning of Eartha is "earth".
From Old English *eorthe*. The name was used by the Puritans in the 17th century.

Edina
Pronunciation: ED-ina
The name Edina is of Old English origin. The meaning of Edina is unknown. The name may possibly be a variation of Edwina, or of Aithne.

Effie
Pronunciation: EFF-ee
Effie is of Greek origin. The meaning of the name Effie is "well spoken". Effie is a diminutive of Euphemia. The name is also used as a nickname for Efrata and Evelyn.

Eileen
Pronunciation: eye-LEEN
The name Eileen is of Irish origin. The meaning of Eileen is unknown. Eileen is an anglicised form of the Irish name Eibhlin.
Diminutive: Eily.

Eithne
Pronunciation: EE-na
The name Eithne is of Irish and Gaelic origin. The meaning of Eithne is either, "little fire" or "kernel". The name is borne by several figures in Irish legend.

Elaine
Pronunciation: ee-LAYNE
The name Elaine is of Greek origin. The meaning of Elaine is "sun ray". Elaine is a French form of the name Helen. In Arthurian legend, the name was borne by a character who fell in love with Lancelot. The name

279

underwent a popular revival in the late 19th century.

Eleanor
Pronunciation: EL-a-nor
Eleanor is of Old French and Old German origin. The meaning of the name Eleanor is "sun ray, other". Eleanor is a French form of the name Helen. The name was brought to Britain in the 12th century by Henry II wife, Eleanor of Aquitaine. Diminutives: Ellie, Nell, Nellie, Nelly.

Elena
Pronunciation: eh-LAYN-ah
Elena is of Greek origin. The meaning of the name Elena is "sun ray". Elena is a variation of the name Helen. The name dates back to the 12th century. The name is considered to be an Italian and Spanish form of Helen.
Elise
Pronunciation: el-LEES
Elise is of French and Hebrew origin. The meaning or the name Elise is "God is my oath". Elise is a French diminutive of Elizabeth. The name became popular in its own right, particularly during the 19th century.

Elizabeth
Pronunciation: ee-LIZ-a-beth
The name Elizabeth is of Hebrew origin. The meaning of Elizabeth is "God is my oath". A biblical name; borne in the Old Testament by the wife of Aaron. In the New Testament the Greek form, Elisabeth was borne by the wife of Zacharias, and mother of John the Baptist. The Greek form of Elisabeth was replaced in the 16th century by Elizabeth, probably due to the reign of

Queen Elizabeth I of England. Diminutives: Bess, Bessie, Bessy, Beth, Eliza, Libby, Lisbeth, Liz, Liza, Lizbeth, Lizzie, Lizzy, Tetty.

Ella

Pronunciation: EL-ah
The name Ella is of Old German origin. The meaning of Ella is "all". The name is derived from the Old German name Alia. The name was introduced to Britain by the Normans. The name was later revived in the 19th century.

Ellen

Pronunciation: EL-en
The name Ellen is of Greek origin. The meaning of Ellen is "sun ray". Ellen is the most common variant of the name Helen. The name is also used as a diminutive of Eleanor. The name was first used as an independent name in the 16th century. Diminutives: Ellie, Nell, Nellie, Nelly.

Eloise

Pronunciation: el-o-WEE
The name Eloise is of Old German origin. The meaning of Eloise is "famous warrior". Eloise is the French variant of the name Louise.

Elsa

Pronunciation: EL-sah
The name Elsa is of Hebrew origin. The meaning of Elsa is "God is my oath". Elsa is originally a German diminutive of the name Elisabeth. The name became a popular first name in its own right.

Emanuela

Pronunciation: e-man-u-elah

The name Emanuela is of Hebrew origin. The meaning of Emanuela is "God is with us". Emanuela is a feminine form of the masculine name Emanuel.

Emily
Pronunciation: EM-i-lee
Emily is of Latin origin. The meaning of the name Emily is "rival, eager". Emily is a feminine form of the Roman family name Aemilius. Boccaccio, a 14th-century writer popularised the name with the form, Emilia. Chaucer used the name in the form Emelye in *The Knight's Tale*. The name was extremely popular during the 18th 19th and 20th centuries.
Diminutives: Millie, Milly.

Emma
Pronunciation: EM-ah
The name Emma is of Old German and Old French origin. The meaning of Emma is "entire, universal". The name was introduced to Britain in the 11th century by Emma of Normandy. The name was a royal name in medieval England. The name was revived in the 18th century, possibly due to Jane Austen's romance novel, *Emma* (1815). Emma has been one of the most favoured names for girls in Britain since the 1970's.

Emmeline
Pronunciation: EM-a-leen
The name Emmeline is of Old French and Old German origin. The meaning of Emmeline is "entire, work". Emmeline is the Old French form of the Old German name Ameline. The name was introduced to Britain by the Normans. The name was made famous by Emmeline Pankhurst, a British political activist and

leader of the British suffragette movement. The Suffragette's helped women to win the right to vote.

Erica
Pronunciation: AIR-a-ka
The name Erica is of Old Norse origin. The meaning of Erica is "complete ruler". Erica is a feminine form of the masculine name Eric. Erica is also the name of a species of plants, which includes heather and rhododendrons. The name was revived during the 19th century, when botanical names became fashionable.

Erin
Pronunciation: AIR-en
Erin is of Gaelic and Irish origin. The meaning of the name Erin is "Ireland". Derived from the Irish Gaelic name Éirinn. Erin is an ancient poetic name for Ireland.

Esmè, Esmèe
Pronunciation: EZ-may
The name Esmè is of Old French origin. The meaning of Esmè is "esteemed". From Latin *aestimatus*. The name was introduced to Scotland from France in the 16th century. The name was originally used for both sexes, it is now mainly given to females.

Esmeralda
Pronunciation: ez-mer-AHL-dah
The name Esmeralda is of Spanish origin. The meaning of Esmeralda is "Emerald". Victor Hugo popularised the name with his heroine in the classic, *The Hunchback of Notre Dame* (1831). Esmeralda

was a gypsy girl loved by Quasimodo.

Estella, Estelle
Pronunciation: EST-el-lah
The name Estella is of Old French origin. The meaning of Estella is "star". Charles Dickens popularised the name within his epic novel, *Great Expectations* (1861). Estelle is the modern French form.

Esther
Pronunciation: ESS-tar
The name Esther is of Persian origin. The meaning of Esther is "star, myrtle". A biblical name; borne in the Old Testament by a young beautiful Hebrew woman. She became the wife of the Persian king Ahasuerus in the 5th century BC after he had rejected his disobedient wife, Vashti. Her story is told in the Old Testament book and in the Apocrypha's Rest of Esther. The name has traditionally been given to girls born during the period of Purim. The name was popular with the Puritans in the 17th century.

Étain
Pronunciation: E-tain
The name Étain is of Irish Gaelic origin. The meaning of Étain is unknown, it could possibly mean "jealously". Étain is a traditional Irish Gaelic name. Borne in Irish legend by a fairy princess whose wooing by the mortal King Eochaidh, was turned into an opera, *The Immortal Hour* (1914).

Ethelinda
Pronunciation: e-thelin-da
The name Ethelinda is of Old English origin. The meaning of Ethelinda is "noble serpent". The name

was revived in the 19th century.

Etta
Pronunciation: ETT-ah
The name Etta is of English origin. The meaning of Etta is "happy".

Eva
Pronunciation: AY-vah
The name Eva is of Hebrew origin. The meaning of Eva "alive". Eva is a Latinate form of the name Harriet Stowe popularised the name with her novel, *Uncle Tom's Cabin* (1852). Eva (Evangeline) was the name of her heroine. Diminutives: Evie, Evita.

Eve
Pronunciation: eve
Eve is of Latin and Hebrew origin. The meaning of the name Eve is "alive". A biblical name; borne in the Old Testament by the first woman on earth. Eve is described as, 'the mother of all living'. Diminutives; Eveleen, Evie.

Evelyn
Pronunciation: EV-e-lyn
Evelyn is of Norman origin. Anglicised form of the Norman French feminine name Aveline. Evelyn is used as both a boy's name, and as a girl's name. The named was adopted as a boy's name in the 17th century. Originally a surname and used as a given name.

F

Fabia
Pronunciation: fah-BIA
The name Fabia is of Latin origin. The meaning of Fabia is "bean". A Latin feminine form of the Roman family name Fabius.

Fabiana
Pronunciation: fah-BE-ann-ah
The name Fabiana is of Latin origin. The meaning of Fabiana is "bean". A Latin feminine form of the Roman family name Fabius.

Fabiola
Pronunciation: fah-bee-OH-lah
The name Fabiola is of Latin origin. The meaning of Fabiola is "bean". A Latin feminine form of the Roman family name Fabius. Fabiola is a feminine diminutive of the masculine name Fabian. Saint Fabiola was a 4th-century member of the Fabius family, who founded the first hospital for sick and needy pilgrims. Queen Fabiola of Belgium was a Spanish princess.

Fadia
Pronunciation: FAD-ee-a
The name Fadia is of Arabic origin. The meaning of Fadia is "savior". Fadia is a feminine form of Fadi.

Fadila
Pronunciation: FAD-il-ah
The name Fadila is of Arabic origin. The meaning of Fadila is "moral excellence". Fadila is a feminine form of Fadile.

Faida
Pronunciation: FAI-da
The name Faida is of Arabic origin. The meaning of Faida is "plentiful".

Faith
Pronunciation: faith

The name Faith is of Middle English origin. The meaning of Faith is "belief". Faith is one of the three great Christian virtues, with hope and charity. The name is also one of the several abstract nouns denoting admirable personal qualities. The name was used throughout the 16th century and popular among the Puritans.

Fallon
Pronunciation: FAL-en
The name Fallon is of Irish and Gaelic origin. The meaning of Fallon is "superiority, leader". An adopted surname, anglicised from the Irish surname O Fallamhain, meaning 'leader'. Originally an occupational surname for a textile worker. The name was popularised by the American television series *Dynasty*.

Fanny
Pronunciation: FAN-ee
The name Fanny is of Latin origin. The meaning of Fanny is "from France". Fanny is diminutive of Frances. The name was extremely popular in the 18th and 19th centuries.

Farah
Pronunciation: FAH-rah
Farah is of Arabic origin. The meaning of the name Farah is "pleasant, joy".

Farrah
Pronunciation: FAH-rah
The name Farrah is a modern coinage of the Arabic name Farah, which means "pleasant, joy". The name was popularised by American actress Farrah Fawcett.

Fatima
Pronunciation: FAH-tee-mah

The name Fatima is of Arabic origin. The meaning of Fatima is "baby's nurse, abstainer". Borne by the Prophet Muhammad's favourite daughter, wife of Haidar, she was the only daughter to bear children.

Fay
Pronunciation: fay
The name Fay is of uncertain origin. The meaning of Fay is "belief, fairy". The name is possibly a diminutive of Faith.

Faye
Pronunciation: faye
The name Faye is of uncertain origin. The meaning of Faye is "belief, fairy". The name is possibly a diminutive of Faith.

Felicity
Pronunciation: fa-LISS-a-tee

The name Felicity is from Old French and Latin origin. The meaning of Felicity is "good fortune, lucky". The name is derived from Latin *Felicitas*. The name was a virtue name and one of the several abstract nouns denoting admirable personal qualities. The name was first used in the 17th century and was popular with the Puritans.

Fern
Pronunciation: fern
The name Fern is of Old English origin. The meaning of Fern is "fern". From Old English *fearn*, denoting a green shade-loving plant. Fern is also used as a nickname for Fernanda.

Ffion
Pronunciation: FEE-on
The name Ffion is of Welsh origin. The meaning of

Ffion is "white, fair". The name is a Welsh form of Fiona.

Fifi
Pronunciation: FEE-fee
The name Fifi is of French origin. The meaning of Fifi is "Jehovah increases". Fifi is French variant of the name Josephine. The name is also used as diminutive for Fiona.

Fina
Pronunciation: FI-na
The name Fina is of Spanish origin. The meaning of Fina is "Jehovah increases". Borne in the 13th century by a woman of San Gimignano, in Tuscany. Fina was a young girl whose claim to be recognized as a saint lay in the perfect resignation with which she accepted bodily suffering. Fina was not martyred, instead she died of a physical disease.

For six years, she lay on a plank in one position, unable to turn or move. Her feast day is 12 March.

Finella
Pronunciation: fin(el)-la
The name Finella is of Gaelic origin. The meaning of Finella is "white, fair". Finella is an Anglicised Scottish form of the Gaelic name Fionnuala.

Finola
Pronunciation: f(i)-no-la
The name Finola is of Gaelic origin. The meaning of Finola is "white, fair". Finola is an Anglicised form of the Gaelic name Fionnuala.

Fiona
Pronunciation: fee-OWN-ah
The name Fiona is of Scottish and Gaelic origin. The meaning of Fiona is

"white, fair". Fiona is a Latin form of Gaelic *fionn*. The name was first by James Macpherson (1736-1796) in his Ossianic poems. William Sharp later used the name Fiona Macleod, as a pen-name for his romantic novels.

Fionnuala
Pronunciation: fya-NOO-lah
The name Fionnuala is of Irish Gaelic origin. The meaning of Fionnuala is "white, fair". Borne in Irish legend; Fionnuala was the daughter of King Lir. Who was transformed into a swan and condemned to wander over the lakes and rivers until Christianity came to Ireland.

Flavia
Pronunciation: FLAH-vee-ah
The name Flavia is of Latin origin. The meaning of Flavia is "yellow hair". Flavia is a feminine form of the Roman family name, Flavius. The name was also borne by several early saints.

Fleur
Pronunciation: F-leur
The name Fleur is of Old French origin. The meaning of Fleur is "Flower".

Flick
Pronunciation: F-li-CK
The name Flick is of Latin origin. The meaning of Flick is "lucky". Flick is also a byname from Felicity.

Flo
Pronunciation: flo
The name Flo is of Latin origin. The meaning of Flo is "flowering, in bloom". Flo is a diminutive of the names Flora and Florence.

Flora
Pronunciation: FLO-ra
The name Flora is of Latin origin. The meaning of Flora is "Flower". From the Roman family name Florus, derived from *flos*. Borne by the Roman goddess of spring and flowers. Her festivals, the Floralia were held on the 28th April- 3rd May. Flora is also the name of a ninth-century Spanish martyr saint. Diminutives: Flo, Florrie.

Florence
Pronunciation: FLOR-ens
Then name Florence is of Latin origin. The meaning of Florence is "flowering, in bloom". Florence is a medieval form of the Latin name Florentius. Florence Nightingale (1820-1910) popularised the name during the 19th century. She was named after the Italian city where she born. The name was later revived in the 20th century.
Diminutives: Flo, Florrie, Foss, Flossie, Floy.

Florrie
Pronunciation: FLOR-ee
The name Florrie is of Latin origin. The meaning of Florrie is "flowering, in bloom". Florrie is a diminutive of the name Florence.

Floss
Pronunciation: flo-ss
The name Floss is of Latin origin. The meaning of Floss is "flowering, in bloom". Floss is a diminutive of the name Florence

Fortune
Pronunciation: for-TUNE
Fortune is of Latin origin. The meaning of the name Fortune is "good fate". Borne in mythology; Roman

goddess of fortune, chance and happiness. The name was adopted in the 17th century by Puritans.

Frances
Pronunciation: FRAN-siss
Frances is of Latin origin. The meaning of the name Frances is "French". Frances is a feminine form of Francis. Diminutives: Fanny, Fran, Francie, Frankie, Frannie.

Francesca
Pronunciation: fran-CHESS-kah
Francesca is of Italian and Latin origin. The meaning of the name Francesca is "French". Francesca is an Italian feminine form of Francisco. Borne in the 13th century by Francesca di Rimini, the daughter of Guido da Polenta, Count of Ravenna. Francesca married Giovanni Malatesta, however she loved his brother Paolo. When Francesca and Paolo were discovered together, they were put to death in c.1289. Her love story has been retold in literature, Dante told the story in his *Inferno v*. Numerous tragic plays have been written on the subject.

Francine
Pronunciation: fran-SEEN
The name Francine is of French and Latin origin. The meaning of Francine is "French". The name is a familiar form of Françoise, which is the French form of Frances.

Francoise
Pronunciation: fran-co-see
The name Francoise is of Spanish and Latin origin. The meaning of Francoise is

"French". Francoise is a Spanish form of the name Frances.

Frederica
Pronunciation: fred-er-EE-kah
The name Frederica is of Old German origin. The meaning of Frederica is "peaceful ruler". Frederica is a Latinate feminine form of the name Frederick.

Freya
Pronunciation: FRAY-ah
Freya is of Old Norse origin. The meaning of the name Freya is "lady, mistress". Borne in Scandinavian mythology; Freya is the goddess of love, marriage and the dead. The fifth day of the week, Friday was named after her.

Frieda
Pronunciation: FREE-dah
The name Frieda is of German origin. The meaning of Frieda is "Lady, peace". Frieda is a diminutive of numerous names that derive from the Old German element *frid*.

Fulgencia
Pronunciation: FUL-gen-cia
The name Fulgencia is of Latin origin. The meaning of Fulgencia is "giving off light".

Fulvia
Pronunciation: FUL-via
The name Fulvia is of Latin origin. The meaning of Fulvia is "dusky".

Fruma
Pronunciation: FRU-ma
The name Fruma is of Yiddish origin. The meaning of Fruma is "deeply religious".

G

Gabriela
Pronunciation: GAB-re-el-AH
Gabriela is of Hebrew origin. The meaning of the name Gabriela is "heroine of God". Gabriela is a feminine form of the name Gabriel. Gabriela is the Latinate form. Gabriella is the Italian form.
Diminutives: Gaby, Gabby.

Gabrielle
Pronunciation: gab-ree-ELL
The name Gabrielle is of Hebrew origin. The meaning of Gabrielle is "heroine of God". Gabrielle is a feminine form of the name Gabriel. Gabrielle is the French form.
Diminutives: Gaby, Gabby.

Gada
Pronunciation: ga-DAH
The name Gada is of Hebrew origin. The meaning of Gada is "fortunate".

Gaea
Pronunciation: GAY-ah
Gaea is of Greek origin. The meaning of the name Gaea is "the earth". Born in mythology; the womanly personification of the earth and mother of the Titans.

Gaetana
Pronunciation: gae-tan-AH
The name Gaetana is of Italian and Latin origin. The meaning of Gaetana is "from Gaeta". Gaeta is a region in southern Italy.

Gaia
Pronunciation: gab-GA-iah
The name Gaia is of Greek origin. The meaning of Gaia is "the earth". Borne in Greek mythology; the goddess of the earth, she gave birth to the sky, mountains and sea.

Gail

Pronunciation: gayl
The name Gail is of Hebrew origin. The meaning of Gail is "father of exaltation". Gail is a diminutive of the name Abigail. The name became a popular first name in its own right. The name came to Britain in the 20th century.

Galina

Pronunciation: ga-LEEN-ah
Galina is of Greek origin. The meaning of the name Galina is "calm". Derived from the Greek name Galen.

Gaynor

Pronunciation: gay-NOR
The name Gaynor is of Welsh origin. The meaning of Gaynor is "white, soft". Gaynor is a medieval English form of the name Guinevere.

Gavrila

Pronunciation: gav-ril-AH
The name Gavrila is of Hebrew origin. The meaning of Gavrila is "heroine of God".

Gemma

Pronunciation: JEM-ah
Gemma is of Latin origin. The meaning of the name Gemma is "jewel, gem". Derived from the Old Italian word for 'jewel'. The name is borne by Saint, Gemma Galgani (1878-1903). She is known as 'The Daughter of Passion'.

Geneva

Pronunciation: JEN-eve-ah
The name Geneva is of Old French origin. The meaning of Geneva is "juniper tree". The name may refer to the Swiss city, or possibly be a variation of the name Jennifer.

Geneviève

Pronunciation: JEN-a-veev

The name Geneviève is of French origin. The meaning of Geneviève is "white wave". Saint Geneviève (c. 422-512) is the patron saint of Paris. She is said to have defended Paris against the depredations of Attila the Hun with prayer. Her feast day is 3rd January.

Georgette

Pronunciation: jorj-ETT

The name Georgette is of French and Italian origin. The meaning of Georgette is "farmer". Georgette is a French feminine form of the masculine name George.

Georgia

Pronunciation: JOR-jah

Georgia is of Greek and Latin origin. The meaning of the name Georgia is "farmer". Georgia is a feminine form of the masculine name George. The name was influenced by the name of the US state, which was named after King George II of England.

Georgina

Pronunciation: jor-JEE-nah

Georgina is of Latin origin. The meaning of the name Georgina is "farmer". Georgina is a feminine form of the name George. The name was popular during the 18th and 19th centuries.

Georgie

Pronunciation: jorj-EE

Georgie is of Greek and Latin origin. The meaning of Georgie is "farmer". Georgie is a diminutive of Georgette, Georgia, Georgiana or Georgina. Georgia is a feminine form of the masculine name George.

Geraldine
Pronunciation: jare-ul-DEEN
The name Geraldine is of Old German and French origin. The meaning of Geraldine is "spear ruler". Geraldine is a feminine form of the name Gerald. The name was coined in the 16th century by Henry Howard, Earl of Surrey. He used the name in his poems to Lady Elizabeth Fitzgerald, 'the Fair Geraldine'.
Diminutives: Geri, Gerry.

Geri
Pronunciation: JER-ee
The name Geri is of English origin. The name is a modern variation of the name Gerry. British singer Geri Halliwell popularised the name during the 1990's.

Germaine
Pronunciation: jer-MAYNE
The name Germaine is of Latin and French origin. The meaning of Germaine is "brother, German". Germaine is a feminine form of the French name Germain. Borne by a 16th-century French saint, Germaine Cousin (1579-1601).

Gerry
Pronunciation: JER-ee
The name Jerry is of uncertain origin. The meaning of Gerry is "spear ruler". Gerry is a diminutive of the name Geraldine.

Gigi
Pronunciation: JEE-jee
Gigi is of French origin. The meaning of the name Gigi is "bright promise". Gigi is a diminutive of the name Gilberte. The name was popularised by Colette's novel *Gigi* (1944).

Gilda
Pronunciation: JILL-dah
The name Gilda is of Old English origin. The meaning of Gilda is "golden, gilded". The name was popularised in the 1940's with the Hollywood film, starring Rita Hayworth *Gilda* (1946). The film starred Rita Hayworth

Gill
Pronunciation: GILL
The name Gill is of uncertain origin. The meaning of Gill is "bright promise, youthful". Gill is a diminutive of the masculine name Gilbert. The name was popular during the Middle Ages.

Gillian
Pronunciation: GILL-ee-an
The name Gillian is of Latin origin. The meaning of Gillian is "youthful". Gillian is a feminine form of the name Julian. The name was popular during the Middle Ages. Diminutives: Gill Gillie, Gilly.

Gina
Pronunciation: GEE-nah
The name Gina is of uncertain origin. Gina is diminutive of girls' names that end in –gina, such as Georgina. The name became a popular first name in its own right.

Ginger
Pronunciation: JIN-jer
The name Ginger is of English origin. The meaning of Ginger is "liveliness, ginger". Ginger is a diminutive if the name Virginia. Ginger is also the name of a pungent root used as a spice. The name was popularised in the 20th century by the Hollywood dancer, Ginger Rogers (1911-1995).

Gisela
Pronunciation: gi-sel-LAH
The name Gisela is of Old German origin. The meaning of Gisela is "pledge, hostage". From Old German, *gisil*.

Gita
Pronunciation: gi-TAH
The name Gita is of Hindi and Sanskrit origin. The meaning of Gita is "song".

Glenn
Pronunciation: gl-ENN
The name Glenn is of Scottish Gaelic origin. The name Glenn is "Glen, valley". Originally an adopted surname. The name is used as both a boy's name and as a girl's name.

Glory
Pronunciation: glo-EE
Glory is of Latin origin. The meaning of the name Glory is "glory". The name is an anglicised form of the Latin name Gloria.

Glyn
Pronunciation: glin
The name Glyn is of Irish and Gaelic origin. The meaning of Glyn is "valley of water". Glyn is a place name. The name is also a variant of Glen. Glyn is used as both a boy's name and as girl's name

Goldie
Pronunciation: GOLD-ee
Goldie is of English origin. Goldie is a modern by name for one who has blonde hair. Hollywood actress Goldie Hawn popularised the name.

Grace
Pronunciation: grayce
Grace is of Latin origin. The meaning of the name Grace

is "blessing, heavenly favour". The name is one of the several abstract nouns denoting admirable personal qualities that became popular first names among the Puritans during the 16th century. The name was revived in the 19th century. Diminutives: Gracie.

Gráinne
Pronunciation: gron-YAH
The name Gráinne is of Irish Gaelic origin. The meaning of Gráinne is "love". Borne in Irish legend; Gráinne was the daughter of King Cormac.

Greta
Pronunciation: GREH-tah
The name Greta is of German origin. The meaning of Greta is "pearl". Greta is a German diminutive of the name Margareta. Hollywood actress, Greta Garbo (1905-1992) popularised the name during the 20th century.

Gretchen
Pronunciation: GREH-chen
Gretchen is of German origin. The meaning of the name Gretchen is "pearl". Gretchen is a German diminutive of the name Margaret. The name became a popular first name in its own right.

Guinevere
Pronunciation: GWIN-a-veer
The name Guinevere is of Welsh origin. The meaning of Guinevere is "fair and smooth". Borne in Arthurian legend by Arthur's unfaithful wife, Queen Guinevere.

Gulielma
Pronunciation: guile-l-MAH

The name Gulielma is of Italian and Old German origin. The meaning of Gulielma is "will helmet". Gulielma is a feminine form of Wilhelm.

Gunhilda

Pronunciation: gun-HIL-dah

The name Gunhilda is of Old Norse origin. The meaning of Gunhilda is "Battle maid".

Gustava

Pronunciation: gust-av-AH

The name Gustava is of Swedish origin. The meaning of Gustava is "staff of the gods". Gustava is a feminine form of the name Gustave, a royal name in Sweden.

Gwen

Pronunciation: gwyn

Gwen is of Welsh origin. The meaning of the name Gwen is "fair, holy, white". Gwen was originally a diminutive of the name Gwendolyn. The name became a popular first name in its own right. The name was popular during the 19th and 20th centuries.

Gwenda

Pronunciation: gwyn-DAH

Gwenda is of Welsh origin. The meaning of the name Gwenda is "fair, good".

Gweyneth

Pronunciation: gwyn-ETH

The name Gweyneth is of Welsh origin. The meaning of Gweyneth is "blessed, happy". The name was popular during the 19th and 20th centuries. Diminutive: Gwyn.

Gwyn

Pronunciation: GW-in

The name Gwyn is of Welsh origin. The meaning of Gwyn is "fair, blessed, holy, white". The name is used as both a boy's name, and as a girl's name.

Gypsy

Pronunciation: GYP-see

The name Gypsy is of Old English origin. The meaning of Gypsy is "Gypsy". The tribe of Romany was called 'gypsy', as they were thought to have originated in Egypt.

H

Hannah

Pronunciation: HAN-ah

Hannah is of Hebrew origin. The meaning of the name Hannah is "God has favoured me". A biblical name; borne by the mother of the prophet Samuel (I Samuel 1). Unable to conceive, she asked God to bless her with a child, and her prayer was answered. Therefore the name connotes, 'God has graced me with a son'. The name was adopted by the Puritans in the 17th century. Hannah was a popular girls' name in the 20th century.

Harriet

Pronunciation: HARE-ee-et

The name Harriet is of Old German origin. The meaning of Harriet is "home leader". The name is an anglicised form of Henriette. Harriet is also a feminine form of the masculine name Henry.

Diminutives: Hal, Hattie, Hatty, Hettie, Hetty.

Hayley

Pronunciation: HAY-ley

The name Hayley is of Old English origin. The meaning of Hayley is "hay meadow". The name is an adopted surname, originally from a place name. The name became popular in 20th century when Mary Hayley Bell and Sir John Mills named their daughter Hayley Mills in 1946. Hayley Mills went on to become a famous Hollywood actress.

Hazel

Pronunciation: HAY-zel

The name Hazel is of Old English origin. The meaning of Hazel is "the hazel tree". The name was introduced as a first name during the 19th century, when Hazel

306

enjoyed a popular surge as a first name as plant names became fashionable. The name also refers to a specific eye colour.

Heather
Pronunciation: HEH-ther
The name Heather is of Middle English Origin. The meaning of Heather is unknown. From Old English *hadre*, which donates as a species of moorland shrub with purple and white flowers that, thrives on peaty barren lands. Heather is one of the most popular of the flower names that became fashionable during the 19th century.

Hebe
Pronunciation: HE-be
The name Hebe is of Greek origin. The meaning of Hebe is "youthful beauty". Borne in Greek mythology; Hebe was a daughter of Zeus and Hera, she was the goddess of youth and cup-bearer to the gods. The name was adopted in the 19th century for a species of plant that is native to New Zealand.

Heidi
Pronunciation: HYE-dee
Heidi is of Old German origin. The meaning of the name Heidi is "exalted nature". The name is a Swiss diminutive of Adelheid, from the Old German name Adelaide. Johanna Spyri popularised the name with her beloved children's novel, *Heidi* (1881). Heidi was the name given to the orphaned heroine.

Helen
Pronunciation: HEL-en

Helen is of Greek origin. The meaning of the name Helen is "sun ray". The name is an Anglicised form of the Greek name Helene. In classical legend Paris abducted Zeus's mortal daughter, Helen of Troy, an act that resulted in the Trojan War. Helen was, 'the face that launched a thousand ships'.
Diminutives: Ena, Hels, Lena, Nell, Nellie, Nelly.

Helena
Pronunciation: HEL-en-a
Helena is of Latin origin. The meaning of Helena is unknown. The name is a Latinate form of Helen. Saint Helena (c. 248-328) was the mother of Constantine the Great. Her purity allowed her to find the True Cross at Jerusalem. Her feast day is 18th August.

Heloise
Pronunciation: HEL-oh-ees
The name Heloise is of French and Old German origin. The meaning of Heloise is "famous warrior". The name was popularised by the true story of the French philosopher Peter Abelard (1079-1142), and his seventeen year old student and lover, Hèloíse. After Abelard's castration, he entered the monastery of Saint Denis. Hèloíse later became a nun.

Henrietta, Henriette
Pronunciation: HEN-ree-ett
The name Henriette is of Old German origin. The meaning of Henriette is "home leader". Henriette is a feminine form of Henry. Henriette is a French form of Henry that was introduced to Britain in the 17th century, after Charles I

married the French Princess Henriette-Marie in 1625. Diminutives: Etta, Ettie, Etty, Hen, Hennie.

Hermione
Pronunciation: her-MY-oh-nee
The name Hermione is of Greek origin. The meaning of Hermione is "daughter of Hermes, messenger". The name is a feminine form Hermes, the Greek messenger of God. Borne in mythology; Hermione was the daughter of Helen and Menelaus. Shakespeare also used the name in *A Winter's Tale* (1611).

Hero
Pronunciation: HE-ro
The name Hero is of Greek origin. The meaning of Hero is unknown. Borne in Greek legend by a priestess of Venus and beloved by Leander. He swam to her nightly across the Hellespont until one night when he accidently drowned. Hero then drowned herself in the same sea as Leander following his death. Shakespeare also used the name Hero in *Much Ado About Nothing* (1598).

Hilary
Pronunciation: HILL-a-ree
The name Hilary is of Latin origin. The meaning of Hilary is "cheerful". Medieval form of the Latin name Hilarius. Borne by a 4th-century saint and a 5th century pope. The name was given to both girls and boys name, although it is increasingly rare for boys.

Holly
Pronunciation: HAH-lee

Holly is of Old English origin. The meaning of the name Holly is "the holy tree". From Old English *holen*, which denotes a species of evergreen plant with prickly leaves. Holly was one of the numerous flower and plant names that became popular first names during the 19th century. The name is often given to girls who are born at Christmas time. Audrey Hepburn popularised the name when Capote's novel, *Breakfast at Tiffany's* (1958) was turned into a film in 1961. Hepburn played the fascinating heroine, Holy Golightly.

Honor
Pronunciation: AHN-er
The name Honor is of Latin origin. The meaning of Honor is "woman of honor". Honor was one of the several abstract nouns denoting admirable personal qualities that became popular among Puritans in the 16th century. The name was used as both a girl's name and as a boy's name.

Honey
Pronunciation: HUN-ee
Honey is of Old English origin. The meaning of the name Honey is "nectar". The name is often used as a nickname for endearment.

Hope
Pronunciation: HO-pe
Hope is of Old English origin. The meaning of the name Hope is "belief". One of the three great Christian virtues (faith, hope, & charity). The name is one of the several abstract nouns that symbolizes admirable personal qualities. The name was popular among the Puritans in the 16th century.

I

Ianthe
Pronunciation: eye-AH-thee
The name Ianthe is of Greek origin. The meaning of Ianthe is "violet flower". Borne in Ovid's *Metamorphoses*, written in the 1st century, Ianthe was a Cretan girl who married Iphis.

Ida
Pronunciation: EYE-dah
Ida is of Greek and Old German origin. The meaning of the name Ida is "hardworking". From Old German *id*, which means 'work'. The name was introduced to Britain by the Norman's. Borne in Greek mythology; a Greek nymph who cared for the infant Zeus on Mount Ida.

Idris
Pronunciation: E-dris
The name Idris is of Arabic and Welsh origin. The meaning of Idris is "fiery leader, Prophet". Borne in Welsh legend by a giant magician, astronomer and prince whose observatory was on Cader Idris. Described in the Koran, the Arabic name was borne by a man described as 'a true man' and 'a prophet', he was also the founder of the first Shiite dynasty (788-974). The name is used as both a boy's name and as a girl's name.

Ilsa
Pronunciation: I-lsa
Ilsa is of German origin. The meaning of the name Ilsa is "God is my oath". Ilsa is a diminutive of the Hebrew name Elisabeth.

Iman
Pronunciation: ee-MAHN

312

The name Iman is of Arabic origin. The meaning of Iman is "belief, faith".

Imogen
Pronunciation: I-mo-gen
The name Imogen is of Irish and Gaelic origin. The meaning of Imogen is "maiden". From the Celtic name Innogen. The name was first used by Shakespeare in his play, *Cymbeline* (1609). Imogen was the name of the heroine.

India
Pronunciation: IN-dee-ah
The name India is of English origin. Originally the name of the country. India was first used a name in Margaret Mitchell's epic novel *Gone With The Wind* (1936).

Ingrid
Pronunciation: ING-rid
The name Ingrid is of Old Norse origin. The meaning of Ingrid is "fair". Borne in Norse mythology; Ing was the God of earth's fertility. The name was popularised by the Hollywood actress Ingrid Bergman (1915-1982).

Iola
Pronunciation: eye-OH-lah
The name Iola is of Greek origin. The meaning of Iola is "violet colored dawn".

Iolana
Pronunciation: eye-oh-LAH-nah
Iolana is of Hawaiian origin. The meaning of the name Iolana is "to soar like the hawk".

Iolanthe
Pronunciation: eye-oh-LAHN-thee
The name Iolanthe is of Greek origin. The meaning of Iolanthe is "violet flower".

Ione
Pronunciation: eye-OHN
The name Ione is of Greek origin. The meaning of Ione is "violet". Ione is also a flower name. The name may have become popular as a first name during the 19th century, when botanical names became fashionable.

Irene
Pronunciation: eye-REEN
The name Irene is of Greek origin. The meaning of Irene is "peace". Borne in Greek mythology; Irene was a goddess of peace and wealth. Saint Irene (4th century) was one of the three sisters martyred for their faith in Macedonia.

Iris
Pronunciation: EYE-riss
Iris is of Greek origin. The meaning of the name Iris is "Rainbow". Borne in Greek mythology; Iris was a goddess of the rainbow and messenger of the gods. She rode on rainbows that formed as a bridge, linking heaven and the earth so that she could deliver messages from Olympus. The name was revived in the 19th century. Iris is also a flower name.

Irma
Pronunciation: IR-ma
The name Irma is of Old German origin. The meaning of Irma is "entire, universal".

Isabel
Pronunciation: iz-a-bel

Isabel is of Hebrew origin. The meaning of the name Isabel is "God is my oath". Isabel is a Spanish variant of the name Elizabeth. The name was brought to Britain from the France in the form of Isabella by Edward II (1296-1358) French wife. The name was popular throughout Britain until the end of the 17th century. Diminutives; Bel, Bell, Bella, Belle, Ib, Ibbie, Ibby, Isa, Iz, Izzie, Izzy, Tibby.

Isabella

Pronunciation: IZ-a-bel-LA
Isabella is of Hebrew origin. The meaning of the name Isabella is "God is my oath". Isabella is a Latinate form of Isabelle. The name has been a popular throughout Britain since the 18th century.

Isadora

Pronunciation: IZ-a-DOR-ah
The name Isadora is of Greek and Latin origin. The meaning of Isadora is "gift of Isis". The name is a feminine form of Isidore. Acclaimed American dancer, Isadora Duncan (1887-1927) popularised the name.

Isla

Pronunciation: EYE-la
The name Isla is of uncertain origins. Isla is the name of a Scottish river.

Isra

Pronunciation: eyes-ra
The name Isra is of Arabic origin. The meaning of Isra is "night journey". The name is a reference to Muhammad's journey to Jerusalem, in which he met Moses and Jesus.

Itzel
Pronunciation: it-zel
The name Itzel is of Spanish origin. The meaning of Itzel is "star of the aurora sky". Itzel is also the name of a Mayan princess.

Ivana
Pronunciation: ee-VAH-nah
Ivana is of Hebrew and Slavic origin. The meaning of the name Ivana is "God is gracious". Ivana is a feminine form of the masculine names Ivan and John.

Ivette
Pronunciation: ee-VET
The name Ivette is of French origin. The meaning of Ivette is unknown. The name is a variant of Yvette.

Ivonne
Pronunciation: ee-VON
Ivonne is of French origin. The meaning of the name Ivonne is unknown. Ivonne is variant of the name Yvonne.

Ivory
Pronunciation: EYE-vree
Ivory is of Latin origin. The meaning of the name Ivory is "creamy white colour". Ivory is the name used for the hard tusk on animals, which is also used for carving fine art and jewelry.

Ivy
Pronunciation: EYE-vee
The name Ivy is of Old English origin. Ivy is a name from nature, an evergreen climbing plant which represents fidelity and eternity.

J

Jacinta

Pronunciation: JAC-in-ta
The name Jacinta is of Spanish origin. The meaning of Jacinta is "hyacinth". Jacinta is Spanish for of the Greek name Hyacinth. The name was originally used for both sexes however, today it is mostly used as a girl's name.

Jacqueline, Jacquelyn

Pronunciation: JAK-ah-lin
The name Jacqueline is of French and Hebrew origin. The meaning of Jacqueline is "he who supplants". Jacqueline is a feminine form of Jacques. The name was introduced to Britain in the 13th century.
Diminutives: Jackie, Jacky, Jacqui.

Jade

Pronunciation: JAY-de
The name Jade is of English origin. The meaning of Jade is "precious stone". Jade is also a jewel name, of a green stone which was believed to have magical powers of providing protection against disorders of the intestines. The name was derived from archaic Spanish *piedra de ijada*, which means, 'stone of the side'.

Jamie

Pronunciation: JAY-mee
The name Jamie is of Hebrew origin. The meaning of Jamie is "he who supplants". Jamie is a diminutive of the masculine name James. The name became a popular first name in its own right. Jamie is used as both a girl's name and as a boy's name.

Jancis

Pronunciation: JAN-cis
The name Jancis is a modern blend of Jan and Frances. The name was

probably first used by Mary Webb in her novel *Precious Bane* (1924).

Jane, Jayne
Pronunciation: jayn
The name Jane is of Hebrew origin. The meaning of Jane is "God is gracious". Jane is a feminine form of the masculine name John, derived from the Old French name Jehane. Henry VIII's (d 1537) third wife, Jane Seymour popularised the name during the 16th century. The name was extremely popular in the 18th and 19th centuries. Charlotte Brontë contributed to the popularity of the name with her renowned novel, *Jane Eyre* (1847).

Janet
Pronunciation: JAN-et
The name Janet is of Scottish origin. The meaning of Janet is unknown. Janet is a feminine form of the masculine name John, originally a medieval diminutive of Jane. The name was popular throughout Scotland and underwent a revival in the 20th century. Diminutives: Jan, Jennie, Jenny.

Janice
Pronunciation: JAN-iss
The name Janice is originally a diminutive of the name Jane. The name was influenced by names that end in –ice, such as Candice and Bernice. The name became popular in its own right during the early 20th century.

Jasmine
Pronunciation: JAZ-min

Jasmine if of Old French and Persian origin. The meaning of the name Jasmine is "Jasmine". From Arabic *Jasamine*, donating a species of an ornamental climbing plant, which has delicate yellow and white flowers. Disney popularised the name with the film *Aladdin* (1990). Princess Jasmine was the name of the heroine.

Jean
Pronunciation: jeen
Jean is of Hebrew origin. The meaning of the name Jean is "God is gracious". Jean is a feminine form of the masculine name John. The name was popular throughout Britain during the 20th century.
Diminutives: Jeanie, Jeannette, Jeannie.

Jena
Pronunciation: JEN-ah
Jena is of Arabic and Sanskrit origin. The meaning of Jena is "little bird, endurance".

Jeanette
Pronunciation: je-NET
The name Jeanette is of Hebrew origin. The meaning of Jeanette is "God is gracious". Jeanette is a diminutive of the Hebrew name Jean. The name became a popular first name in its own right.

Jeanne
Pronunciation: je(an)-ne
The name Jeanne is of French and Hebrew origin. The meaning of Jeanne is "God is gracious". Jeanne is a feminine form of the masculine name John.
Diminutives: Jeannette, Jeannine.

Jemima

Pronunciation: je-MYE-mah

Jemima is of Hebrew origin. The meaning of the name Jemima is "dove". A biblical name; borne in the Old Testament by the eldest of Job's daughters. The name was adopted by the Puritans. Beatrix Potter popularised the name with her heroine, Jemima Puddleduck.

Jennifer

Pronunciation: JEN-ee-fer

The name Jennifer is of English origin. The meaning of Jennifer is "fair and smooth". Jennifer is a variant of Guinevere. The name was popular throughout Britain during the 20th century.

Jessica

Pronunciation: JESS-a-kah

The name Jessica is of Hebrew origin. The meaning of Jessica is "He sees". The name may be a Shakespearean invention for the daughter of Shylock in *The Merchant of Venice* (1596). Diminutives: Jess, Jessie.

Jessie

Pronunciation: JESS-ee

The name Jessie is of Hebrew origin. The meaning of Jessie is "He sees". Jessie is a Scottish diminutive of the name Janet. The name dates back to the 18th century. Jessie is also a diminutive of the name Jessica.

Jillian

Pronunciation: JIL-ee-an

The name Jillian is of unknown origin. Jillian is a modern variation of the name Gillian. Diminutives: Jill, Jilly.

Jinny
Pronunciation: JIN-ee
Jinny is of uncertain origin. The name is a variation of Jenny or a diminutive of the name Virginia.

Joan
Pronunciation: jone
The name Joan is of Hebrew origin. The meaning of Joan is "God is gracious". Joan is a feminine form of the masculine name John. Borne by the only female pope, supposedly of the 13th century. However, her existence is still in dispute. The name was replaced by Jane by the 17th century. Hollywood actress Joan Crawford popularised the name during the 20th century.

Joanna
Pronunciation: joh-AN-ah
Joanna is of Latin origin. The meaning of Joanna is "God is gracious". Joanna is a feminine form of the masculine name John. Derived from the Latin name Johanna. A biblical name; borne by several women who were disciples of Christ. The Puritans adopted the name. The name was later revived in the 18th century.
Diminutive: Jo, Joey.

Joanne
Pronunciation: JOH-anne
The name Joanne is of uncertain origin. From the Old French name Johanne, derived from the Latin name Johanna. The name was first used as a first name in French-speaking communities in the US. The name became popular

during the 20th century. Diminutives: Jo, Joey.

Jocasta
Pronunciation: JO-cast-ah
The name Jocasta is of Greek origin. The meaning of Jocasta is "shining moon". Borne in Greek mythology; Jocasta was a daughter of Meneceus and Queen consort of Thebes, Greece. She was also the wife of Laius, mother of Oedipus, and both mother and grandmother of Antigone, Eteocles, Polynices and Ismene. She unknowingly became the wife of her own son, when the truth was revealed she hung herself.

Jocelin, Joceline
Pronunciation: JOS-e-lin
The name Jocelin is of Old German origin. The meaning of Jocelin is "one of the Goths". The name was introduced to Britain by the Normans. Jocelin is used as both a boy's name, and as a girl's name. Diminutives: Joss, Jossy.

Jocelyn
Pronunciation: JOS-e-lyn
The name Jocelyn is of Old German origin. The meaning of Jocelyn is "one of the Goths". The name was introduced to Britain by the Normans. Jocelyn is used as both a boy's name, and as a girl's name. Diminutives: Joss, Jossy.

Johanna
Pronunciation: joh-HAHN-ah
Johanna is of Latin and Hebrew origin. The meaning of the name Johanna is "God is gracious". The name is originally a Latinate and

feminine form derived from Johannes (John).

Jordan
Pronunciation: JOR-dan
Jordan is of Hebrew origin. The meaning of the name Jordan is "down-flowing". From the name of the river in the Middle East where Christ was baptized by John the Baptist. The name has been used as a first name since the Crusades. The name underwent a popular revival in the 1980's. Jordan is used as both a boy's name, and as a girl's name.

Josephine
Pronunciation: JOH-sa-feen
The name Josephine is of Hebrew origin. The meaning of Josephine is "Jehovah increases". Josephine is a feminine form of the masculine name Joseph. Napoleon Bonaparte's wife, Empress Josèphine (1763-1814) popularised the name across Europe. Diminutives: Fifi, Jo, Joey, Josa, Josette, Josie, Josy, Posie, Posy.

Joy
Pronunciation: joy
The name Joy is of Old French origin. The meaning of Joy is "joy". The name is a direct adoption of the English vocabulary. The name was used during the Middle Ages and was popular with the Puritans. The name was later revived in the 19 century.

Judith
Pronunciation: JOO-dith
The name Judith is of Hebrew origin. The meaning of Judith is "Jewess, from Judea". A biblical name; borne in the Old Testament by a wife of Esau. Judith was a central figure in the Apocrypha's

Book of Judith. The name popular during the 18th and 20th centuries. Diminutives: Jodi, Jodie, Jody, Jude, Judi, Judy.

Judy

Pronunciation: JOO-dee
The name Judy is of Hebrew origin. The meaning of Judy is "Jewess, from Judea". Judy is a diminutive of the name Judith.

Julia

Pronunciation: joo-lee-AH
The name Julia is of Latin origin. The meaning of Julia is "Jove's child" Julia is a feminine form of the Roman family name Julius. Shakespeare used the name in *The Two Gentlemen of Verona* (1594). The name was extremely popular in Britain during the 18th century. Diminutives: Jules.

Juliana

Pronunciation: joo-lee-AH-NAH
The name Juliana is of Latin origin. The meaning of Juliana is "youthful, Jove's child". Juliana is a feminine form of Julian, the name dates back to the Middle Ages.

Julianne

Pronunciation: joo-lee-AH-ne
The name Julianne is a 20th-century coinage of uncertain origin. Julianne is a combination of the names Anne and Julie.

Julie

Pronunciation: JOO-lee
The name Julie is of French origin. The meaning of Julie is "youthful, Jove's child". Julie is a French form of the Latin name Julia. The name was first used in Britain in

the 20th century. Julie became one of the most popular girl's names during the 1070's.

Julienne
Pronunciation: JOO-lee-ene
The name Julienne is of French origin. The meaning of Julienne is "youthful, Jove's child". Julienne is a French feminine form of the masculine name Julian.

Juliet
Pronunciation: joo-lee-ET
The name Juliet is of Latin origin. The meaning of Juliet is "youthful, Jove's child". Juliet is a diminutive of the name Julia. Shakespeare popularised the name with the infamous love story, Romeo *and Juliet* (1595).

June
Pronunciation: joon
June is the sixth month of the year. The name was possibly derived from the Latin Iunius. The name is often associated with the Latin name Juno. June is known as the bridal month. June was the most successful of the names that were taken from the months of the year. The name was first adopted as a first name in the early 20th century.

Juno
Pronunciation: joo-NO
The name Juno is of Latin origin. The meaning of Juno is "queen of heaven". Borne in Roman mythology; Juna was a Roman goddess, wife and sister of Jupiter and the queen of heaven. She is identified with the Greek goddess Hera, as patron of women and marriage.

Justine

Pronunciation: juss-Tine

The name Justine is of Latin origin. The meaning of Justine is "fair, upright". Justine is a feminine form of the masculine name Justin. Originally a French from of the Latinate name Justina. Lawrence Durrell popularised the name with his novel, *Justine* (1957).

K

Kacie
Pronunciation: KAY-see
The name Kacie is of American origin. The meaning of Kacie is "alert, vigorous". Kacie is a variant of the name Casey.

Kadenza
Pronunciation: KAD-en-za
The name Kadenza is of Latin origin. The meaning of Kadenza is "with rhythm".

Kady
Pronunciation: KAY-dee
The name Kady is of American origin. The meaning of Kady is unknown. Kady is a variant of the name Katy.

Kai
Pronunciation: kye
Kai is of Hawaiian origin. The meaning of the name Kai is "the sea".

Kaila
Pronunciation: KYE-lah
The name Kaila is of Hebrew and Hawaiian origin. The meaning of Kaila is "the laurel crown".

Kaitlin
Pronunciation: KAYT-len
Kaitlin is of Irish origin. The meaning of the name Kaitlin is "pure". Kaitlin is a phonetic form of the name Caitlin, an Irish form of Catherine.

Kamala
Pronunciation: KAM-al-ah
The name Kamala is of Sanskrit origin. The meaning of Kamala is "pink". Kamala is a feminine form of the masculine name Kamal. In classical Hindu texts, Kamala is a byname of the goddess of Lakshmi. The name is also borne by the wife of Shiva.

Karen
Pronunciation: KARE-en
The name Karen is of Danish origin. The meaning of the name Karen is "pure". Karen is a variation of the name Katherine. Karen became one of the most popular girls' names in Britain during the 1970's.

Kate
Pronunciation: KAY-te
The name Kate is a variation of Katherine. The name has become a popular first name by its own right.

Katherine, Katharine
Pronunciation: KATH-er-rin
Katherine is of Greek origin. The meaning of the name Katherine is "pure". Katherine is a Latin form of Catherine. Kathrine is the English spelling, Katharine is the Scottish spelling. The early Latin forms Katerina and Caterina became Katharine and Catherine.

Kathleen
Pronunciation: kath-LEEN
The name Kathleen is of Irish origin. The meaning of Kathleen is "pure". Kathleen is a variation of Catherine, which was influenced by the Irish Gaelic name Caítlin. The name was first used outside of Ireland in the 19th century.

Kathryn
Pronunciation: KATH-ryn
The name Kathryn is of Greek origin. The meaning of Kathryn is "pure". Kathryn is a variant of the names Catherine and Kathrine.

Katrina
Pronunciation: ka-TREE-nah

Katrina Is of Greek origin. The meaning of the name Katrina is unknown. Katrina is a variation of the names Catriona and Catrina.

Katya
Pronunciation: KAT-ya
Katya is of Greek and Russian origin. The meaning of the name Katya is "pure". Katya is a Russian form of the Greek name Katherine.

Kay, Kaye
Pronunciation: kay
The name Kay is of Greek origin. The meaning of Kay is "pure". Diminutives of Katherine and Kathleen. The name became a popular first name in its own right.

Kayleigh
Pronunciation: kay-LEE
The name Kayleigh is of Irish and Gaelic origin. The meaning of Kayleigh is "slim and fair". Kayleigh is a variant of the names Cayla and Kaylee.

Kellie, Kelly
Pronunciation: KELL-ee
The name Kelly is of Irish and Gaelic origin. The meaning of Kelly is "strife, warlike". Originally an Irish surname. The name is an anglicised form of the ancient Irish Gaelic name Ceallach.

Kendall
Pronunciation: KEN-dal
The name Kendall is of Old English origin. The meaning of the Kendall is "the Kent River valley". An adopted surname, from a Cumbrian place name, Kendal. The name is used as both a boy's name, and as a girl's name. Kendal has been used as a

given name since the 19th century.

Kerenza
Pronunciation: KER-en-za
The name Kerenza is of English origin. The meaning of Kerenza is "love, affection". Kerenza is a variant of the Cornish name Kerensa.

Kerry
Pronunciation: KARE-ee
The name Kerry is of Irish and Gaelic origin. The meaning of Kerry is "black". Kerry is also a place name of an Irish county. The name was first used by Irish immigrants to Australia for their sons. Kerry is used as both a girl's name and as a boy's name.

Khadija
Pronunciation: kah-DEE-jah
The name Khadija is of Arabic origin. The meaning of Khadija is "early baby". Khadijah bint-Khuwaylid was the first wife of Prophet Muhammad and mother of all his children. She was named in Koran as one of the four perfect women.

Kiara
Pronunciation: kee-AR-ah
Kiara is of Irish origin. The meaning of the name Kiara is "black". Kiara is a variant of the Irish name Ciara. The name is also a feminine form of Kieran.

Kiera
Pronunciation: kee-RAH
The name Kiera is of Irish origin. The meaning of Kiera is "black, lord". Kiera is a variant of the Irish name Ciara and is a modern feminine form of Ciaran. Kiera is also a variant of the Greet name Kira.

Kim

Pronunciation: KIM

The name Kim is of English origin. The meaning of Kim is "gold". Originally a diminutive of Kimball or Kimberley. The name is used as both a boy's name and as a girl's name.

Kimberley

Pronunciation: KIM-ber-lee

The name Kimberley is of English origin. The meaning of Kimberley is "Cyneburg's field". Kimberley is used as both a girl's name and as a boy's name.

Kira

Pronunciation: KEER-ah

Kira is of Greek origin. The meaning of the name Kira is "Lord". Kira is a variant of the name Kyra.

Kitty

Pronunciation: KIH-tee

The name Kitty is of Greek origin. The meaning of Kitty is "pure". Kitty is a diminutive of the Greek name Katherine. The name has been used a first name since the 15th century. The name was also used as a slang term for a woman of dubious morals during the 17th century.

Kirsten

Pronunciation: KERS-ten

Kirsten is of Latin and Scandinavian origin. The meaning of the name Kirsten is "follower of Christ". Kirsten is a Scandinavian form of the name Christine.

Kirstie, Kirsty

Pronunciation: KERS-tee

The name Kirsty is of Scottish origin. The meaning of Kirsty is "follower of Christ".

Scottish diminutives of Christina or Christine.

Kristen
Pronunciation: KRISS-ten
Kristen is of Latin origin. The meaning of the name Kristen is "follower of Christ". Kristen is a variant of Christine.

Kristin
Pronunciation: KRISS-tin
Kristin is of Latin origin. The meaning of the name Kristin is "follower of Christ". Kristin is a variant of Christina and Christine. The name is also a feminine form of Christianus.

Kylie
Pronunciation: KYE-lee
The name Kylie is of Australian origin. The meaning of Kylie is "boomerang". The name was probably coined as a feminine form of the masculine name Kyle. The name was most popular during the 1980's. The name was made famous by Australian actress and singer, Kylie Minogue.

Kynthia
Pronunciation: kyn-THIA
The name Kynthia is of Greek origin. The meaning of Kynthia is "from Mount Kynthos". Kynthia is a variant of the Greek name Cynthia.

Kyoko
Pronunciation: kee-OH-koh
Kyoko is of Japanese origin. The meaning of the name Kyoko is "mirror".

Kyra
Pronunciation: KEER-ah
Kyra is of Greek origin. The meaning of the name Kyra is "Lord". Kyra is a feminine form of the masculine name Kyros.

L

Lacey
Pronunciation: LAY-see
Lacey is of Old French origin. The meaning of the name Lacey is unknown. Originally a nobleman's surname. The name was brought to Britain by the Normans.

Ladonna
Pronunciation: la-DAH-nah
The name Ladonna is of Italian origin. The meaning of Ladonna is "Lady". Ladonna is a modern form of the Italian name Donna.

Laetitia
Pronunciation: le-TISH-ah
The name Laetitia is of Latin origin. The meaning of Laetitia is "joy".
Diminutives: Lettie, Letty, Tisha.

Laila
Pronunciation: LAY-lah
The name Laila is of Arabic origin. The meaning of Laila is "night beauty".

Lakeisha
Pronunciation: lah-KEE-shah
Lakeisha is of uncertain origin. The meaning of the name Lakeisha is "cassia tree". Lakeisha is an elaborated form of the name Keisha.

Laine
Pronunciation: layn
The name Laine is of English origin. The meaning of Laine is "path, roadway". Laine is a variant of the surname Lane. The name is also used as a short form of the name Marlaine and Melanie.

Lainey
Pronunciation: layn-EE
The name Lainey is of French origin. The meaning

336

of Lainey is "bright, shining light". Lainey is a diminutive of the Old French name Elaine.

Lakshmi
Pronunciation: la-KSH-mi
The name Lakshmi is of Hindi and Sanskrit origin. The meaning of Lakshmi is "good sign, good omen". Borne by the goddess of beauty, good fortune, and wealth. Lakshmi is the wife of Vishnu and the mother of Kama.

Lana
Pronunciation: LAHN-ah
Lana is of modern coinage. The name is possibly a variant of the Old German name Alana, which means "precious". American actress Lana Turner (1921-1995) popularised the name.

Lara
Pronunciation: LAR-ah
Lara is of Latin origin. The meaning of the name Lara is "protection". Lara is a diminutive of the name Larissa. Lara is also a Spanish surname and a place name. Boris Pasternak popularised the name in his novel, *Dr Zhivago* (1957).

Larissa
Pronunciation: la-RISS-ah
Larissa is of Latin origin. The meaning of the name Larissa is "cheerful". The name was borne by a Greek martyr of the Eastern Church.

Laura
Pronunciation: LAW-rah
The name Laura is of Latin origin. The meaning of Laura is "the bay, the laurel plant". Laura is a feminine form of *laurus*. The love

poet Petrarch (1304-1374) addressed his sonnets to a Laura.

Laurel
Pronunciation: LAWR-el
The name Laurel is of Latin origin. The meaning of Laurel is "the bay, the laurel plant". A nature name derived from the name of the tree.

Lauren
Pronunciation: LAWR-en
The name Lauren is of Latin origin. The meaning of Lauren is "the bay, the laurel plant". Lauren is a variant of the name Laura. The name is also a feminine form of the masculine name Lawrence. Hollywood actress Lauren Bacall (1924-2014) popularised the name during the 20th century.

Lavinia
Pronunciation: la-vee-NEE-ah
The name Lavinia is of Latin origin. The meaning of Lavinia is unknown. Borne in mythology by the daughter of Latinus, king of the Latini. Lavinia became the wife of Aeneas and the ancestress of Romulus and Remus. The name was popular during the Renaissance, and later revived in the 18th century.

Layla
Pronunciation: LAY-la
The name Layla is of Arabic origin. The meaning of Layla is "wine". Layla is a variation of the Arabic name Leila.

Leah
Pronunciation: LAY-ah
Leah is of Hebrew origin. The meaning of the name Leah is "delicate, cow". A

biblical name; borne by Jacob's first wife and the mother of Jacob's twelve sons (Genesis 29). The name was revived by the Puritans,

Leanne, Leanna
Pronunciation: lee-AN-ah
The name Leanne is of English origin. The meaning of Leanne is unknown. The name is either a combination of the name Lee and Anna or possibly a variation of the name Liane.

Leanora
Pronunciation: LEE-nor-ah
The name Leanora is of Italian origin. The meaning of Leanora is "compassion, light". Leanore is the Italian form the Old German name Eleanor.

Leda
Pronunciation: LEE-dah
The name Leda is of Greek origin. The meaning of Leda is "joy, happiness". Borne in Greek mythology; Leda was the Queen of Sparta and the mother of Helen of Troy and Clytemnestra.

Lee
Pronunciation: LEE
Lee is of Old English origin. The meaning of the name Lee is "wood, meadow, clearing". An adopted surname and place name. Lee was first used as a first name in the 19th century, probably in honour of the Confederate general Robert E. Lee (1807-1870). The name is used as both a boy's name and as a girl's name.

Leila
Pronunciation: LEE-lah
The name Leila is of Arabic origin. The meaning of Leila is "night beauty".

Lena
Pronunciation: LEE-nah
The name Lena is originally a byname from female names ending in –lena, such as Helena. The name became a popular first name in its own right.

Leona
Pronunciation: LEE-oh-nah
Leona is of Latin origin. The meaning of the name Leona is "Lion". Leona is a feminine form of the masculine name Leon.

Leonie
Pronunciation: LEE-oh-nee
Leonie is of Latin origin. The meaning of the name Leonie is "Lion". Leonie is a feminine form of the masculine name Leon. Leonie is the French form.

Leonora
Pronunciation: lee-a-NOR-ah
The name Leonora is of Greek and Italian origin. The meaning of Leonora is "compassion, light". Leonora is the Italian form of the name Eleanor. Beethoven popularised the name is his opera *Fidelio* (1814). Diminutives: Leo, Nora, Norah.

Lesley
Pronunciation: les-LEE
The name Lesley is of Scottish origin. The meaning of Lesley is "Holly garden". Originally a Scottish surname derived from a place called Lesslyn in Aberdeenshire. Lesley is a variant of the name Leslie.

Liesel
Pronunciation: LIE-sel
The name Liesel is German and Hebrew origin. The meaning of Liesel is "God is my oath". Liesel is a

German diminutive of the name Elizabeth.

Lili
Pronunciation: LIL-ee
Lili is of German and Hebrew origin. The meaning of the name Lili is "lily, God is my oath". Lili is a German diminutive of the name Elizabeth. The name became a popular first name in its own right.

Lilian
Pronunciation: LIL-e-an
The name Lilian is of Latin origin. The meaning of Lilian is "lily". Lilian is also a variant of the name Lily. Diminutives: Lily.

Lily
Pronunciation: LIL-ee
Lily is of Greek and Latin origin. The meaning of the name Lily is "lily". From Greek *leirion*, which denotes a species of slender plants with trumpet shaped flowers. The lily is a symbol of innocence and purity. The name became popular during the 19th century, when botanical names became fashionable.

Lina
Pronunciation: LY-na
The name Lina is of Arabic and Latin origin. The meaning of Lina is "palm tree". Lina is a diminutive of names that end with –lina, such as Selina.

Linda
Pronunciation: LIN-dah
The name Linda is of Spanish origin. The meaning of Linda is "pretty". Linda is also a byname for the names Belinda and Melinda. Diminutives: Lin, Lindie, Lindy.

Lindsay

Pronunciation: LIN-d-say

Lindsay is of Old English origin. The meaning of the name Lindsay is "Lincoln's marsh". Sir Walter de Lindesay brought the name to Scotland from Lindsey, Lincolnshire. The name is used as both a boy's name and as a girl's name.

Lisa

Pronunciation: LEE-sah

Lisa is of Hebrew origin. The meaning of the name Lisa is "God is my oath". Lisa is a variation of the name Liza. The name was popular throughout the 20th century.

Livia

Pronunciation: LIV-iah

Livia is of Latin origin. The meaning of the name Livia is "olive, tree". Livia is a feminine form of the Roman clan name Livius.

Lois

Pronunciation: LOH-iss

The name Lois is of Greek origin. The meaning of Lois is "superior". A biblical name; borne in the New Testament by the grandmother of Timothy.

Lola

Pronunciation: LOH-lah

The name Lola is of unknown origin. The meaning of Lola is "sorrows". Lola is a Spanish diminutive of the name Dolores.

Lolita

Pronunciation: LOH-e-tah

The name Lolita is of unknown origin. The meaning of Lolita is "sorrows". Lolita is a Spanish diminutive of the name Dolores.

Lorna

Pronunciation: LOR-nah

The name Lorna is of Scottish origin. The meaning of Lorna is unknown. The name was invented by R D Blackmore for his novel *Lorna Doone* (1869). The name was possibly derived from an area of Argyll, Scotland called Lorne.

Lorraine
Pronunciation: lor-AYN
The name Lorraine is of French origin. The meaning of Lorraine is "from Lorraine". Originally an adopted French surname derived from the district of Alsace-Lorraine.

Louisa
Pronunciation: LOH-e-sah
The name Louisa is of Latin origin. The meaning of Louisa is "famous warrior". Louisa is Latinate feminine form of the name Louis. The name was popular during the 17th century.
Diminutives: Lou, Louie, Lulu.

Louise
Pronunciation: loo-EEZ
The name Louise is of Old German and French origin. The meaning of Louise is "famous warrior". Louise is a French feminine form of the masculine name Louis. Saint Louise (16th century) was the co-founder of the nursing order Daughter of Charity. The name was adopted in Britain during the 17th century.
Diminutives: Lou, Louie, Lulu.

Lucia
Pronunciation: LOU-cee-ah
Lucia is of Italian and Latin origin. The meaning of the name Lucia is "light". Lucia

is a feminine form of the Latin name Lucius.

Lucilla
Pronunciation: LOO-sil-lah
The name Lucilla is of Latin origin. The meaning of Lucilla is "light". Lucilla is a Latin byname for Lucia. The name was borne by several saints. The name was popular with the Romans and later revived in the 19th century.

Lucille
Pronunciation: loo-SEEL
Lucille is of French origin. The meaning of Lucille is "light". Lucille is the French form. The name was made popular by American actress Lucille Ball (1911-1989).

Lucinda
Pronunciation: loo-SEEN-dah
The name Lucinda is of Latin origin. The meaning of Lucinda is "light". Lucinda is a variant of the Latin name Lucy.

Lucy
Pronunciation: LOO-see
The name Lucy is of Latin origin. The meaning of Lucy is "light". Lucy is an anglicised form of the Old French name Lucie. The name is borne by a fourth-century saint. Saint Lucy is patroness of sight.
Diminutives: Loose, Luce.

Lulu
Pronunciation: LOO-loo
The name Lulu is of Spanish and German origin. The meaning of Lulu is "famous warrior". Lulu is a byname of Luisa, Luise and Louise. The name became a popular first name in its own right.

Lydia

Pronunciation: LED-ee-ah

The name Lydia is of Greek origin. The meaning of Lydia is "woman of Lydia, from Lydia", a town in Asia Minor. A biblical name; borne by a woman who was converted to Christianity by Saint Paul (16:14).

Lyn, Lynn

Pronunciation: lyn

The name Lyn is of uncertain origin. The meaning of Lyn is "pretty". Lyn is a variant of the name Linda.

Lynette

Pronunciation: le-NET

The name Lynette is of Welsh origin. The meaning of Lynette is "idol, nymph". Originally adopted from the medieval French form of Eluned. Lord Tennyson (1859-1885) popularised the modern form of the name in *Idylls of the King.*

Lyra

Pronunciation: LY-rah

The name Lyra is of Greek origin. The meaning of Lyra is "lyre". Lyra is a variant of the Greek name Lyris.

M

Mackenzie
Pronunciation: ma-KEN-zee
The name Mackenzie if of Gaelic and Irish origin. The meaning of Mackenzie is "son of the wise ruler". An adopted Scottish surname, from Gaelic Mac Coinnich. Mackenzie is used as both a boy's name, and as a girl's name.

Madelaine
Pronunciation: MAD-el-aine
The name Madelaine is of French and Hebrew origin. The meaning of Madelaine is "woman from Magdala". Magdala is a village by the Sea of Galilee. Madelaine is a medieval French form of the name Magdalene.

Magdalen, Magdalene
Pronunciation: MAG-da-len
The name Magdalen is of Hebrew origin. The meaning of Magdalen is "woman from Magdala". Magdala is a village by the Sea of Galilee. A biblical name; borne by Saint Mary Magdalene, a reformed prostitute and follower of Jesus.

Mahalia
Pronunciation: ma-HAL-yah
The name Mahalia is of Hebrew origin. The meaning of Mahalia is "tenderness".

Maia, Maya
Pronunciation: MA-ia
Maia is of Greek origin. The meaning of the name Maia is "great, mother". Maia is a variation of the name Mary. Borne in Greek mythology; Maia was a beautiful nymph and mother of Hermes. In Roman mythology, she is

347

eldest and most beautiful of the Pleiades. The month of May was named in honour of her. In Buddhist philosophy, Maya gave birth to Buddha in the shape of a little white elephant.

Mallory
Pronunciation: MALL-or-ee
The name Mallory is of Old French origin. The meaning of Mallory is "unfortunate". The name is used as both a boy's name and as a girl's name.

Márie
Pronunciation: mar-EE
The name Márie is of Irish Gaelic origin. The meaning of Márie is unknown.

Maisie
Pronunciation: MAY-zee
Maisie if of English origin. The meaning of the name Maisie is "pearl". Maisie is a diminutive of the names Margaret, Marjorie and Mary.

Manon
Pronunciation: MAN-awn
The name Manon is of French origin. The meaning of Man is "star of the sea". Manon is a French diminutive of the name Marie.

Manuela
Pronunciation: mahn-WAY-lah
The name Manuela is of Spanish and Hebrew origin. The meaning of Manuela is "God is with us". Manuela is a feminine form of the name Manuel.

Mara, Marah
Pronunciation: MAHR-ah
The name Mara is of Hebrew origin. The meaning of Mara is "bitter". A biblical name; adopted by Naomi, mother-in-law of

Ruth. She claimed the name Mara after the death of her husbands and sons.

Marcella, Marcelle
Pronunciation: mar-SELL-ah

Marcella is of Latin origin. The meaning of the name Marcella is "dedicated to Mars". Marcella is a feminine form of a Roman family name Marcellus. Marcelle is the French form. Saint Marcella from the 4th century was killed during the sack of Rome.

Marcia
Pronunciation: MAR-shah

Marcia is of Latin origin. The meaning of the name Marcia is "dedicated to Mars". Marcia is a feminine form of the Roman family name Marcius. Diminutives: Marcie, Marcy.

Maretta
Pronunciation: mar-ee-et-AH

The name Maretta is is of Scottish origin. The meaning of Maretta is "star of the sea". Maretta is an anglicised form of Mairead and the Scottish Gaelic form of the name Margaret.

Margaret
Pronunciation: MARG-ar-et

The name Margaret is of Greek origin. The meaning of Margaret is "pearl". Derived from the Latin name Margarita, which was derived from Greek *margaron*. Saint Margaret of Antioch was a 3rd-century virgin martyr, is renowned for fighting the devil in the shape of a dragon. Diminutives: Daisy, Madge, Maggie, Marge, Margie, Margy, Marji, Marjie, May, Meg, Meggie, Peg, Peggy.

Margarita

Pronunciation: MARG-ar-ee-TAH

The name Margarita is of Spanish origin. The meaning of Margarita is "pearl". Margarita is a Spanish form of Margaret. The name became a popular first name in its own right.

Margherita

Pronunciation: MARG-er-ee-TAH

The name Margherita is of Italian origin. The meaning of Margherita is "pearl". Margherita is an Italian form of Margaret. The name became a popular first name in its own right.

Marguerite

Pronunciation: mar-gue-rite

The name Marguerite is of French origin. The meaning of Marguerite is "pearl". Marguerite is French variation of the name Margaret. The name was first adopted during the 19th century. Diminutives: Margot.

Maria

Pronunciation: mah-REE-ah

Maria is of Latin origin. The meaning of the name Maria is "star of the sea". Maria is Latinate form of the name Mary. The name was revived during the 20th century, possibly due to the popularity of the American musical, *West Side Story*.

Mariah

Pronunciation: mah-ri-AH

Mariah is of Latin origin. The meaning of the name Mariah is "star of the sea". Mariah is a variant of the name Maria. The name dates back to the 19th century. The name was popularised by American singer Mariah Carey.

Marian

Pronunciation: mar-ee-AHN

The name Marian is of French origin. The meaning of Marian is "star of the sea". Marian is a French diminutive of the name Marie. The name became a popular first name during the Middle Ages. The name was later revived in the 19th century.

Marie

Pronunciation: mah-REE

The name Marie is of French origin. The meaning of Marie is "star of the sea". Marie is a French form of the Latin name Maria. The name became a popular first name in its own right.

Mariella

Pronunciation: mar-EE-el-AH

Mariella is of German origin. The meaning of the name Maiella is "star of the sea". Mariella is originally a German diminutive of the name Mary.

Marietta

Pronunciation: MAR-e-ett-AH

The name Marietta is of Italian origin. The meaning of Marietta is "star of the sea". Marietta is an Italian diminutive of the name Mary. Mariette is the French form.

Marilyn

Pronunciation: MARE-a-lin

Marilyn is of English origin. The meaning of the name Marilyn is "star of the sea". Marilyn is a variation of the name Mary. The name was popularised in the 20th century by Hollywood actress Marilyn Monroe (1926-1962).

Marina
Pronunciation: mah-REE-nag
The name Marina is of Latin origin. The meaning of Marina is "from the sea". Possibly derived from Latin *marinus*, or from a Latin family name that is related to Marius. The name was borne by the 14th-century martyr of the Greek Church. Shakespeare used the name in *Pericles, Prince of Tyre* (1619).

Marissa
Pronunciation: ma-RISS-ah
The name Marissa is of Latin origin. The meaning of Marissa is "of the sea", Marissa is a diminutive of the name Mary.

Marlene
Pronunciation: mar-LEEN
The name Marlene is of German origin. The meaning of Marlene is "star of the sea". The name was introduced to Britain by Lili Marlene. German and Hollywood actress Marlene Dietrich (1901-1992) popularised the name during the 20th century.

Marnie
Pronunciation: marn-EE
Marnie is of Scandinavian origin. The meaning of the name Marnie is "from the sea". Marnie is a variant of the Latin name Marina. The name is also a diminutive of Marna.

Martha
Pronunciation: MAR-tha
Martha is of Aramaic origin. The meaning of the name Martha is "Lady". A biblical name; borne in the New Testament by the sister of Lazarus and Mary of

Bethany. She is the patron saint of the helping professions. The name was revived by the Puritans.

Martina, Martine
Pronunciation: mar-TEEN-ah
The name Martina is of Latin origin. The meaning of Martina is "dedicated to Mars". Martina is a feminine form of the masculine name Martin. Martina is the Latinate form, Martine is the French form. The name was borne by two saints.

Mary
Pronunciation: MARE-ee
The name Mary is of Latin origin. The meaning of Mary is "star of the sea". Mary is a medieval Anglicization of the French name Marie. A biblical name; borne by the virgin mother of Christ, Mary became the object of great worship in the Catholic Church. Mary Magdalene and Mary of Bethany are also mentioned in the Bible. Diminutives: Maidie, Maisie, Mamie, May, Mimi, Minnie, Moll, Molly, Poll, Polly.

Matilda
Pronunciation: mah-TIL-dah
The name Matilda is of Old German origin. The meaning of Matilda is "mighty in battle, strength". From Old German *mahti*. The name was introduced to Britain in the 11th century by Queen Matilda, wife of William the Conqueror. Diminutives: Mattie, Matty, Tilda, Tilly.

May
Pronunciation: may

The name May is of English origin. The meaning of May is "the fifth month". The name is derived from the Latin Maius. May is of the names of months that were adopted as first names in the early 20th century. May is a diminutive of the name Mary.

Maybelle
Pronunciation: MAY-belle
The name Maybelle is of English origin. The meaning of Maybelle is "lovable". Maybelle is a variant of the English name Mabel.

Maxine
Pronunciation: mak-SEEN
The name Maxine if of Latin origin. The meaning of Maxine is "greatest". Maxine if a feminine form of the name Max.

Megan
Pronunciation: MEG-an
Megan is of Welsh origin. The meaning of the Megan is "pearl". Megan is a Welsh diminutive of Meg.

Mehetabel
Pronunciation: meh-et-a-bel
The name Mehetabel is of Hebrew origin. The meaning of Mehetabel is "God makes happy". A biblical name; borne by a figure mentioned in the Old Testament.

Melanie
Pronunciation: MEL-a-nee
The name Melanie is of French and Greek origin. The meaning of Melanie is "black, dark". The name is derived from the French form of the Latin name Melania. The name is borne by two Roman saints. The name was introduced to Britain in the 17th century. Margaret Mitchell

popularised the name in her epic novel, *Gone With The Wind* (1936). Melanie Wilkes is wife of Ashely Wilkes and Scarlet O'Hara's best friend.

Melba
Pronunciation: MEL-bah
The name Melba is of Australian origin. The name is derived from the Australian place name Melbourne. The name was possibly created as a surname by diva Nellie Melba (1861-1931).

Melinda
Pronunciation: ma-LIN-dah
The name Melinda is of Latin origin. The meaning of Melinda is "sweet". The name is an 18th-century coinage, a combination of the names Mel and Linda. The name was also influenced by the name Greek name Melissa and is often associated with bees, honey and sweetness.

Melissa
Pronunciation: ma-LISS-ah
Melissa is of Greek origin. The meaning of the name Melissa is "bee, honey". Borne in Greek mythology by a princess of Crete, who introduced mankind to honey. Diminutives: Mel.

Melody
Pronunciation: MEL-a-dee
The name Melody is of Greek origin. The meaning of Melody is "song, music". Melody is a direct adoption from the English vocabulary, which denotes a musical tune. The name was first used in the 13th century.

Mercedes
Pronunciation: mer-SAY-dees

Mercedes is of Spanish origin. The meaning of the name Mercedes is "mercies". Derived from Maria de Las Mercedes, a Spanish title for the Virgin Mary. Mercedes is also the name of the German luxury car. Diminutives: Mercy, Sadie.

Mercy
Pronunciation: MER-see
Mercy is of English origin. The meaning of the name Mercy is "compassion". The name is a direct adaptation from the English vocabulary. The virtue name was adopted by the Puritans in the 17th century. Mercy is also a diminutive of the name Mercedes.

Merlin
Pronunciation: MER-lin
Merlin is of Welsh origin. The meaning of the name Melvin is "sea fortress".

From Latinate form, Merlinus, of the Old Welsh name Myrddin. Borne in Arthurian legend by magician Merlin Ambrosius. The name is used as both a boy's name and as a girl's name.

Mia
Pronunciation: MEE-ah
Mia is of Latin and Scandinavian origin. The meaning of the name Mia is "star of the sea". Mia is a Scandinavian diminutive of the Latin name Maria. The name was popularised in the 20th century by Hollywood actress Mia Farrow.

Michaela
Pronunciation: mih-KAY-lah
The name Michaela is of Hebrew origin. The meaning of Michaela is "who is like God?" Michaela is a feminine form

of the masculine name Michael.

Michelle
Pronunciation: mee-SHELL
Michelle is of French and Hebrew origin. The meaning of the name Michelle is "who is like God?" Michelle is a feminine form of the French name Michel. The name was popularised by the Beatles in the 20th century.
Diminutives: Chelle, Mich, Michy, Shell, Shelley, Shelly.

Mignon
Pronunciation: mig-NON
The name Mignon is of French origin. The meaning of Mignon is "cute, dainty".

Millie, Milly
Pronunciation: mill-EE
Millie is of Latin and Old German origin. The meaning of Millie is "rival, bee, honey". Millie is a diminutive of the names Camila, Mildred and Millicent.

Mimi
Pronunciation: MEE-mee
Mimi is of French origin. The meaning of the name Mimi is "star of the sea". Mimi is a diminutive of the name Mary.

Mina
Pronunciation: MEE-nah
The name Mina is of German origin. The meaning of the name Mina is "love". Mina is a diminutive of the names Philomena and Wilhelmina.

Minerva
Pronunciation: mi-NER-vah
The name Minerva is of Latin origin. The meaning of Minerva is "the mind".

Borne in mythology; Minerva was the Roman goddess of wisdom, arts, crafts and war. She is equivalent to the Greek goddess Athena.

Minna
Pronunciation: min-NAH
The name Minna is of Old German origin. The meaning of Minna is "determined protector". Minna is a diminutive of the name Wilhelmina.

Minnie
Pronunciation: min-EE
Minnie is of uncertain origin. The meaning of Minnie is "star of the sea, determined protector". Minnie is a diminutive of the names Mary and Wilhelmina. The name became a popular first name in its own right. Walt Disney made popularised the name in the 20th century, by using it for the name of Mickey Mouse's girlfriend.

Mirabella
Pronunciation: mira-bel-LAH
The name Mirabella is of Latin origin. The meaning of Mirabella is "wonderful". The name was popular in medieval Britain.

Miranda
Pronunciation: mer-ANN-dah
The name Miranda is of Latin origin. The meaning of Miranda is "worthy of admiration". The name was used by Shakespeare in *The Tempest* (1612). Miranda was the name of the innocent heroine, raised and educated on an isolated island by her magician father.

Miriam

Pronunciation: MEER-ee-em

The name Miriam is of Hebrew origin. The meaning of Miriam is "star of the sea". Miriam is an old-fashioned form of the name Mary. A biblical name; borne by the sister of Moses and Aaron. The name was adopted by the Puritans. The name was later revived in the 18th century.

Mitzi

Pronunciation: MIT-zee

Mitzi is of German origin. The meaning of the name Mitzi is "star of the sea". Mitzi is originally a German diminutive of the Latin name Maria.

Modesty

Pronunciation: MAH-dess-tee

The name Modesty is of Latin origin. The meaning of Modesty is "modest, without conceit". Modesty is a virtue name.

Mohana

Pronunciation: mo-HAN-ah

The name Mohana is of Sanskrit origin. The meaning of Mohana is "attractive, enchanting".

Moira

Pronunciation: MOY-rah

The name Moira is of English origin. The meaning of Moira is "star of the sea". Moria is the Irish Gaelic form of the name Mary.

Moll

Pronunciation: moll

The name Moll is of Latin origin. The meaning of Moll is "star of the sea". Moll is a diminutive of the names Mary and Molly.

Molly
Pronunciation: moll-EE
The name Molly is of Latin origin. The meaning of Molly is "star of the sea". Molly is a diminutive of the names Mary.

Mona
Pronunciation: MOH-nah
The name Mona is of Irish Gaelic origin. The meaning of Mona is "aristocratic, noble". Mona is an anglicised form of the Irish Gaelic name Muadhnait. Mona is sometimes used as a diminutive of the name Monica. The name is also an Italian short form of Madonna. Leonardo da Vinci popularised the name with his famous painting, *Mona Lisa*.

Monica
Pronunciation: MAH-ni-kah
Monica is of Latin origin. The meaning of the name Monica is "advisor, alone". Borne by the mother of Saint Augustine, she prayed for her son and saved him from self-destruction. American sitcom, Friends (1994-2004) popularised the name with its character Monica Geller.

Monique
Pronunciation: mon-EEK
The name Monique is of French and Latin origin. The meaning of Monique is "advisor". Monique is French form of the Latin name Monica.

Morwenna
Pronunciation: mor-WEN-ah
The name Morwenna is of Welsh origin. The meaning

of Morwenna is "maiden". The name is borne by a 5th century Cornish saint.

Myra
Pronunciation: MYE-rah
The name Myra is of Greek origin. The meaning of the name Myra is "myrrh". The name was a poetic and literary invention by the English poet Fulke Greville (1554-1628). The name was popular during the 19th century.

N

Nadia

Pronunciation: NAH-d'-yah

The name Nadia is of Russian origin. The meaning of Nadia is "hope". The name is an Anglicization of Nadya, diminutive of the Russian name Nadezhda. The name is popular in Russia.

Nadine

Pronunciation: nay-DEEN

Nadine is of Russian origin. The meaning of the name Nadine is unknown. The name is a French diminutive of Nadia. The name was first used in the 20th century, when Diaghilev's Ballets Russes was established in Paris.

Naida

Pronunciation: NAY-da

The name Naida is of Greek origin. The meaning of Naida is "water nymph".

Nancy

Pronunciation: NAN-cee

Nancy is of Hebrew origin. The meaning of the name Nancy is "grace". The name is originally a diminutive of the name Constance. However, during the 18th century the name was regarded as a diminutive of Anne. Diminutives: Nan, Nance.

Naomh

Pronunciation: nay-OHM

The name Naomh is of Irish Gaelic origin. The meaning of the Naomh is "holy".

Naomi

Pronunciation: nay-OH-mee

The name Naomi is of Hebrew origin. The meaning of Naomi is "pleasant". A biblical name; borne in the Old Testament an ancestress of Jesus and mother in law to Ruth. The name has long been popular with Jewish families.

Natalia, Natalya
Pronunciation: NAT-al-ee-a
Natalia is of Russian origin. The meaning of the name Natalia is "birthday". Derived from Latin *natale domini*. The name refers to the birthday of Christ. Saint Natalia was Saint Adrian's wife. Diminutives: Talia, Talya, Tally.

Natalie
Pronunciation: NAT-a-lee
The name Natalie is of Latin origin. The meaning of Natalie is "birthday". The name is a French form of Natalya. The name dates back to the 20th century when Diaghilev's Ballet Russes was first established in Paris.

Natasha
Pronunciation: na-TAH-shah
The name Natasha is of Russian origin. The meaning of Natasha is "birthday". Natasha is a diminutive of the name Natalya. The name became a popular first name in its own right. The name became famous with Leo Tolstoy's epic novel *War and Peace* (1865-9). Natasha was the name of the heroine. Diminutives: Tash, Tasha.

Neila
Pronunciation: NEE-lah
The name Neila is of Hebrew origin. The meaning of Neila is "closing". The name is a feminine form of the masculine name Neil.

Nelinia
Pronunciation: NEL-ee-nee-a
The name Nelinia is of Scottish origin. The meaning of Nelinia is "Champion". Nelinina is a feminine form of the masculine name Neil.

Neima
Pronunciation: NEE-ma
The name Neima is of Hebrew origin. The meaning of Neima is "melody".

Neiva
Pronunciation: NEE-vah
The name Neiva is of Spanish origin. The meaning of Neiva is "snow". Neiva is a feminine variant of the word, nieve.

Neka
Pronunciation: NEE-ka
The name Neka is of Native American Indian origin. The meaning of Neka is "wild goose".

Nelia
Pronunciation: NEE-lee-a
Nelia is of Latin origin. The meaning of the name Nelia is "horn". Nelia is a diminutive of the Latin name Cornelia.

Nell
Pronunciation: N-ell
The name Nell is a diminutive of the Old French & Old German name, Eleanor. The meaning of the name Nell is "horn, sun ray". Nell can also be a variant for the names Helen, Ellen and Nelly. Diminutives: Nellie, Nelly.

Nelly
Pronunciation: NEL-ee

365

Nelly is of English origin. The meaning of the name Nelly is "sun ray". Nelly is a diminutive of the names Helen and Eleanor.

Nemera
Pronunciation: NEM-er-a
The name Nemera is of Hebrew origin. The meaning of Nemera is "leopard".

Neneca
Pronunciation: NE-ne-KA
The name Neneca is of Spanish origin. The meaning of Neneca is "industrious". Neneca is a variant of the Old German name Amelia.

Neoma
Pronunciation: NE-oo-ma
The name Neoma is of Greek origin. The meaning of Neoma is "new moon".

Nera
Pronunciation: NEE-ra
The name Nera is of Hebrew origin. The meaning of Nera is "candle".

Nereida
Pronunciation: ne-RAY-dah
Nereida is of Greek and Spanish origin. The meaning of the name Nereida is "sea nymph". Borne in Greek mythology; the Nereids were mermaids of the sea.

Nerissa
Pronunciation: NEE-riss-a
The name Nerissa is of Italian origin. The meaning of Nerissa is "black haired".

Nerola
Pronunciation: NE-rol-a
The name Nerola is of Italian origin. The meaning of Nerola is "orange flower".

Nerys

Pronunciation: NER-iss
The name Nerys is of Welsh origin. The meaning of Nerys is "noblewoman".

Nessa

Pronunciation: NESS-a
The name Nessa is of Scottish Gaelic origin. The meaning of Nessa is unknown. Nessa is a diminutive of the Greek name Agnes. The name was borne in Scottish legend by the mother of Conchobhar. Nessa is also used as a variant of the Greek name Vanessa.

Nettie

Pronunciation: NEH-tee
The name Nettie is of English origin. The meaning of Nettie is unknown. Nettie is a diminutive of all girls' names ending –net.

Niamh

Pronunciation: NI-amh
The name Niamh is of Irish Gaelic origin. The meaning of Niamh is "brightness". Borne in Irish mythology by the lover of Oisín was carried off to the land of eternal youth.

Nicola

Pronunciation: NIC-o-la
Nicola is of Greek origin. The meaning of the name Nicola is "people of victory". The name is a Latinate and Italian feminine form of the name Nicholas. Diminutives: Nic, Nik, Nicki, Nicky, Niki,, Nikki, Nico.

Nicole

Pronunciation: ni-KOHL
The name Nicole is of Greek origin. The meaning of Nicole is "people of victory". The name is a

French feminine form of the name Nicholas.

Nigella
Pronunciation: NI-gel-la
The name Nigella is of English origin. The meaning of Nigella is "Champion". Nigella is a Latinate feminine form of the name Nigel.

Nikita
Pronunciation: nih-KEE-tah
Nikita is of Greek origin. The meaning of the name Nikita is "unconquered". Nikita is a Russian masculine name, derived from the Greek name Aniketos. The name was borne by an early pope. The name is regarded as a girl's name in the English-speaking world; however it is still in use as a boy's name in Russia.

Nina
Pronunciation: NEE-nah
The name Nina is of Spanish and Hebrew origin. The meaning of Nine is "little girl". The name was originally a diminutive of girls' names that ended with –nina. The name became a popular first name in its own right. Christopher Columbus named one of his three ships Nina.
Diminutive: Ninka.

Nisha
Pronunciation: NEE-shah
The name Nisha is of Hindi origin. The meaning of Nisha is "night",

Nissa
Pronunciation: NISS-a
The name Nissa is of Hebrew origin. The meaning of Nissa is "to test".

Nixie
Pronunciation: NIX-ee
The name Nixie is of Old German. The meaning of the name Nixie is "water sprite".

Noelani
Pronunciation: no-ah-LAH-nee
The name Noelani is of Hawaiian origin. The meaning of Noelani is "mist of heaven".

Noelle
Pronunciation: noe-ELL
Noelle is of Old French origin. The meaning of the name Noelle is "Christmas". Noelle is a feminine form of Noel.

Nokomis
Pronunciation: n(o)-KO-mis
The name Nokomis if of Native American Indian origin. The meaning of Nokomis is "daughter of the moon".

Nolan
Pronunciation: NO-lan
The name Nolan is of Irish and Gaelic origin. The meaning of Nolan is "Champion". Nolan is an adopted surname.

Nona
Pronunciation: NOH-nah
The name Nona is of Latin origin. The meaning of Nona is "ninth". The name was originally given to a family's ninth baby.

Nora
Pronunciation: NOR-ah
Nora is of English origin. The meaning of the name Nora is "woman of honor". In Scotland, Nora is used as a feminine form of the name Norman.

Nordica
Pronunciation: NOR-dic-a
The name Nordica is of Latin origin. The meaning of Nordica is "from the North".

Noreen
Pronunciation: nor-EEN
The name Noreen is of Irish origin. The meaning of Noreen is unknown. Noreen is a variant of the name Nora.

Norell
Pronunciation: no-RELL
The name Norell is of Scandinavian origin. The meaning of Norell is "from the North". The name is originally a surname.

Norma
Pronunciation: NOR-mah
Norma is of Latin origin. The meaning of the name Norma is "the standard, norm". The name was possibly invented by Felice Romani. The name became popular in the 19th century, after Vincenzo Bellini's 1832 tragic opera, *Norma*. The name was popularised by Hollywood actress Norma Jeane Mortenson, also known as Marilyn Monroe (1926-1962).

Nova
Pronunciation: NOH-vah
The name Nova is of Latin origin. The meaning of Nova is "new". In astronomy, a nova is a star that releases bursts of energy.

Nuala
Pronunciation: NOO-la
The name Nuala is of Irish origin. The meaning of Nuala is unknown. The name was originally a diminutive of Fionnuala. The name is now widely

used as a first name in its own its own right.

Nura
Pronunciation: NOOR-ah
The name Nura is of Arabic and Aramaic origin. The meaning of Nura is "light".

Nydia
Pronunciation: NIH-dee-ah
The name Nydia is of Latin origin. The meaning of Nydia is "nest". Taken from the word *nidus*. The name was popularised by Edward Bulwer-Lytton's epic novel, *The Last Days of Pompeii* (1834). Nydia was the name of a blind woman who died whilst saving her beloved one.

Nina
Pronunciation: NEE-nah
The name Nina is of English origin. The meaning of Nine is unknown. Nine is a feminine form of Nyles.

Nyree
Pronunciation: ny-REE
The name Nyree is of Maori origin. The meaning of the Nyree is unknown. The name dates back to before Christ.

Nysa
Pronunciation: NY-sa
The name Nysa is of Greek origin. The meaning of Nysa is "ambition".

O

Oceana
Pronunciation: oh-see-AH-nah
The name Oceana is of Greek origin. The meaning of Oceana is "ocean". The name is a feminine form of *Oceanus*.

Octavia
Pronunciation: ock-TAHV-yah
The name Octavia is of Latin origin. The meaning of Octavia is "eighth". The name is a feminine form of Octavius, from Latin *octavus*. Octavia was sometimes given to the eighth or child or daughter.

Odele
Pronunciation: OH-del
The name Odele is of Greek origin. The meaning of Odele is "song". The name is also possibly a variant of Adele.

Odelia
Pronunciation: oh-DEEL-yah
The name Odelia is of Hebrew origin. The meaning of Odelia is "praise God". Borne by an 8th-century French saint.

Odessa
Pronunciation: oh-DESS-ah
The Odessa is of Greek origin. The meaning of Odessa is "long journey". The name is a variant of Odysseus.

Odila
Pronunciation: oh-DIL-a
The name Odila is of Old German origin. The meaning of Odila is "fortunate in battle".

Ofra
Pronunciation: OF-ra
The name Ofra is of Hebrew origin. The meaning of Ofra

is "fawn". The name is variant of Ophrah.

Oksana
Pronunciation: OK-sana
The name Oksana is of Hebrew and Russian origin. The meaning of Oksana is "praise God".

Ola
Pronunciation: Oh-lah
The name Ola is of Old Norse origin. The meaning of Ola is "ancestor's relic". Ola is a variant of the Greek name Olesia.

Oleisa
Pronunciation: oh-LEE-sa
Oleisa is of French origin. The meaning of the name Oleisa is "God is my oath". Oleisa is a variant of the Hebrew name Elizabeth.

Olena
Pronunciation: oh-LEE-na
The name Olena is of Greek and Russian origin. The meaning of the name Olena is "sun ray". The name is a variant of Helen.

Olesia
Pronunciation: OL-ee-SEE-a
Olesia is of Greek origin. The meaning of the name Olesia is "man's defender".

Olethea
Pronunciation: oh-lee-THEE-ah
The name Olethea is of Greek origin. The meaning of Olethea is "truth". Olethea is a variant of the Greek name Alethea.

Olga
Pronunciation: OL-gah
The name Olga is of Old Norse and Scandinavian origin. The meaning of Olga is "blessed, holy". The name is a Russian form of Helga.

Saint Olga was a 10th century Christian and Princess from Kiev.

Olina
Pronunciation: oh-LEE-nah
The name Olina is of Hawaiian origin. The meaning of Olina is "joyous".

Olinda
Pronunciation: oh-LIN-dah
The name Olinda is of Greek origin. The meaning of Olinda is "wild fig".

Olivia
Pronunciation: oh-LIV-ee-ah
The name Olivia is of Latin origin. The meaning of Olivia is "olive tree". The name is possibly a Latinate feminine form of Oliver. The name was used by Shakespeare in his play *Twelfth Night* (1602). Saint Olivia was venerated in Italy as patron the saint of olive trees.

Olwen
Pronunciation: OL-wen
The name Olwen is of Welsh origin. The meaning of Olwen is "white footprint". Borne in the medieval story of *Culhwch and Owen*, Olwen was so beautiful that wherever she stepped four white flowers would suddenly appear.

Olympia
Pronunciation: oh-LIM-pee-ah
Olympia is of Greek origin. The meaning of the name Olympia is "from Mount Olympus". The name is a modern adaptation of the ancient name, Peloponnesus, which was the site of the early Olympic games.

Ondine
Pronunciation: ON-dine
The name Ondine is of Latin origin. The meaning of Ondine is "little wave".

Ondrea
Pronunciation: ON-dree-ah
The name Ondrea is of Czechoslovakian origin. The meaning of Ondrea is unknown. Ondrea is a variant of the name Andrea.

Oneida
Pronunciation: ON-ee-da
The name Oneida is of Native American Indian origin. The meaning of Oneida is "long awaited".

Onella
Pronunciation: ON-el-la
The name Onella is of Greek origin. The meaning of Onella is "light".

Oona
Pronunciation: OO-nah
The name Oona is of Irish and Scottish origin. The meaning of Oona is "one". The name is an anglicised form of the Irish Gaelic name Úna.

Opal
Pronunciation: OH-pel
The name Opal is of Hindi and Sanskrit origin. The meaning of Opal is "gem". Opal is a type of semi-precious stone. The gemstone is suitable for an a baby born in October. Opals have been associated with bad luck for centuries.

Ophelia
Pronunciation: oh-FEEL-yah
The name Ophelia is of Greek origin. The meaning of Ophelia is "help". Ophelia is a feminine form of Greek *ophelos*. Shakespeare used the name is his play, *Hamlet* (1601).

Ophelia was the ill-fated lover of Hamlet. The name was popular during the 19th century.

Ophrah
Pronunciation: OHF-rah
Ophrah is of Hebrew origin. The meaning of the name Ophrah is "young deer, gazelle". A biblical name; borne by several male figures. The name is now used as both a boy's name and as a girl's name.

Oracia
Pronunciation: OR-a-cee-a
Oracia is of Spanish origin. The meaning of the name Oracia is unknown. The name is a feminine form of the Latin clan name, Horace.

Oralee
Pronunciation: OR-a-lee
The name Oralee is of Hebrew origin. The meaning of Oralee is "my light". Oralee is a variant of the English name Auralee.

Oriana
Pronunciation: or-ee-AHN-ah
The name Oriana is of Latin origin. The meaning of Oriana is "Sunrise". From Latin *oriri*. The name first appeared in the 14th-century romance, *Amadis de Gaul*.

Orla
Pronunciation: OR-lah
The name Orla is of Irish, Gaelic and Celtic origin. The meaning of Orla is "Princess".

P

Paloma
Pronunciation: pa-LOH-mah
Paloma is of Latin origin. The meaning of the name Paloma is "dove". Paloma is a Spanish name.

Pamela
Pronunciation: PAM-eh-lah
The name Pamela was invented by the poet Sir Philip Sidney (1554-86). He used the name for his heroine in his book, Arcadia (1590). Samuel Richardson popularised the name with his novel, *Pamela* (1740).

Pandora
Pronunciation: pan-DOE-ah
Pandora is of Greek origin. The meaning of the name Pandora is "all gifts". Borne in Greek mythology; Pandora was the beautiful, but foolish first mortal, created by the Greek god of fire to avenge the theft of fire by Prometheus. Pandora was given charge of a mysterious box and told never to open it up. However Pandora could not resist opening the box, and in doing so she released all of humankind's ills into the world, followed by one counterpart, Hope.

Paris
Pronunciation: PARE-iss
The name Paris is of Greek origin. In Greek mythology, Paris was the name of the young prince of Troy, whose love affair with Helen caused the Trojan war. Paris is used as both a boy's name and as a girl's name. The name was also an English given surname for immigrants from the capital of France.

Pascale
Pronunciation: PAS-cale

The name Pascale is of French and Hebrew origin. The meaning of Pascale is "pertaining to Easter". Pascale is the feminine form of the French name Pascal. Early Christians often gave the name to children born at Passover.

Patience
Pronunciation: PAY-shuns
The name Patience is of English origin. The meaning of the name Patience is "enduring, forbearing". Patience is one of the several abstract nouns denoting admirable qualities. The name was popular among Puritans in the 16th century.

Patricia
Pronunciation: pa-TRISH-ah
The name Patricia is of Latin origin. The meaning of Patricia is "noble". Patricia is a feminine form derived from *patricius*, which means 'nobleman'. The name is also a feminine form of Patrick.
Diminutives: Pat, Patsy, Pattie, Patty, Tricia, Trish.

Patsy
Pronunciation: PAT-see
The name Patsy is of Latin origin. The meaning of Patsy is "noble, patrician". Patsy is a diminutive of the name Patricia.

Paula
Pronunciation: PAW-lah
The name Paula is of Latin origin. The meaning of Paula is "small". Paula is a feminine form of the masculine name Paul. A 4th-century Saint Paula founded a number of convents in and around Bethlehem.

Paulette
Pronunciation: PAWL-ette

The name Paulette is of Latin origin. The meaning of Paulette is "small". Paulette is a French diminutive form of the Latin name Paula.

Paulina
Pronunciation: pawl-EEN-ah
The name Pauline is of Latin origin. The meaning of Paulina is "small". Paulina is Latinate diminutive form of the name Paula.

Pauline
Pronunciation: pawl-EEN
The name Pauline is of Latin origin. The meaning of Pauline is "small". The name is a French form of Paulina.

Penelope
Pronunciation: pen-NELL-a-pee
Penelope is of Greek origin. The meaning of the name Penelope is "weaver". Borne in Greek mythology; Penelope was the wife of Odysseus. She passed his ten-year absence in spinning, loyally fending off all suitors. She was the model of domestic virtues. The name has come to signify a loyal, and intelligent woman.
Diminutives: Pen, Penny.

Pepita
Pronunciation: p(e)-pi-ta
The name Pepita is of Spanish origin. The meaning of Pepita is "Jehovah increases". Pepita is a feminine form of Joseph.

Peta
Pronunciation: PET-ah
The name Peta is of Spanish and Greek origin. The

meaning of Peta is "rock". Peta is a variant of the Spanish name Papita. The name is also a variant of the Greek name Petra. Peta is a modern feminine form of the masculine name Peter.

Petra
Pronunciation: PEH-trah
The name Petra is of Greek origin. The meaning of Petra is "rock". Petra is a feminine form of the masculine name Peter, derived from Greek *petra*.

Petrova
Pronunciation: PET-rova
The name Petrova is Greek and Russian origin. The meaning Petrova is "rock". Petrova is a Russian feminine form of the name Peter.

Petula
Pronunciation: pe-tu-LAH
Petula is of Latin origin. The meaning of the name Petula is "to ask, to seek". Possibly derived from the Latin *petulare*.

Philippa
Pronunciation: FIL-lip-ah
The name Philippa is of Greek origin. The meaning of Philippa is "horse lover". Philippa is a feminine form of the masculine name Philip. Diminutives: Phil, Phillie, Philly, Pip, Pippa, Pippi, Pippy.

Philomena
Pronunciation: pa-LOH-mah
Philomena is of Greek origin. The meaning of Philomena is "beloved". The name was borne by two early Roman saints. Diminutives: Mena, Mina, Phil, Phillie, Philly.

Phoebe

Pronunciation: FEE-bee

Phoebe is of Greek origin. The meaning of the name Phoebe is "bright, radiant". Borne in Greek mythology; it was the title given to the Greek goddess of the moon, Artemis. The name became popular in the 18th century.

Pia

Pronunciation: PEE-ah

The name Pia is of Latin origin. The meaning of Pia is "pious". The name is a feminine form of the Latin adjective *pius*.

Pilar

Pronunciation: pee-LAR

The name Pilar is of Spanish origin. The meaning of Pilar is "pillar". From Nuestra Señora del Pilar, which means, 'Our Lady of the Pillar'? In the Catholic tradition, it is a reference to a legendary appearance of the Virgin Mary standing on a pillar at Saragossa.

Pippa

Pronunciation: PIPP-a

Pippa is of Greek origin. The meaning of the name Pipa is "lover of horses". Pippa is a diminutive of the Greek name Phillipa.

Polly

Pronunciation: PAH-lee

The name Polly is of English and Irish origin. The meaning of Polly is "star of the sea". Polly is a variant of the name Molly, which is a nickname for Mary.

Pollyanna

Pronunciation: POLL-ee-ann-a

The name Pollyanna was invented by Eleanor Porter for the heroine in her children's book, *Pollyanna*

(1913).

Poppy
Pronunciation: POP-ee
The name Poppy is of Latin origin. The meaning of Poppy is unknown. From Latin *papaver*, donating a species of flower that has papery leaves.

Posy
Pronunciation: POH-see
The name Posy is of English origin. The meaning of Posy is "a bunch of flowers". Posy is also used a nickname for Josephine.

Primrose
Pronunciation: PRIM-rose
The name Primrose is of Latin origin. The meaning of Primrose is "first rose". From Latin *prima rosa*. Primrose is also a botanical name of a 19th-century yellow flower which blooms early in spring, particularly on banks and in woodlands.

Princess
Pronunciation: PRIN-sess
The name Princess if of English origin. Princess is a title name used by Royalty.

Priscilla
Pronunciation: pris-SILL-ah
Priscilla is of Latin origin. The meaning of the name Priscilla is "ancient". Priscilla is a feminine diminutive of the Roman family name Priscus. A biblical name: Priscilla was a first-century Christian missionary. The name was adopted by the Puritans. Diminutives: Cilla, Pris.

Prudence
Pronunciation: PROO-dens
The name Prudence is of Latin origin. The meaning of Prudence is "caution, discretion". The name was

popular during the 16th, 17th and 19th centuries.

Prunella
Pronunciation: PRU-nell-a
The name Prunella is of Latin origin. The meaning of Prunella is "small plum".

Psyche
Pronunciation: p-sy-che
The name Psyche is of Greek origin. The meaning of Psyche is "breath, of the soul". Borne in mythology; Psyche was a mortal girl who fell in love with Cupid.

Purity
Pronunciation: PUR-it-ee
The name Purity if of Middle English origin. Purity is a virtue name.

Q

Qiturah
Pronunciation: KWIT-ur-ah
The name Qiturah is of Arabic origin. The meaning of Qiturah is "incense, scent".

Queenie
Pronunciation: KWE-nee
The name Queenie is of English origin. The meaning of Queenie is "Queen". From Old *cwen*, which means 'woman'. Queenie was a name used to by contemporaries to refer to Queen Victoria. The name was popular during the 20th century.

Quenby
Pronunciation: KWIN-bee
The name Quenby is of Old English origin. The meaning of Quenby is "Queen's settlement". Quenby is also a place name.

Querida
Pronunciation: kare-EE-sah
The name Querida is of Spanish origin. The meaning of Querida is "beloved".

Questa
Pronunciation: KWES-ta
The name Questa is of French origin. The meaning of Questa is "one who seeks".

Quiana
Pronunciation: kee-AHN-ah
The name Quiana is of American origin. The meaning of Quiana is "silky". The name is also possibly a variant of the name Hannah or Ayana.

Queta
Pronunciation: KAY-tah
The name Queta is of Spanish origin. The

meaning of Queta is unknown.

Quilla
Pronunciation: KWIL-la
The name Quilla is of Middle English origin. The meaning of Quilla is "feather".

Quincey
Pronunciation: KWIN-cey
Quincey is of Old French origin. The meaning of the name Quincey is "estate of the fifth son". Adopted surname, originally a baronial name from Cuinchy in northern France. Quincey can be used as a both a girl's name, and as a boy's name.

Quinn
Pronunciation: KWIN
The name Quinn is of Irish and Gaelic origin. The meaning of Quinn is "counsel". An adopted Irish surname, from the Gaelic name O Cuinn, meaning 'decedent of Conn'. Quinn has been used a given name from very ancient times. Quinn is used as both a girl's name and as a boy's name.

Quintina
Pronunciation: KWIN-te-na
Quintina is of Latin origin. The meaning of the name Quintina is "fifth".

Quirina
Pronunciation: KW-ree-na
The name Quirina is of Latin origin. The meaning of Quirina is "Warrior".

R

Rachana
Pronunciation: ra-SHA-nah
Rachana is of Hindi origin. The meaning of the name Rachana is "creation".

Rachel
Pronunciation: RAY-cehl
The name Rachel is of Hebrew origin. The meaning of Rachel is "ewe, female sheep". A biblical name; borne in the Old Testament by the wife of Jacob, and mother of Benjamin and Joseph. She was described as being 'beautiful in form and countenance'. She died whilst giving birth to Benjamin. The name was popularised in hit TV series, *Friends* (1994-2004).
Diminutives: Rach, Rae.

Radha
Pronunciation: RAD-ha
The name Radha is of Hindi and Sanskrit origin. The meaning of Radha is "success". In Hindu religion, Radha was the name of a cowherd who became the favourite consort of Krishna.

Rae
Pronunciation: ray
The name Rae is of Hebrew origin. The meaning of Rae is "ewe, female sheep". Rae is a diminutive of the name Rachel.

Rafaela
Pronunciation: rah-fah-AY-lah
The name Rafaela is of Spanish origin. The meaning of Rafaela is "God has healed". Rafaela is a feminine form of the masculine name Raphael.

Raphaela
Pronunciation: rah-fah-AY-lah

The name Raphaela is of Spanish origin. The meaning of Raphael is "God has healed". Raphael is a feminine form of the masculine name Rephael.

Ramona
Pronunciation: ra-MOH-nah
The name Ramona is of Spanish and Old German origin. The meaning of Ramona is "protecting hands". Ramona is a feminine form of the masculine name Roman, the Spanish form of Raymond.

Raquel
Pronunciation: rah-KELL
Raquel is of Spanish and Portuguese origin. The meaning of the name Raquel is "ewe, female sheep". Raquel is a Spanish form the name Rachel.

Rebecca
Pronunciation: ree-BEK-ah
The name Rebecca is of Hebrew origin. The meaning of Rebecca is "to bind". Rebecca is a Latin form of the Hebrew name Rebekah. The name was popularised in the 20th century, possibly due to Daphne du Maurier's novel *Rebecca* (1938). The novel was later made into a film by Alfred Hitchcock in 1940. Diminutives: Becca, Becky.

Regan
Pronunciation: REE-gan
Regan is of Gaelic origin. The meaning of the name Regan is unknown. Shakespeare used the name for one of the king's three daughters in *King Lear* (1606).

Renata
Pronunciation: REN-at-ah
The name Renata is of Latin origin. The meaning of Renata is "Reborn". Renata is a Latinate form of the name Renèe. The name was adopted by the Puritans.

Rene, Renie
Pronunciation: REN-ee
The name Rene is of Greek origin. The meaning of Rene is "peace". Rene is a diminutive of the Greek name Irene.

Rhiannon
Pronunciation: ree-ANN-on
The name Rhiannon is of Welsh origin. The meaning of Rhiannon is "goddess, great queen". Borne in mythology; by a figure in the *Mabinogian*, the collection of Welsh legends.

Rhoda
Pronunciation: ROH-da
The name Rhoda is of Greek and Latin origin. The meaning of Rhoda is "rose". From Greek *rhodon*. A biblical name; borne by a servant girl who was one of the early Christian disciples. The name was popular during the 18th and 19th centuries.

Rhona
Pronunciation: ROH-nah
Rhona is of uncertain origin. Rhona is a feminine form of the masculine name Ronald.

Rica
Pronunciation: REE-kah
The name Rica is of Old Norse origin. The meaning of Rica is "complete ruler". Rica is a diminutive of any girl's name ending –rica, such as Erica or Frederica.

Rika

Pronunciation: re-KAH

The name Rika is of Old Norse origin. The meaning of Rika is "complete ruler". Rika is a diminutive of any girl's name ending –rica, such as Erica or Frederica.

Rita

Pronunciation: REE-tah

The name Rita is of Spanish origin. The name is originally a diminutive of Margarita, the Spanish form of Margaret. The Italian Saint Rita is regarded as the patron saint of unhappy marriages and desperate cases.

Roberta

Pronunciation: roh-BER-tah

The name Roberta is of Old English and Old German origin. The meaning of Roberta is "bright fame". Roberta is a feminine form of the masculine name Robert. Diminutives: Bobbie, Bobby.

Robin

Pronunciation: RAH-bin

Robin is of English origin. The meaning of the name Robin is unknown. The name is a 20th-century adoption of a well establish boy's name for girls. Robyn is also used a nickname for males named Robert. Robyn is also the name of a red-breasted songbird.

Róisín

Pronunciation: ROE-sheen

The name Róisín is of Irish Gaelic origin. The meaning of Róisín is "little rose".

Romaine

Pronunciation: ROE-may-ne

The name Romaine is of French origin. The meaning of Romaine is "woman of Rome".

Ros
Pronunciation: ros
The name Ros is of Old German origin. The meaning of Ros is "gentle horse, horse protector". Ros is a diminutive of Rosalind, Rosamund or any name beginning with Ros-.

Rosa
Pronunciation: ROH-za
Rosa is of Latin origin. The meaning of the name Rosa is "rose". Rosa is a Latinate form of Rose.

Rosalie
Pronunciation: ROH-za-lee
The name Rosalie is of French origin. The meaning of Rosalie is "rose garden". Rosalie is a French name derived from the Latin name Rosa. Saint Rosalie was a 12th-century virgin martyr of Palermo, Sicily.

Rosalind
Pronunciation: RAH-za-lind
The name Rosalind is of Old German origin. The meaning of Rosaline is "gentle horse". Shakespeare popularised the name in *As You Like It* (1603). Rosalind was the name of the heroine. Diminutives: Ros, Roz.

Rosaline
Pronunciation: ROZ-a-lin
The name Rosaline is of French origin. The meaning of Rosaline is "gentle horse". Rosaline is a variation of the name Rosalind.

Rosamond
Pronunciation: ROH-za-mond

The name Rosamond is of Old German origin. The meaning of Rosamond is "horse protector". The name dates back to the Middle Ages.

Rosamund
Pronunciation: ROH-za-mund
The name Rosamund is of French origin. The meaning of Rosamund is "horse protector". The name was associated with the Latin *rosa mundi*, which means, 'rose of the world'. An epithet that was given to the Virgin Mary. Diminutives: Ros, Rosa, Roz.

Rosanna
Pronunciation: ROSE-an-ah
The name Rosanna is an 18th-century coinage combining the names Rose and Anna together.

Rosanne
Pronunciation: ROSE-anne
The name Rosanne is a 19th-century coinage combining the names Rose and Anne together.

Rose
Pronunciation: rohz
The name Rose is of Latin origin. The meaning of Rose is "rose". Rose is derived from Latin, *rosa*. The name denotes a shrub of the genus rosa, fragrant flowers with thorny stems. The name was introduced to Britain by the Normans in the 11th century. Diminutives: Rosie.

Rosemary
Pronunciation: ROHZ-mare-ee
The name Rosemary is of Latin origin. The meaning of Rosemary is "dew of the sea". Rosemary is also the

name of a fragrant herb.
Diminutives: Romey, Romy.

Rosetta
Pronunciation: ROE-set-ah
Rosetta is of Latin origin. The meaning of the name Rosetta is "rose". Rosetta is a variation of the name Rose. Originally an Italian diminutive, that dates back to the 19th century.

Rosheen
Pronunciation: ROE-she-n
The name Rosheen is of Irish Gaelic origin. The meaning of Rosheen is "little rose". Rosheen is an Anglicization of the Irish Gaelic name Roísín.

Rosie
Pronunciation: ROSE-ee
The name Rose is of Latin origin. The meaning of Rosie is "rose". Rosie is a diminutive of all names that contain the element, 'Rose'.

Rosina
Pronunciation: ROS-in-ah
The name Rosina is of Latin origin. The meaning of Rosina is "rose". Originally a Spanish diminutive, Rosina is a variation of the name Rose.

Rowan
Pronunciation: ROH-an
The name Rowan is of Gaelic origin. The meaning of Rowan is "red berry tree". Rowan is used as both a girl's name and as a boy's name.

Rowena
Pronunciation: roh-EEN-ah
The name Rowena is of Old German origin. The meaning of Rowena is "fame and happiness". Rowena is also possibly a variation of the Welsh name Rhonwen.

Roxanne

Pronunciation: roks-ANN

Roxanne is of Persian origin. The meaning of the name Roxanne is "Dawn". The name is borne by a Persian wife of Alexander the Great. Diminutive: Roxy.

Ruby

Pronunciation: ROO-bee

The name Ruby is of English origin. The meaning of Ruby is "the red gemstone". From Latin *rubus*. Ruby is the name of a precious red stone, considered by the Ancients to be an antidote to poison and a protection from the plague. Some people consider Rubies to be bad luck. Rubies are the birthstone of July.

Ruth

Pronunciation: rooth

The name Ruth is of Hebrew origin. The meaning of Ruth is "friend". A biblical name; borne in the Old Testament by the loyal wife of Boaz. Ruth was the young Moabite widow and daughter-in-law of Naomi. The name was popular during the 17th century. Diminutives: Ruthi, Ruthie.

S

Sabrina

Pronunciation: sa-BREE-nah

Sabrina is of Celtic origin. The meaning of Sabrina is unknown. Sabrina is a Roman name for the River Severn. Borne in mythology; the name of the illegitimate daughter of King Locrine of Wales. She was drowned in the river Severn by her father's ex-wife, Gwendolen. The Old Man of the Sea took pity on her and turned her into a river goddess.

Sadie

Pronunciation: SAY-dee

The name Sadie is of Hebrew origin. The meaning of Sadie is "Princess". Sadie is a diminutive for Sarah and Mercedes. The name was first used as a first name at the beginning of the 20th century.

Saffron

Pronunciation: SAFF-ron

Saffron is of Arabic origin. Derived from Arabic *zafaran*. Saffron is the most expensive of all spices. Saffron is also a bright orange/yellow colour dye.

Sally

Pronunciation: SAL-ee

The name Sally is of Hebrew origin. The meaning of Sally is "Princess". Sally is a diminutive of Sarah, often used in its own right. The name was popular in the 18th and 20th centuries.
Diminutives: Sal.

Samantha

Pronunciation: sa-MAN-thah

The name Samantha is of English origin. The meaning of Samantha is "listen, God heard". American Actress Samantha Eggar popularised the name during the 1960's with the hit TV show, *Bewitched*.

Sanchia
Pronunciation: san-CHIA
The name Sanchia is of Spanish origin. The meaning of Sanchia is "holy, sacred". Sanchia is a variant of the Latin name Sancia. The name was introduced into Britain during the 13th century.

Sandie, Sandy
Pronunciation: SAN-dee
Sandy is of uncertain origin. The meaning of the name Sandy is "man's defender". Diminutives of Alexandra, Cassandra and Sandra.

Sandra
Pronunciation: SAN-drah
The name Sandra is of English origin. The meaning of Sandra is "man's defender". Sandra is a variation of the Alexandra, via the Italian form, Alessandra.

Saorise
Pronunciation: seer-sha
The name Saorise is of Irish Gaelic origin. The meaning of Saorise is "freedom".

Sapphire
Pronunciation: SAFF-ire
The name Sapphire is of English origin. From Old French *safir*, derived from Greek *sappheiros*. Sapphire is a jewel name and the birthstone for September. A Sapphire is a transparent blue precious stone.

Sara, Sarah
Pronunciation: SARE-ah
The name Sarah is of Hebrew origin. The meaning of Sarah is "Princess". A biblical name; borne by the wife of Abraham and mother of Isaac, whom she conceived

when she was 90 years old. Originally called Sarai, she was given the name Sarah at God's command. Sarah lived an adventurous and nomadic life. She was described as being exceptionally beautiful. The name became popular in the 16th century.

Sarina
Pronunciation: sa-REE-nah
The name Sarina is of Latin origin. The meaning of Sarina is "Princess". Sarina is a variant of the Hebrew name Sarah.

Sarita
Pronunciation: sa-RE-ta
The name Sarita is of Hebrew origin. The meaning of Sarita is "Princess". Sarita is a variant of the Hebrew name Sarah.

Sasha
Pronunciation: SAH-shah
Sasha is of Greek and Russian origin. The meaning of the name Sasha is "man's defender". Sasha is a Russian diminutive of the name Alexandra. Sasha is used as both a girl's name and as a boy's name.

Saskia
Pronunciation: SAS-kee-a
Saskia is of Danish and Old German origin. The meaning of the name Saskia is "the Saxon people". Saskia was the name of the wife of the Dutch painter, Rembrandt (17th century).

Scarlett
Pronunciation: SCAR-let
The name Scarlett is of Old French origin. The meaning of Scarlett is "red". An adopted surname derived originally from Old French

escarlate, which means 'scarlet cloth'. Margaret Mitchell popularised the name in her epic novel, *Gone With The Wind* (1936). Scarlett O' Hara was the name of the heroine.

Selena, Selina
Pronunciation: sa-LEEN-ah
The name Selina is of uncertain origin. The meaning of Selina is "the moon". The name was first used in Britain during the Middles Ages.

Selma
Pronunciation: SEL-mah
The name Selma is of Old German and Arabic origin. The meaning of Selma is "safe, peace".

Serena
Pronunciation: ser-REE-nah
Serena is of Latin origin. The meaning of the name Serena is "calm, serene".

From Latin *serenus*, meaning 'calm'. Borne by a Christian saint.

Shannon
Pronunciation: SHAN-en
Shannon is of Gaelic origin. The meaning of the name Shannon is "old". Originally an adopted surname, derived from Ireland's principal river.

Sharon
Pronunciation: SHARE-en
The name Sharon is of Hebrew origin. The meaning of Sharon is "a fertile plain". A biblical place name, from the plain of Sharon in the Holy Land. The name was adopted by the Puritans.

Sheba
Pronunciation: SHEE-bah
The name Sheba is of Hebrew origin. The meaning of Sheba is

"promise". Sheba is a diminutive of Bathsheba, which is associated with the Queen of Sheba. She visited Solomon in search of information about his God. Balkis, Queen of Sheba, also appears in the Koran. Sheba is the name of a kingdom in southern Arabia noted for its great wealth.

Sheila
Pronunciation: SHEE-lah
The name Sheila is of Irish and Gaelic origin. The meaning of Sheila is "blind". Sheila is an anglicised form of the Irish Gaelic name, Síle.

Shelley
Pronunciation: SHEL-ee
The name Shelley is of Old English origin. The meaning of Shelley is "sloped meadow". An adopted surname and place name from Old English, meaning 'wood on a slope'. Shelley is also used a nickname for Michelle, Rochelle and Shirley. Shelley is used as both a girl's name and as a boy's name.

Sheridan
Pronunciation: SHARE-a-den
The name Sheridan is of Irish and Gaelic origin. The meaning of Sheridan is "seeker". An adopted Irish surname, from O Sirideain. The name was popularised by Irish playwright Richard Brinsley Sheridan (1751-1861). The name is used as both a boy's name and as a girl's name.

Sherry
Pronunciation: SHARE-ee
The name Sherry is of English origin. The meaning of Sherry is "darling, dear".

403

From French chèrie. The name is also a short form of the Hebrew name Sharon.

Shona
Pronunciation: SH-o-na
The name Shona is of Gaelic and Hebrew origin. The meaning of Shona is "God is gracious". Shona is a Gaelic feminine form of the name John.

Sian
Pronunciation: shaahn
The name Sian is of Welsh origin. The meaning of Sian is "God's grace". Sian is a Welsh variant of the name Jane.

Siena
Pronunciation: see-EN-ah
Siena is of Latin origin. The meaning of the name Siena is "from Siena". Originally a place name of the city, Siena in Italy. Siena is also the name of reddish shade of brown.

Sidney, Sydney
Pronunciation: SID-nee
Sidney is of Old English origin. The meaning of the name Sidney is "wide meadow". Sidney is an adopted surname and place name. The name has been used as a first name since the 17th century. Charles Dickens boosted the popularity of the name when he used it for his hero in *A Tale Of Two Cities* (1859). Australian city of Sydney was named in honour of Thomas Townshend. The name is used as both a boy's name and as a girl's name.

Silvia
Pronunciation: SIL-vee-ah
The name Silvia is of Latin origin. The meaning of Silvia is "wood, forest".

From the Latin name Silvius. Shakespeare used the name in *The Two Gentlemen of Verona* (1594).

Simone
Pronunciation: sih-MOHN
The name Simone is of Hebrew origin. The meaning of Simone is "hear, listen". Simone is a feminine form of the masculine name Simon. Simone is used as both a girl's name and as a boy's name.

Sinèad
Pronunciation: sha-NADE
The name Sinèad is of Irish Gaelic origin. The meaning of Sinèad is "God is gracious". Sinèad is an Irish Gaelic form of the name Janet.

Siobhan
Pronunciation: sha-VAHN
The name Siobhan is of Irish Gaelic and Hebrew origin. The meaning of Siobhan is "God is gracious". Siobhan is an Irish Gaelic form of the name Joan.

Sky, Skye
Pronunciation: sky
The name Sky is of English origin. Sky is one of several nature names that became popular when nature names were made fashionable during 1960's. Skye is associated to the Isle of Skye in Scotland. Sky is used as both a girl's name and as a boy's name.

Skyler
Pronunciation: SKY-ler
Skyler is of Dutch origin. The meaning of the name Skyler is "fugitive".

405

Sonia

Pronunciation: SOHN-yah
The name Sonia is of Greek origin. The meaning of Sonia is "wisdom". Sonia is a Russian variation of the name Sophia. Stephen McKenna popularised the name with his novel, *Sonia* (1917).

Sonja

Pronunciation: SON-ja
The name Sonja is of Greek origin. The meaning of Sonja is "wisdom". Sonja is a Russian variation of the name Sophia.

Sophia

Pronunciation: so-FEE-ah
Sophia is of Greek origin. The meaning of the name Sophia is "wisdom". The name was introduced to Britain in the 17th century by the granddaughter of James I.

Sophie

Pronunciation: so-FEE
Sophie is of French origin. The meaning of the name Sophie is "wisdom". The name was introduced to Britain in the 17th century by the granddaughter of James I.

Sorcha

Pronunciation: SAW-kha
The name Sorcha is of Irish and Gaelic origin. The meaning of Sorcha is "bright".

Sorrel

Pronunciation: s(or)-rell
The name Sorrel is of Old French and Old German origin. The meaning of Sorrel is "sour". From the Old French plant name, *surele*, derived from *sur*, which means 'sour'. This refers to the acid taste of its leaves.

Stacey, Stacie, Stacy

Pronunciation: ST-aa-cee

The name Stacey is of Greek origin. The meaning of Stacey is "Resurrection". Stacey is a diminutive of the Greek name Anastasia, and of the name Eustacia.

Stella

Pronunciation: STELL-ah

The name Stella is of Latin origin. The meaning of Stella is "star".

Stephanie

Pronunciation: STEFF-a-nee

The name Stephanie is of Greek origin. The meaning of Stephanie is "garland, crown". Stephanie is a feminine form of the masculine name Stephan. Diminutives: Steff, Steffi, Steffie, Steph, Stephie.

Stevie

Pronunciation: STE-vie

The name Stevie is of Greek origin. The meaning of Stevie is "garland, crown". The name is originally a diminutive of Stephen. The name is used as both a girl's and as a boy's name.

Summer

Pronunciation: SUH-mer

The name Summer is of Old English origin. Summer is one of several names derived from nature. The name was popularised during the 1960's when nature names became fashionable.

Susanna, Susannah, Suzanna

Pronunciation: SU-zan-ah

The name Suzanna is of Hebrew origin. The meaning of Suzanna is "lily". From the Hebrew name Shushannah.

T

Tabitha
Pronunciation: TAB-i-thah
The name Tabitha is of Aramaic origin. The meaning of Tabitha is "gazelle". A biblical name; borne by a New Testament figure, the Aramaic name of Dorcas. She was a kind woman noted for her good work, who was resurrected by St Peter.

Tacy
Pronunciation: TAY-cee
The name Tacy is of Latin origin. The meaning of Tacy is "silence". The name may possibly a short form of Anastasia.

Taffy
Pronunciation: TAFF-ee
The name Taffy is of Welsh origin. The meaning of Taffy is "loved one".

Tahira
Pronunciation: TA-hi-ra
Tahira is of Arabic origin. The meaning of the name Tahira is "virginal, pure".

Taima
Pronunciation: ta(i)-MAH
The name Taima is of Native American Indian origin. The meaning of Taima is "pearl of thunder".

Talia
Pronunciation: TAL-yah
The name Talia is of Hebrew and Aramaic origin. The meaning of Talia is "heaven's dew". The name is a variant of Taliah. Talia is also a short form of the name Natalia.

Tallulah
Pronunciation: TAL-oo-lah
The name Tallulah is of Native American Indian origin. The meaning of Tallulah is "running water, leaping water". The

Choctaws lived near the Tallulah waterfall.

Tamara
Pronunciation: TAM-a-rah
Tamara is of Hebrew origin. The meaning of the name Tamara is "date palm". The name is a Russian variant of Tamar, borne by a 12th-century Queen of Georgia. Diminutives: Tammie, Tammy.

Tamsin
Pronunciation: TAM-sin
The name Tamsin is of English origin. The meaning of Tamsin is unknown. Tamsin is a short form of the Aramaic name Thomsaina, the feminine form of Thomas. The name dates back to the Middle Ages.

Tania, Tanya
Pronunciation: THAN-ya
The name Tania is of Russian origin. The meaning of Tania is unknown. Tania is a Russian diminutive of Tatiana.

Tansy
Pronunciation: TAN-see
The name Tansy is of Greek origin. The meaning of Tansy is "eternal life". From old French *tanesie*, derived from Greek *anthanasi*, which means 'immortal'. Tansy is also the name of a bitter tasting, aromatic herb. The name was adopted as a first name in the 1960's.

Tara
Pronunciation: TAH-rah
Tara is of Gaelic and Sanskrit origin. The meaning of the name Tara is "hill, star". Ancient Tara is the name of a place in County Meath, 'stone of

destiny' where Irish kings resided. The name was popularised by the Hollywood film, *Gone with the Wind* (1939). Tara is the name of Scarlett O'Hara's family estate. Borne in Hindu mythology; Tara is one of the names of the wife of Shiva. In Mahayana Buddhism, Tara is the name of the wife of Buddha.

Tatiana
Pronunciation: tat-YAH-nah
Tatiana is of Latin and Russian origin. The meaning of the name Tatiana is "of the family of Tatius". From the feminine for of the Latin name Tatianus. Tatiana is also the name of a 3rd-century saint.

Tegan
Pronunciation: TEA-gan
The name Tegan is of Welsh origin. The meaning of Tegan is "beautiful".

Teresa
Pronunciation: ter-REE-sah
The name Teresa is of Greek origin. The meaning of Teresa is "late summer". The first bearers of the name might possibly have been from the Greek island of Therasia. The name is popular among Roman Catholic saints. Saint Thèrese of Lisieux (1873-97) was a young Carmelite nun who wrote her autobiography whilst she lay dying of tuberculosis. Mother Teresa founded an order of nuns, the Missionaries of Charity, whose sisters help people in need around the world. Mother Teresa's hard work earned her the title, 'the saint of the gutters'.

Theresa

Pronunciation: ter-REE-sah
The name Theresa is of Greek origin. The meaning of Theresa is "late summer". The first bearers of the name might possibly have been from the Greek island of Therasia. The name is popular among Roman Catholic saints.

Tess

Pronunciation: TESS
The name Tess is of Greek origin. The meaning of Tess is "late summer". Tess is diminutive of Teresa and Theresa, the name became popular in its own right. Tomas Hardy popularised the name with his famous novel, *Tess of the d'Ubervilles* (1891).

Tessa

Pronunciation: TESS-ah
Tessa is of English origin. The meaning of the name Tessa is "fourth child". Tessa is diminutive of Teresa and Theresa, the name became popular in its own right.

Thea

Pronunciation: THEE-ah
Thea is of Greek origin. The meaning of the name Thea is "goddess". Thea is a short form of Althea, Mathea and Dorothea.

Theodora

Pronunciation: thee-a-DOR-ah
The name Theodora is of Greek origin. The meaning of Theodora is "God's gift". Theodora is a feminine form of the masculine name Theodore.

Tiana

Pronunciation: tee-AHN-ah

Tiana is of Latin and Russian origin. The meaning of the name Tiana is 'of the family of Tatius'. Tiana is a diminutive of Tatiana.

Tiffany
Pronunciation: TIF-a-nee
The name Tiffany is of Greek origin. The meaning of Tiffany is "revelation of God.". Tiffany is variant of the Greek name Theophania. The name refers to manifestations of God, particularly Epiphany. In many Christian countries, females who are born on 6th January (the Feast of Epiphany) are given some form of this name. The name was made popular by the New York jeweler, Tiffany & Co.

Tilda
Pronunciation: TIL-da
The name Tilda is German origin. The meaning of Tilda is "mighty in battle". Tidla is a diminutive of the Old German name Matilda.

Tilly
Pronunciation: TILL-ee
The name Tilly is German origin. The meaning of Tilly is "mighty in battle". Tilly is a diminutive of the Old German name Matilda. Tilda is also a variant of the name Tilda.

Tina
Pronunciation: TEE-nah
The name Tina is of Latin origin. The meaning of Tina is "follower of Christ". Originally a diminutive for Christiana, the name is now used in its own right.

Toni
Pronunciation: TOH-nee
The name Toni is of English origin. The meaning of Toni

is unknown. Toni is a diminutive of Antonia, Antonina and Antoinette.

Tonia, Tonya
Pronunciation: TOHN-yah
The name Tonia is of French origin. The meaning of Tonia is unknown. Tonia is French feminine diminutive of the name Antoine.

Tracie, Tracy, Tracey
Pronunciation: T-race-ee
The name Tracie is of Greek origin. The meaning of Tracie is "late summer". Variations of Teresa. The name was popularised by the character of Tracey Lord in the film *The Philadelphia Story* (1940).

Trina
Pronunciation: TREEN-nah
Trina is of Scandinavian origin. The meaning of the name Trina is "pure". Trina is diminutive for the Greek name Katrina.

Trinity
Pronunciation: TRIN-ee-tee
The name Trinity is of Latin origin. The meaning of Trinity is "triad". The name refers to the Holy Trinity in Christian faith.

Trista
Pronunciation: TRISS-tah
Trista is of English origin. The meaning of the name Trista is "tryst". Trista is a feminine form of the masculine name Tristan.

Tristana
Pronunciation: TRIST-an-ah
The name Tristana is of Welsh origin. The meaning of Tristana is "tryst". Tristana is a feminine form

of the masculine name Tristan.

Trixie
Pronunciation: TRIKS-ee
The name Trixie is of English origin. The meaning of Trixie is "blessed, voyager". Trixie is a diminutive of Beatrix.

Troy
Pronunciation: TR-oy
The name Troy is of Irish and Gaelic origin. The meaning of Troy is "descendant of the footsoldier". An adopted surname that was given to those who migrated to England from Troyes in France, after the Norman conquest of 1066. Troy is also associated with the ancient city In Asia Minor where the Trojan wars were fought. The name is used as both a boy's name and as a girl's name.

Trudi, Trudie, Trudy
Pronunciation: TROO-dee
The name Trudi of Old German origin. The meaning of the name Trudi is "strength, strong spear". The name is frequently used as a nickname for people called Gertrude, Hiltrud and Ermintrude.

Tryphena
Pronunciation: T-ryphe-na
The name Tryphena is of Greek origin. The meaning of Tryphena is "delicacy". A biblical name; Tryphena appears in one of Paul's epistles to the Romans.

Tuesday
Pronunciation: TUES-day
The name Tuesday is of Old English origin. Tuesday is a day of the week. The name was popularised by the hit TV series and Hollywood film *The Addams Family*. Tuesday Addams was the

daughter of Mortica and Gomez Addams.

Tulia

Pronunciation: TU-lee-a
Tulia is of Spanish and Latin origin. The meaning of the name Tulia is unknown. Derived from an ancient Roman family name, *Tullius.*

Tyler

Pronunciation: TYE-ler
The name Tyler is of English origin. The meaning of Tyler is "a worker in roof tiles". Originally an occupational name. Tyler is used as both a girl's name and as a boy's name.

Tyra

Pronunciation: TEER-ah
The name Tyra is of Old English origin. The meaning of Tyra is "Thor's battle". The name was made famous by supermodel Tyra Banks.

U

Uberta
Pronunciation: OO-ber-TA
The name Uberta is of Italian origin. The meaning of Uberta is "shining intellect". Uberta is variant of the Old German name Huberta.

Udele
Pronunciation: OO-del-e
The name Udele is of Old English origin. The meaning of Udele is "wealthy".

Ula
Pronunciation: oo-LA
Ula is of Celtic and Hawaiian origin. The meaning of the name Ula is "gem of the sea, wealthy".

Ulani
Pronunciation: uwl-an-EE
The name Ulani is of Hawaiian origin. The meaning of Ulani is "cheerful".

Ulima
Pronunciation: uwl-li-MA
The name Ulima is of Arabic origin. The meaning of Ulima is "wise".

Ulla
Pronunciation: uwl-LA
The name Ulla is of Old Norse origin. The meaning of Ulla is "will, determination".

Ulrica
Pronunciation: uwl-REE-kah
The name Ulrica is of Old German origin. The meaning of Ulrica is "power of the wolf". The name is a feminine form of Ulric.

Ultima
Pronunciation: uwl-ti-MA
The name Ultima is of Latin origin. The meaning of Ultima is "farthest point".

Ulva
Pronunciation: uwl-VA
The name Ulva is of Old German origin. The meaning of Ulva is "Wolf".

Ulyssa
Pronunciation: yoo-LISS-ah
The name Ulyssa is of Latin origin. The meaning of Ulyssa is unknown. The name is a feminine form of the masculine name Ulysses.

Uma
Pronunciation: OO-mah
The name Uma is of Hindi and Sanskrit origin. The meaning of Uma is "flax, turmeric". Borne by the goddess what mediates between Brahma and the other gods. Uma is also a byname for the Indian goddess Sakti, wife of Shiva. The Hebrew meaning of the name Uma is "nation".

Una
Pronunciation: OO-nah
Una is of Latin origin. The meaning of Una is "one". Anglicised form of the Irish Gaelic name, Ũna. The name was borne in Irish legend by the mother of Conn Cètchathach.

Udine
Pronunciation: un-DEE-ne
The name Udine if of Latin origin. The meaning of Udine is "little wave". Borne in mythology, Udine is the name of the spirit of the waters.

Unique
Pronunciation: yoo-NEEK
Unique is of Latin origin. The meaning of the name Unique is "only on".

Unity
Pronunciation: yoo-ni-TEE
The name Unity is of Middle English origin. The

meaning of Unity is "oneness". The name was used by the Puritans.

Urania

Pronunciation: yoo-ran-IA
The name Urania is of Greek origin. The meaning of Urania is "heavenly". Borne in Greek mythology; Urania was the eldest of Zeus' and Mnemosyne's nine daughters. Zeus and Mnemosyne slept together for nine consecutive nights and birthed nine Muses, Urania was one of them. Urania was in charge of astronomy, she is often associated with universal love and the Holy Spirit. Urania inherited Zeus' majesty and power, and the beauty and grace of her Mnemosyne.

Urbana

Pronunciation: ur-BAN-a
The name Urbana is of Latin origin. The meaning of Urbana is "of the city". The name is a feminine form of Urban.

Uriela

Pronunciation: YOO-rie-la
The name Uriela is of Hebrew origin. The meaning of Uriela is "God's light".

Urit

Pronunciation: YOO-rit
The name Urit is of Hebrew origin. The meaning of Urit is "brightness".

Ursula

Pronunciation: UR-soo-lah
The name Ursula is of Latin and Scandinavian origin. The meaning of Ursula is "little bear". Several legends claim that Saint Ursula was a 4th-century British princess who went on

pilgrimage to Rome with her maiden companions, they were all massacred by the Huns at Cologne. Disney made the name famous in their film, *The Little Mermaid (1989)*. Ursula is the name of the evil octopus.

Usha
Pronunciation: oo-shah
The name Usha is of Hindi and Sanskrit origin. The meaning of Usha is "Dawn". Borne in mythology, Usha was the daughter of heaven and the sister of night.

V

Val
Pronunciation: VAL
The name Val is a diminutive of Valda, Valentina, Valerie, or Valma.

Valda
Pronunciation: VAL-da
The name Valda is of Old German origin. The meaning of Valda is "renowned ruler". Valda is a feminine form of the name Waldemar.

Valen
Pronunciation: VA-len
Valen is a variant of the Latin name Valentine. The meaning of the name is "strong", "healthy". Valen is used as a both a boy's name and a girl's name.

Valencia
Pronunciation: vah-LEN-cee-ah
The name Valencia is of Latin origin. The meaning of Valencia is "strong". The name is a feminine form of Valentinus.

Valentina
Pronunciation: val-en-TEE-nah
The name Valentina is of Latin origin. The meaning of Valentina is "strong". The name is a feminine form of Valentine.

Valeria
Pronunciation: val-ER-e-a
Valeria is of Latin origin. The meaning of the name Valeria is "to be healthy". Valeria is a variant of the Latin name Valerie.

Valerie
Pronunciation: VAL-er-ee
The name Valerie is of Latin origin. The meaning of Valerie is "strong, healthy". The name is a French form of the Latin name Valeria. Valerie is a feminine form

of Valerius, a Roman family clan name. The name was borne by a 3rd-century saint.

Valeska
Pronunciation: VAL-esk-a
The name Valeska is of Slavic origin. The meaning of Valeska is "splendid leader". The name is a feminine form of Vladislav.

Valkyrie
Pronunciation: VALK-y-ree
The name Valkyrie is of Scandinavian origin. The meaning of Valkyrie is unknown. Borne in mythology; Valkyrie was an attendant of Odin.

Valley
Pronunciation: VAL-ee
The name Valley is of a diminutive of Valerie. Valley is also a geography name, for a low spot in a landscape.

Vallombrosa
Pronunciation: VALL-om-bros-a
The name Vallombrosa is of Italian origin. The meaning of Vallombrosa is "shady valley". Vallombrosa is also a place name of a forest resort near Florence, Italy.

Valonia
Pronunciation: VAL-o-ne-a
The name Valonia is of Latin origin. The meaning of Valonia is "shallow valley". Valonia is also a place name.

Valora
Pronunciation: VAL-o-ra
The name Valora is of Latin origin. The meaning of Valora is "brave, courageous".

Vanda
Pronunciation: VAN-da

Vanda is of Italian and Czechoslovakian origin. The meaning of the name Vanda is "the tribe of vandals". The name became popular in the 20th century.

Vanessa
Pronunciation: va-NESS-ah
The name Vanessa is of Greek origin. The meaning of Vanessa is "Butterfly". The name was invented by the author Jonathan Swift (1667-1745) for his friend Esther Vanhomrigh for *Gulliver's Travels*. He combined the first syllable of her Dutch surname name with Essa.

Vania
Pronunciation: VAHN-yah
Vania is of Latin origin. The meaning of the name Vania is "brings good news". The name is a variant of Ivana.

Vanita
Pronunciation: va-NEE-tah
The name Vanita is of Hindi origin. The meaning of Vanita is "woman".

Vanity
Pronunciation: VAN-ih-tee
The name Vanity is of French origin. The meaning of Vanity is "inflated in pride".

Vanna
Pronunciation: VAN-ah
The name Vanna is of Cambodian origin. The meaning of Vanna is "golden". Vanna is the feminine form of the name John.

Vanora
Pronunciation: VAHN-or-a
The name Vanora is of Old Welsh origin. The meaning of Vanora is "white wave".

Varda
Pronunciation: VAR-da
The name Varda is of Hebrew origin. The meaning of Varda is "rose".

Vashti
Pronunciation: VA-sh-tee
The name Vashti is of Persian origin. The meaning of Vashti is "beautiful". A biblical name; Vashti was the wife of King Ahasuerus of Persia. The king replaced his wife with Esther after she refused to display her beauty before his guests.

Vasilia
Pronunciation: VAS-il-a
The name Vasilia is of unknown origin. The meaning of Vasilia is "royal, kingly". Vasilia is a feminine form of the Greek name Basil.

Veda
Pronunciation: VEE-da
Veda is of Sanskrit origin. The meaning of the name Veda is "knowledge". The Vedas are the four sacred books of the Hindus.

Vedette
Pronunciation: VEE-dett
The name Vedette is of Italian origin. The meaning of Vedette is "sentry".

Vega
Pronunciation: VEE-ga
The name Vega is of Arabic origin. The meaning of Vega is "falling venture". Vega is also the name of the brightest star in the group of stars named, Lyra.

Velika
Pronunciation: VEL-ee-ka
The name Velika is of Slavic origin. The meaning of Velika is "great".

Velma
Pronunciation: VEL-ma
Velma is of English origin. The meaning of the name Velma is "determined protector". Velma is possibly a variant of the name Selma.

Velvet
Pronunciation: VEL-vet
The name Velvet is of English origin. The meaning of Velvet is unknown. Velvet is also the name of a soft fabric, which is associated with luxury.

Venerada
Pronunciation: VEN-er-ada
The name Venerada is of Spanish origin. The meaning of Venerada is "venerated".

Venetia
Pronunciation: ve-NEE-shah
The name Venetia is of Latin origin. The meaning of Venetia is "city of canals". From the Latin name for the city of Venice in Northern Italy. Venetia is also associated with the Roman goddess of love and fertility, Venus.

Venus
Pronunciation: VEE-nus
The name Venus is of Latin origin. The meaning of Venus is "love, fertility". Borne in Roman mythology; Venus is the Roman goddess of love and fertility.

Vera
Pronunciation: VEER-ah
Vera is of Russian and Slavic origin. The meaning of the name Vera is "faith". The name is often used as a nickname for Veronica and Guinevere.

Verbena

Pronunciation: VERB-en-a

The name Verbena is of Latin origin. The meaning of Verbena is "holy plants". The name was originally used to refer to the olive and myrtle plants, which had spiritual significance to the Romans.

Verena

Pronunciation: VER-ee-na

Verena is of Latin origin. The meaning of the name Verena is "true".

Verity

Pronunciation: VARE-i-tee

The name Verity is of Latin origin. The meaning of Verity is "truth". From the Latin word *veritas*. The name was adopted by the Puritans.

Verona

Pronunciation: VER-o-na

The name Verona is a short form of Veronica. The origin of the name is disputed. Verona is also the name of a northern Italian city.

Veronica

Pronunciation: ver-RON-ni-kah

Veronica is of Latin origin. The meaning of the name Veronica is "true image". From Latin *vera icon*. Saint Veronica was an Italian mystic. According to legend, St Veronica wiped the face of Jesus on his way to the cross. A 'true image' of Christ's face was left on the cloth. The name is a Latin form of the Greek name Berenice. The name was first used in Britain in the 17th century, the name was popular with Catholic families. Diminutives: Ronnie, Vero.

Veronique

Pronunciation: VER-on-i-k
The name Veronique is of French origin. The meaning of Veronique is "victory bringer". The name is a French form of Veronica.

Victoria

Pronunciation: vit-TOR-ee-ah
Victoria is of Latin origin. The meaning of the name Victoria is "victory". Victoria is a feminine form of Latin *victorius*. Borne in mythology; Victoria was a goddess who smiled on the people of ancient Rome for centuries. The name was adopted by early Christians. The name has been associated with Royalty after Queen Victoria (1819-1901) was given the name by her German mother.
Diminutives: Vic, Vicki, Vickie, Vicky, Vikki, Vita, Tori, Toria, Tory.

Viola

Pronunciation: VI-o-la
The name Viola is of Latin origin. The meaning of Viola is "violet". Viola is a variant of the Latin name Violet. The name was used by Shakespeare in *Twelfth Night* (1602).

Violet

Pronunciation: VYE-a-let
The name Violet is of Latin origin. The meaning of Violet is "purple". From Latin *viola*. Violet is the name of a low growing plant with purple or white flowers. The name became popular in the 19th century when flower names became fashionable.

Violetta

Pronunciation: VYE-el-et-a
The name Violetta is a variant of the Latin name Violet. The meaning of Violetta is "purple".

Vivian

Pronunciation: VIV-ian

The name Vivian is of Latin origin. Old French form of the Latin name Vivianus, from *vivus* which means "alive", "lively". The meaning of the name Vivian is "full of life" Vivian is used as both a boy's name and as a girl's name.

Vivien

Pronunciation: VIV-e-en

Vivien is of Latin origin. The meaning of the name Vivien is "alive, lively". From the Roman family name Vivianus. Borne in Arthurian legend; Vivien was the Lady of the Lake and the mistress of Merlin. She stole Lancelot when he was a child and raised him herself.

W

Wallis
Pronunciation: WAL-is
The name Wallis if of Old English origin. The meaning of Wallis is "from Wales". Wallis is a variant of the name Wallace. The Duchess of Windsor, Wallis Simpson popularised the name.

Wanda
Pronunciation: WAHN-dah
The name Wanda is of Slavic origin. The meaning of Wanda is "the tribe of the Vandals". An ancient Slavonic tribe named *The Vandals*, were well known for their destructive behavior, which led to the modern term 'vandalism'. The name Wanda was popularised in Ouida's novel, *Wanda* (1883).

Wanetta
Pronunciation: WAN-ett-a
The name Wanetta is of Old English origin. The meaning of Wanetta is "pale-skinned".

Warda
Pronunciation: WAR-da
The name Warda is of Old German origin. The meaning of Warda is "Guardian".

Wava
Pronunciation: WAY-vah
The name Wava is of Slavic origin. The meaning of Wava is "stranger". Wave is a Russian form of the name Barbara.

Waverly
Pronunciation: WAY-ver-lee
The name Waverly is of Old English origin. The meaning of Waverly is "meadow of quivering aspens". Waverly is also a place name.

Wendell
Pronunciation: WEN-dell

The name Wendell is of Old German origin. The meaning of Wendell is "wanderer".

Wendy
Pronunciation: WEN-dee
Wendy is of English origin. The meaning of the name Wendy is "friend". The name was created by J M Barrie for the heroine of *Peter Pan* (1904). Wendy was a nickname which was given to him by a friend's daughter.

Weslee
Pronunciation: WEZ-lee
The name Weslee is of Old English origin. The meaning of Weslee is "western meadow". Weslee is a feminine form of the name Wesley.

Whitley
Pronunciation: WHIT-lee
The name Whitley is of Old English origin. The meaning of Whitley is "white meadow". Whitley is also a place name.

Whitney
Pronunciation: WHIT-nee
Whitney is of Old English origin. The meaning of the name Whitney is "white island". Whitney is also a place name. Originally used as a boy's name, Whitney became a popular first name for females in the early 1980's.

Wilda
Pronunciation: WIL-da
The name Wilda is of Old English and Old German origin. The meaning of Wilda is "untamed".

Wilhelmina
Pronunciation: WIL-ah-men-ah

The name Wilhelmina is of Old German origin. The Meaning of Wilhelmina is "determined protector".

Willa
Pronunciation: WIL-ah
The name Willa is of Old German origin. The meaning of Willa is "determined protector". Willa is a feminine form of the name William.

Willow
Pronunciation: WIL-oh
The name Willow is of English origin. The meaning of Willow is "grace". Willow is the name of a species of tree, known for its grace.

Wilma
Pronunciation: WIL-ma
The name Wilma is of Old German origin. The meaning of Wilma is "determined protector". Wilma is a short form of the name Wilhelmina. The name became famous with Hanna-Barbera's cartoon serious, The Flintstones. Wilma Flintstone was a Stone Age housewife.

Wilona
Pronunciation: WIL-oo-na
The name Wilona is of Old English origin. The meaning of Wilona is "longed for".

Winifred
Pronunciation: WIN-a-fred
The name Winifred is of Old English and Welsh origin. The meaning of Winifred is "blessed, peace". Borne by a martyred Welsh Princess, Winifred was traditionally known as the patron saint of virgins.

Winona
Pronunciation: wyw-NOH-nah
The name Winona is of Native American Indian origin. The meaning of Winona is "eldest daughter". From Sioux Indian. The name was made famous by Hollywood actress Winona Ryder.

Winsome
Pronunciation: WIN-sum
The name Winsome is of Old English origin. The meaning Winsome is "agreeable".

Winter
Pronunciation: WIN-ter
The name Winter is of Old English origin. The meaning of Winter is unknown. Winter is also the name of one of the four seasons, Spring, Summer, Autumn, Winter.

Wren
Pronunciation: WREN
The name Wren is of Old English origin. The meaning of Wren is unknown. Wren is also the name of a small brown songbird.

Wyanet
Pronunciation: WHY-an-et
The name Wyanet is of Native American Indian origin. The meaning of Wyanet is "beautiful".

Wyetta
Pronunciation: WHY-ett-a
The name Wyetta is of Old English origin. The meaning of Wyetta is "war strength". Wyetta is a feminine form of the Old English name Wyatt.

Wynne
Pronunciation: WYN-ee
The name Wynne comes from the Welsh word, *gwen*, which means "fair, holy,

blessed, white". The meaning of the name Wynne is "friend". Wynne is also a variant of the name Wynn. Wynne is used as both a girl's name and as a boy's name.

Wyome
Pronunciation: WY-o-me
The name Wyome is of Native American Indian origin. The meaning of Wyome is "wide plain".

X

Xanthe

Pronunciation: ZAN-thah
The name Xanthe is of Greek origin. The meaning of Xanthe is "yellow, blonde". From Greek *xanthos*.

Xaviera

Pronunciation: zay-vee-HER-ah
The name Xaviera is of Arabic and Basque origin. The meaning of Xaviera is "bright, splendid". The name is a feminine form of the masculine name, Xavier.

Xeni

Pronunciation: SHEH-nee
The name Xeni is of Guatemalan origin. The meaning of Xeni is "protector of plants". Derived from the name Xeniflóres.

Xenia

Pronunciation: ZAYN-yah
The name Xenia is of Greek origin. The meaning of Xenia is "hospitable".

Xylia

Pronunciation: ZYE-lee-ah
The name Xylia is of Greek origin. The meaning of Xylia is "woodland".

Y

Yaffa
Pronunciation: YA-ffa
The name Yaffa is of Hebrew origin. The meaning of Yaffa is "lovely".

Yakira
Pronunciation: ya-KEE-ra
The name Yakira is of Hebrew origin. The meaning of Yakira is "precious".

Yalena
Pronunciation: yal-EE-na
The name Yalena is of Greek and Russian origin. The meaning of Yalena is "sun ray". Yalena is a variant of the name Helen.

Yaminah
Pronunciation: yah-mi-NAH
The name Yaminah is of Arabic origin. The meaning of Yaminah is "suitable".

Yannick
Pronunciation: YANN-ick
Yannick if of French and Hebrew origin. The meaning of the name Yannick is "God is gracious". The name is used as both a boy's name and as a girl's name. Yannick is variant of the name John.

Yara
Pronunciation: YAH-rah
The name Yara is of Brazilian and Arabic origin. The meaning of Yara is "small butterfly".

Yarina
Pronunciation: ya-RI-na
The name Yarina is of Russian origin. The meaning of Yarina is "peace". Yarina is a variant of the Greek name Irene.

Yarmila
Pronunciation: yar-MIL-LA

441

The name Yarmila is of Slavic origin. The meaning of Yarmila is "trader".

Yasmin, Yasmine
Pronunciation: yahz-MEEN
The name Yasmin is of Arabic and Persian origin. The meaning of Yasmin is "jasmine flower". The name is a variation of Jasmine.

Yesenia
Pronunciation: yeh-SEE-nee-ah
Yesenia is of Spanish origin. The meaning of Yesenia is unknown. Yesenia is variant of Llesenia.

Ynez
Pronunciation: ee-NEZ
The name Ynez is of French and Spanish origin. The meaning of Ynez is "chaste". Ynez is a variant of the Greek name Agnes.

Yoana
Pronunciation: yo-ANA
The name Yoana is of Hebrew origin. The meaning of Yoana is "God is gracious". The name is a variant of Joanna and a feminine form of the masculine name John.

Yoko
Pronunciation: YO-ko
The name Yoko is of Japanese origin. The meaning of Yoko is "good, positive".

Yolanda
Pronunciation: yoh-LAHN-dah
Yolanda is of Greek and Spanish origin. The meaning of the name Yolanda is "violet flower".

Yolande
Pronunciation: yoh-LAHN-dee

The name Yolande is of Latin origin. The meaning of Yolande is "violet flower". A variation of the French name Iolanthe derived from the Italian name Violanta.

Yonina

Pronunciation: yo-ni-NA
The name Yonina is of Hebrew origin. The meaning of Yonina is "dove".

Yosepha

Pronunciation: yo-se-pha
The name Yosepha is of Hebrew origin. The meaning of Yosepha is "Jehovah increases". The name is a Feminine form of the name Joseph.

Yseult

Pronunciation: yse-(u)-lt
The name Yseult is of French origin. The meaning of Yseult is "fair lady". The name is also a variant of the name Isolde.

Yudit

Pronunciation: YU-dit
The name Yudit is of Hebrew origin. The meaning of Yudit is "praise".

Yuliya

Pronunciation: yu-li-ya
The name Yuliya is of Russian origin. The meaning of Yuliya is "youthful". The name is a variant of Julia.

Yumiko

Pronunciation: yoo-mee-koh
Yumiko is of Japanese origin. The meaning of the name Yumiko is "arrow child".

Yuriko

Pronunciation: yoo-ree-koh
The name Yuriko is of Japanese origin. The meaning of Yuriko is "lily child".

Yvette

Pronunciation: ee-VET
The name Yvette is of French origin. The meaning of Yvette is "yew". The name is a feminine form of the French name Yves.

Yvonne

Pronunciation: ee-VAHN
The name Yvonne is of French and Old German origin. The meaning of Yvonne is "yew". A feminine form of the French name Yves.

Z

Zahavah
Pronunciation: ZA-hav-AH
The name Zahavah is of Hebrew origin. The meaning of Zahavah is "gilded".

Zaida
Pronunciation: ZAY-dah
The name Zaida is of Arabic origin. The meaning of Zaida is "prosperous".

Zaina
Pronunciation: ZAY-nah
Zaina is of Greek origin. The meaning of the name Zaina is "beauty". Zaina is a variant of the name Xenia.

Zalika
Pronunciation: za-LEE-kah
The name Zalika is of Swahili origin. The meaning of Zalika is "well born".

Zandra
Pronunciation: ZAHN-dra
The name Zandra is of Spanish origin. The meaning of Zandra is "man's defender". Zandra is a diminutive of the Greek name Alexandra.

Zaneta
Pronunciation: zah-NEE-tah
The name Zaneta is of Spanish origin. The meaning of Zaneta is unknown. Borne by a saint.

Zara
Pronunciation: ZR-ah
The name Zara is of Arabic origin. The meaning of Zara is "radiance". The name is possibly taken from the Hebrew meaning, 'bright as the dawn'. Zara is a diminutive of the name Sarah.

Zarina
Pronunciation: za-REEN-ah

Zarina is of Persian origin. The meaning of the name Zarina is "golden".

Zea
Pronunciation: ZEE-a
The name Zea is of Latin origin. The meaning of Zea is "grain".

Zarya
Pronunciation: ZAR-ya
The name Zarya is of Slavic origin. The meaning of Zarya is "protector of warriors". Borne in mythology, Zarya is a water priestess and protector of the warriors.

Zefira
Pronunciation: ZE-fir-a
The name Zefira is of Hebrew origin. The meaning of Zefira is "morning".

Zelda
Pronunciation: ZEH-dah
Zelda is of Old German origin. The meaning of the name Zelda is "dark battle". Originally used as a nickname of the Old German name, Griselda.

Zelenia
Pronunciation: ZEL-een-ia
The name Zelenia is of Greek origin. The meaning of Zelenia is "the moon". Zelenia is a variant of the Greek name Selena.

Zena
Pronunciation: ZEE-na
The name Zena is of Greek origin. The meaning of Zena is "guest, stranger". The name is a variant of Xenia.

Zelma
Pronunciation: ZEL-mah

The name Zelma is of Old German origin. The meaning of Zelma is "helmet of God". Zelma is a variant of the name Selma.

Zenobia
Pronunciation: ze-NOH-bee-ah
Zenobia is of Greek origin. The meaning of the name Zenobia is "life of Zeus". Borne by a 3rd-century queen of Palmyra in the Arabian desert. The name was revived in the 19th century.

Zetta
Pronunciation: ZEE-ta
The name Zetta is of Hebrew origin. The meaning of Zetta is "olive".

Zoe
Pronunciation: ZOH-ee
Zoe is of Greek origin. The meaning of the name Zoe is "life". Originally a Greek Jewish translation of the Hebrew name Eve, meaning 'life'. The name was borne by a 3rd-century Roman martyr. The name was adopted in Britain in the 19th century, the name has been in regular since.

Zola
Pronunciation: ZO-la
The name Zola is of Italian origin. The meaning of Zola is "lump of earth". The name is possibly a variation of the Greek name Zoe. Zola was adopted as a first name in the late 20th century.

Zora
Pronunciation: ZOR-ah
The name Zora is of Slavic origin. The meaning of Zora is "dawn". Variation: Zorah.

Banned baby names around the world

Although the UK and USA have some of the most liberal rules in the world when it comes to baby names, other countries have created lists of banned names that you cannot name your child in their country.

The 2016 Book of Baby Names have put together some of the funniest and most bizarre banned baby names from around the world.

Mexico

The Mexian State of Sonora released a long list of names that are banned for reasons being that they are 'derogatory, pejorative, discriminatory or for simply lacking in meaning.' The list of prohibited names in Sonora include;

All Power	Petronilo
Batman	Pocahontas
Burger King	Privado
Cesárea	Rambo
Christmas Day	Robocop
Circuncisión	Rocky
Email	Rolling Stone
Espinacia	Terminator
Facebook	Sonora querida
Harry Potter	Telesforo
Hermione	Tránsito
Hitler	Twitter

Iluminada	Usnavy
James Bond	Virgen
Lady Di	Verulo
Masiosare	Yahoo
Micheline	Zoila Rosa

Saudi Arabia

Saudi Arabia released their list of banned baby names which include any names that have royal connotations such as prince or princess, names of prophets, western names are also included in the list. The list of forbidden baby names in Saudi Arabia include;

Abdul Naser	Loland
Al Mamlaka (The Kingdom)	Malaak (Angel)
Alice	Malika (Queen)
Amir (Prince)	Maline
Aram	Maya
Basmala (utterance of the name of God)	Nabi (Prophet)
Barrah	Nabiyya (Female Prophet)
Baseel	Nardeen
Bayan	Naris
Binyamin (Arabic for Benjamin)	Randa
Elaine	Rital
Iman	Rama (Hindu God)
Inar	Sandy

Jibreel (Angel Gabriel)	Sumuw (Highness)
Kibrial	Tabarak (Blessed)
Lareen	Tilaj
Lauren	Yara
Linda	Wireelam

Australia

Australian government have 'proposed names will not be registered if they are obscene or offensive, unreasonably long, contain symbols without phonetic significance or are not in the public interest for some other reason.' Some of the baby names banned in Australia include the following;

Batman	Maryjuana
Bonghead	Medicare
(Blankspace)	Ned Kelly
Chief Maximus	Osama
Circumcision	Panties
Chow Tow	Pieandsauce
Dick Head	Post Master General
G-Bang	President
Goose	#ROFL
Hitler	Ranga
Ice-T	Scrotum
Ikea	Shithead
iMac	Spinach
Jesus Christ	Smelly
Lol	Snort

Lucifer	Virgin
Martian	

Germany

German guidelines state that names must indicate the gender of the child and must not be likely to lead to humiliation. You are forbidden to use surnames or the names of objects or products as first names. In order to protect the child, the name must not be absurd or degrading in any way. Local registrars decide which names to approve and which ones to reject.

A Turkish couple who were living in Germany were refused the permission to call the child Osama Bin Laden. Gender Neutral names are also rejected such as the name Matti.

Amongst some of the banned baby names in Germany are;

Agfa	Osama Bin Laden
Atom Fired	Pillula
Gramopho	Puhbert
Bierstübl	Satan
Cain	Schnucki
Hitler	Schroeder
Judas	Sputnik
Lenin	Stompie
MC Donald	Troublemaker
Ogino	The number 'Pi'

| Omo | Woodstock |

China

In China, a couple tried to name their child Wang @. The symbol in Chinese is pronounced "ai-ta", which means "Love him". The parents claimed that the @ symbol echoed the love that they had for the child.

Malaysia

Malaysian authorities have also banned the use of numbers in baby names, Japanese car names and royal titles. A list of banned baby names has been published. Included on the list is the Canonese monikers Sor Chai which means Insane, Chow Tow, meaning Smelly Head. The use of Woti has also been discouraged as a baby name as it means sexual intercourse.

New Zealand

A court in New Zealand took over the guardianship of a young girl named, Talula Does The Hula From Hawaii so that they could change her name. The judge condemned the name and the rising trend of parents using wacky baby names, claiming that it would lead to bullying.

Another couple in New Zealand were banned from naming their twins Fish and Chips, although the name Number 16

Bus Shelter was approved by authorities.

Include on the list of banned baby names in New Zealand include;

Anal	Majesty
Baron	Major
Bishop	Messiah
Duke	President
Judge	Prince
King	Princess
Knight	Queen
Lady	Royale
Lucifer	

Portugal

Portugal has put a ban on parents using nicknames on their Childs birth certificates. This means the name Tom would be rejected however the full name Thomas would be accepted.

Amongst the banned names in Portugal are;

Albuquerque
Ashanti
Ben-Hur
Brilhante
Britta Nórdica
Do Sorriso
Faruk

Mar E Sol (Portuguese for sean & sun)
Nazareth Fernades
Nirvana
Olaf
Portugal
Sandokan
Satélite
Sayonara (Japanese for goodbye)
Viking
Zingara (Italian for gypsy)

BIBLOGRAPHY

Cresswell, Julia
Bloomsbury Dictionary of First Names
Bloomsbury, London, 1992

Cross. F. L and Livingstone E A, ed
Oxford Dictionary of the Christian Church
Oxford University Press, 1997

Drunkling, Leslie
First names first
J M Dent & Sons Ltd, London 1977

Fergusson, Rosalind
Choose Your Baby's name
Penguin, London 1987

Hall, James
Dictionary of Subjects and Symbols in Art
John Murrary, 1992

Hanks, Patrick and Falvia Hodges
A Concise Dictionary of First Names
Oxford University Press, Oxford, 1997

Holy Bible
Cambridge University Press

Macleod, Iseabail and Terry Freedman
The Wordsworth Dictionary of First Names

Wordsworth Editions Limited, London, 1995

Office for National Statistics
Baby Names, England and Wales
Publish 2014

Pickering, David
The Penguin Dictionary of First Names
Penguin, 2004

Room, Adrian
Brewer's Names
Cassell, London, 1992

Stafford, Diane
The Big Book of 60, 000 Baby Names
Sourcebooks, Inc, 2006

Strong, James
Strong's Concordance of the Bible
Thomas Nelson 1980

Withycombe, E G
Oxford Dictionary of English Christian Names
Oxford University Press, Oxford 1977

Printed in Great Britain
by Amazon.co.uk, Ltd.,
Marston Gate.